ATROCITY
ON THE
ATLANTIC

ATROCITY
ON THE
ATLANTIC

**Attack on a Hospital Ship
During the Great War**

NATE HENDLEY

DUNDURN
PRESS

Publisher and acquiring editor: Kwame Scott Fraser | Editor: Dominic Farrell
Cover designer: Karen Alexiou
Cover image: ©Imperial War Museum (Art.IWM ART 5605); background: Unsplash/Kiwihug

Library and Archives Canada Cataloguing in Publication

Title: Atrocity on the Atlantic : attack on a hospital ship during the Great War / Nate Hendley.
Names: Hendley, Nate, author.
Description: Includes bibliographical references and index.
Identifiers: Canadiana (print) 2023055427X | Canadiana (ebook) 20230554288 | ISBN 9781459751347 (softcover) | ISBN 9781459751354 (PDF) | ISBN 9781459751361 (EPUB)
Subjects: LCSH: Llandovery Castle (Hospital ship) | LCSH: Hospital ships—Canada— History—20th century. | LCSH: World War, 1914-1918—Naval operations, Canadian. | LCSH: World War, 1914-1918— Naval operations, German. | LCSH: World War, 1914-1918—Naval operations—Submarine. | LCSH: Submarines (Ships)—Germany—History—20th century. | LCSH: World War, 1914-1918—Atrocities.
Classification: LCC VG450 .H46 2024 | DDC 359.8/364097109041—dc23

We acknowledge the support of the Canada Council for the Arts and the Ontario Arts Council for our publishing program. We also acknowledge the financial support of the Government of Ontario, through the Ontario Book Publishing Tax Credit and Ontario Creates, and the Government of Canada.

Care has been taken to trace the ownership of copyright material used in this book. The author and the publisher welcome any information enabling them to rectify any references or credits in subsequent editions.

The publisher is not responsible for websites or their content unless they are owned by the publisher.

Printed and bound in Canada.

Dundurn Press
1382 Queen Street East
Toronto, Ontario, Canada M4L 1C9
dundurn.com, @dundurnpress

This book is dedicated to everyone who was on board the hospital ship *Llandovery Castle* on the night of June 27, 1918.

Contents

Introduction

The *Llandovery Castle* was a British passenger liner that was converted into a hospital ship during the First World War. Chartered by the Canadian government in March 1918, the ship brought thousands of seriously ill and injured men home to Canada to recuperate.

On the evening of June 27, 1918, while heading back to Britain to pick up more patients, the *Llandovery Castle* was torpedoed by U-boat *86*, a German submarine. The ship sank within minutes off the coast of Ireland. Since the *Llandovery Castle* was on a return voyage, it wasn't carrying patients. Between the British crew and members of the Canadian Army Medical Corps (CAMC) there were 258 people on board, and most of them made it into lifeboats.

The commander of the submarine that torpedoed the *Llandovery Castle* was convinced it was carrying American pilots, in violation of the Hague Conventions, a set of international treaties regulating wartime conduct. Upon realizing he was mistaken, the sub commander tried to murder all the survivors, since sinking hospital ships also contravened Hague rules.

One lifeboat with twenty-four passengers escaped. Its occupants bore witness to the torpedo attack and the attempt to murder the shipwrecked survivors.

The *Llandovery Castle* sinking aroused global condemnation, and those responsible for it were prosecuted at the Leipzig War Crimes Trials — the little-known attempt to bring German war criminals to justice after the First

World War. The judicial ruling on the *Llandovery Castle* case established a hugely important legal precedent that has guided future war crimes trials since.

For all that, the *Llandovery Castle* soon vanished from popular memory, remembered mostly for the fact that fourteen female nurses on the ship drowned.

This book will recount the sinking of the ship and the details of the trial held after the war in an attempt to hold the men on the U-boat accountable. It will discuss the significance of the verdict reached in that trial on future war crimes trials. Finally, it will explain why this notorious atrocity was forgotten and examine the resurgence of interest in the *Llandovery Castle* that marked the one-hundredth anniversary of the sinking.

There are no imagined conversations in this book: any quotes contained in it have been taken from newspaper accounts, witness testimony, court decisions, letters, diaries, interviews, memos, and other sources, all of which are listed in the back.

The metric system was not in use in Canada when the events in this book took place. For the sake of consistency, I have generally used the imperial system (inches, feet, miles) when citing measurements.

I hope that this book will spark further interest in a doomed ship, the brave men and women on it, and the legacy of an attack that was once described as "the very worst thing that Germany has yet done at sea."

CHAPTER ONE

"Do You Think There Is Any Hope for Us?"

N o one saw the torpedo coming. If it left a wake in the water, nobody noticed. The explosives-laden warhead detonated on the port side of His Majesty's Hospital Ship (HMHS) *Llandovery Castle* near the No. 4 hold, devastating the engine room. Several stokers were killed or incapacitated, and the ship lights instantly went out. After the emergency generator kicked in, the lights flickered on again, providing some dim illumination in the darkness.

It was 9:30 p.m. ship-time, Thursday, June 27, 1918, and the *Llandovery Castle* was heading back to Britain from Canada to pick up another transport of wounded Canadian soldiers. These men would be returned to Canada for a long convalescence. When the torpedo struck, the *Llandovery Castle* was approximately 114 miles southwest of Fastnet Rock, the southern most place in Ireland.

Captain Edward Sylvester felt a tremendous shock from the explosion. At first, he didn't realize the ship had been torpedoed. The *Llandovery Castle* was travelling at 13.6 knots — 13.6 nautical miles (15.64 regular miles) per hour — on a calm sea. There had been no warnings about German submarines (*Unterseeboots*, or U-boats for short) in the area.

If momentarily perplexed by the cause of the blast, Captain Sylvester immediately realized that the ship he commanded was sinking fast. He rang the engine room with the thought of ordering the sailor in charge to stop and then reverse the engines. The idea was to halt the ship's forward momentum, which was accelerating the flood of water through the hole made by the torpedo.

There was no response from the engine room. Presumably, everyone in the room was dead or seriously injured. The hospital ship continued plowing ahead, rapidly filling with water. At five hundred feet long and weighing 11,423 tons, the *Llandovery Castle* was relatively big, but the single torpedo had managed to inflict tremendous damage.

"About three minutes after the explosion, the carpenter reported the ship was hit in the No. 4 hold and would not remain afloat. I then gave orders to lower all the boats and send them away," Captain Sylvester later explained.

Sylvester was an experienced captain in his midfifties. As a young man, he had trained on His Majesty's Ship (HMS) *Worcester* and then taken a job with the Union Steam Ship Company. The Union Steam Ship Company merged with the Castle Mail Packets Company in 1900 to become the Union-Castle Mail Steamship Company. The latter operated a vast fleet of passenger ships and other vessels. Sylvester stayed on as captain of the *Llandovery Castle* when it was chartered by the Canadian government in March 1918 to transport wounded men back home.

Captain Sylvester was responsible for the 258 people on board, a total that included 164 crew members and ninety-four Canadian Army Medical Corps (CAMC) personnel. The CAMC treated injured troops. Their ranks included doctors, orderlies, and fourteen nursing sisters — the name given to female Canadian military nurses at the time.

The *Llandovery Castle* could accommodate hundreds of patients, but this was a return voyage, so the ship wasn't carrying any when it was hit. Regardless, the ship was supposed to be off-limits. Under the Hague Conventions of 1907, which reinforced previous international treaties regarding warfare, hospital ships could be stopped, boarded, and searched, but they could not be attacked. To guarantee this status, hospital ships were not allowed to carry guns, armed soldiers, or war supplies.

Following Hague rules, the *Llandovery Castle* was painted white, with horizontal green stripes along each side interspersed with large red crosses. The ship flew a Red Cross flag, a white flag with a red cross at the centre, and was as brightly lit as a Christmas tree, with white-and-green electric lights. Unlike war vessels, hospital ships were supposed to make themselves as visible as possible. The ship's name had been passed on to German authorities, so they could add it to a list of vessels to avoid, in theory at least.

Germany had ratified the Hague Conventions, including the agreement to refrain from attacking hospital ships, before the war started, but that meant little to Oberleutnant zur See (first lieutenant at sea) Helmut Patzig. He was the commander of U-86. His sub had been stalking the *Llandovery Castle* for hours, slowly manoeuvring into position to launch a torpedo.

Born in Danzig (now in Poland and called Gdansk) in 1890, Patzig joined the Imperial German Navy in 1910. While he initially served on a battleship, Patzig asked to be transferred to the navy's fledgling U-boat division a year after the war broke out. This was a risky move since submarines, which were relatively new weapons at the time, had a tendency to sink or experience severe mechanical issues. No matter: Patzig thrived in this environment and became watch officer of U-55 in 1915. He served on the same sub until September 1917.

By the time Patzig took command of U-86 in January 1918, he had earned the Iron Cross First and Second Class. In the months leading up to the *Llandovery Castle* ambush, he sank over a dozen vessels.

Patzig knew perfectly well that the *Llandovery Castle* was a hospital ship (his own crew would later testify they recognized the ship's hospital lights from a distance). Like many of his colleagues, however, the first lieutenant was convinced such ships routinely violated Hague rules by transporting soldiers and war supplies. The German Imperial Admiralty felt the same way and permitted attacks on hospital ships — albeit only in the Mediterranean Sea and in a zone running from the English Channel to the North Sea.

The *Llandovery Castle* carried nineteen lifeboats, which could accommodate roughly fifty people apiece. The ship also had smaller rafts that could be used in dire emergencies. Given that there were no patients on board, there should have been plenty of available lifeboat space. However, the torpedo blast damaged most of the lifeboats on the port side, rendering them unseaworthy. Also, because the ship was sinking so quickly, it wasn't clear if any lifeboats could get away.

Standing on the bridge, Captain Sylvester barked orders into a megaphone as Lieutenant Colonel Thomas Macdonald, commander of the CAMC personnel, helped launch lifeboats, which were secured to ropes that hung from davits — cranes used to lower or raise lifeboats along the side of the ship.

The *Llandovery Castle* kept plowing forward, however, enormously complicating the lifeboat-launching process. Seawater continued to pour in, causing the deck to slope, making it "a matter of great difficulty" to get the lifeboats underway, as a subsequent report put it. Still, there was no panic on board, as the crew and medical staff made their way to the lifeboats.

In the wireless room, a Marconi operator desperately tried to send out a distress call. Telegram networks that transmitted messages tapped out in Morse code had been around for decades. "Wireless telegraphy" on board ships was something new, however. In a wireless system, messages were conveyed via radio waves, not cables. This technology enabled long-distance communication to and from vessels after they left port.

Italian engineer Guglielmo Marconi — the man who developed the "wireless" system — famously tapped a Morse code message from Europe to Newfoundland, without the need of an undersea cable. The *Llandovery Castle* was only trying to send a message for a fraction of that distance to receivers in Ireland or Great Britain. However, the ship's wireless telegraphy system had been damaged by the torpedo and no messages got through. Eventually, the operator gave up and left, to try to find a lifeboat. Nobody outside the immediate area knew that the *Llandovery Castle* had been torpedoed and was sinking fast.

Sylvester raced to his cabin to grab some items before the ship went down. These included "an electric torch" — that is, a battery-powered lamp or flashlight — and a tin of tobacco. He had a pipe on him and figured the tobacco might come in handy for later. Fully equipped, he dashed back to the deck to supervise the lifeboats.

Witnesses said that at least three lifeboats from the starboard side of the ship and two from the port side made it to the water. A government report later concluded that almost everyone on board managed to get into a lifeboat "save those killed by the explosion."

Private William Pilot was on his third round-trip back to England on the *Llandovery Castle* when the ship was hit. Born in 1893 in St. John's, Newfoundland, Pilot had enlisted in late 1914, in Toronto. He was shipped to the United Kingdom in May the following year, where he ended up in the Canadian Corps Cyclist Battalion. Bicycle troops served as dispatch riders, transporting messages — a vital task when shellfire destroyed radio and telegram cables. Pilot was injured on October 8, 1916, in Courcelette, France. "While carrying stretcher, was wounded in right leg below knee joint inner side. Shrapnel fragment removed. No fracture," states his medical case sheet.

Pilot recovered and was sent back in action. In March 1918, he joined the medical staff of the *Llandovery Castle* as an orderly, a job that could entail heavy physical work. Among other duties, orderlies might be called on to move patients on stretchers and ease them in and out of bed or on and off

Orderly William Pilot of the Canadian Army Medical Corps.

examination tables. Orderlies also helped prep patients for surgery, ran baths for them, and assisted doctors and nurses when needed.

Pilot would later detail his experience on the sinking ship in a diary, handwritten in a neat, cursive style in dark ink: "Quite a mess up with lifeboats being smashed or swamped. After being in two finally climbed aboard ship again although decks were underwater. Then got away on a raft with two sailors."

The rafts could fit around twenty to thirty people. Pilot and his companions floated inside one of them, waiting for rescue.

Private Shirley Taylor of Saint John, New Brunswick, found himself in a similar position. Taylor was below decks in his "sleeping quarters," as a report put it, when the torpedo struck. Taylor rushed to the port side of the ship to access his pre-assigned lifeboat but found it was wrecked. He ran to the other side of the ship to try his luck there. He observed Lifeboat No. 9 dangling over the side, so he slid down a rope and clambered aboard. A deckhand joined him. The lifeboat tipped, spilling Taylor and everyone else into the water. Although it was late June, the ocean was frigid. Being immersed in the North Atlantic could lead to hypothermia and then death within minutes. The private clung to an oar, then a crate, alternating between shouts and loud whistles to gain the attention of anyone in an upright lifeboat.

Private Frederick Cooper, who was born in Great Britain like many of his CAMC colleagues, was walking on the starboard deck when the attack occurred. The explosion tossed him against the ship railings. Cooper quickly grasped that the ship was in serious trouble and rushed to find a lifebelt. He saw a lifeboat suspended in air over the side of the ship, the ropes and pulleys jammed up. Crew members managed to untangle the ropes and lower the lifeboat, with about twenty people, onto the water. The lifeboat promptly collided with another lifeboat and several people were tossed overboard. Private Cooper looked about for a way to save himself.

For Acting CAMC Sergeant Arthur Knight, the situation must have seemed horribly familiar. Knight was born in Brighton, England, and came to Canada in 1910. He worked as a brass finisher at a London, Ontario, firm that made caskets then joined the Canadian Expeditionary Force

(CEF) — Canada's military mission in Europe — on September 27, 1915. Twenty-nine years old at enlistment, Knight served in a field ambulance unit then at Moore Barracks, Shorncliffe, in the United Kingdom before being transferred to a hospital ship called the *Letitia*.

Like the *Llandovery Castle*, the *Letitia* was a former liner that had been turned into a hospital ship to take badly wounded Canadians home. On the first day of August 1917, the *Letitia* slammed into rocks in the waters outside Halifax Harbour. It was foggy, as it so often is on the East Coast, and the harbour pilot, whose job was to board ships and bring them safely into harbour, didn't see the hazard in time. The *Letitia* stuck fast on the rocks, with 546 patients plus the crew on board. Fortunately, no one was hurt in the accident.

A fleet of rescue vessels raced to the scene and took off all the injured men. The captain and some crew briefly stayed on board, but when it became apparent the ship was too wrecked to be towed ashore, they also departed in rescue boats. One crewman was somehow left behind by mistake. He tried to swim to shore, but drowned, becoming the only fatality connected to the incident. The *Letitia* remained jammed on the shoal for months, then finally broke in two and slid underwater.

There was little chance of any rescue ships arriving to save the *Llandovery Castle* passengers, however.

Having survived one hospital ship disaster already, Sergeant Knight was determined to beat doom again. He raced to Lifeboat No. 5, which was dangling precariously from the davits. Knight climbed into the lifeboat, which contained eight crew members and all fourteen nursing sisters from the ship.

Two of the nurses in the lifeboat were in bedclothes. The rest were wearing their unforms, which featured blue tops with high necklines and wrist-length sleeves, white veils, and white aprons that descended to the ankles. All the nursing sisters wore lifebelts, the Great War equivalent of a personal floatation device.

With difficulty, the men working the ropes managed to lower Lifeboat No. 5 onto the ocean. Getting away from the ship, which was still sinking and moving forward at the same time, was another matter. The lifeboat ropes had become tangled and couldn't be unfastened. As it bounced on the ocean waves, the lifeboat remained stuck to the hull of the *Llandovery Castle*. Sergeant Knight grabbed an axe and hacked at the ropes as others pulled and tugged to loosen the binds.

"I broke two axes trying to cut ourselves away but was unsuccessful," Knight later reported.

Lifeboat No. 5 banged against the steel hull of the ship. People inside the lifeboat pushed against the hull with oars. These efforts failed and all the oars snapped or broke. Then, miraculously, the ropes slackened, and the lifeboat drifted away from the sinking ship. With no workable oars, however, the lifeboat remained dangerously close to the *Llandovery Castle*.

Big ships can create a whirlpool when they sink, dragging down smaller craft or swimmers. This is what happened to Lifeboat No. 5. "We were carried towards the stern of the ship when suddenly the poop deck seemed to break away and sink. The suction drew us quickly into the vacuum," recalled Sergeant Knight.

According to Knight, the nursing sisters accepted their fate with stoic resolve: "I estimate we were together in the boat about eight minutes. In that whole time, I did not hear a complaint or a murmur from one of the sisters. They were supremely calm and collected. There was not a cry for help or any outward evidence of fear. In the entire time, I only overheard one remark," said Knight.

Nursing Sister Margaret Fraser, the matron or leader of the nurses, looked at Knight and asked, "Sergeant, do you think there is any hope for us?"

"No," he replied.

Caught in the suction, the lifeboat tipped and all the passengers spilled into the ocean. Knight caught a glimpse of the nursing sisters flailing in the water. He was the only surviving witness to their last moments.

Knight was dragged under the surface, rose, then smacked his head on a heavy piece of floating debris. The dazed sergeant sank again, only to be jarred by a powerful, new explosion. The blast was likely caused by the cold ocean water splashing against the ship's red-hot boilers. The explosion likely saved Knight's life, as it propelled him back to the surface. Floating there, he shivered and tried to get his bearings.

Ship's purser Henry Evans also witnessed the death throes of Lifeboat No. 5. He was in his cabin when the attack occurred. Hearing the torpedo explode, he rushed on deck and helped launch lifeboats. At one point, Evans slid down a rope-ladder into a lifeboat, but the small craft swamped, and the purser fell into the ocean. Kept buoyant by his lifebelt, Evans tried to swim to Lifeboat No. 5. He never reached it. In the water, he watched as it capsized, overwhelmed by the vortex of the sinking ship.

"There were some sisters and men in the boat," Evans later testified, referring to the doomed nurses.

Evans swam away, as other lifeboats floundered in the whirlpool stirred up by the *Llandovery Castle* going under the water. People grabbed debris and screamed for help. A small handful of lifeboats managed to stay afloat, and those in them were madly rowing them away from the scene.

Sergeant Knight seized a floating piece of wood to keep himself from sinking. Knight was so cold and disoriented that he didn't even notice that U-*86* had surfaced and was cruising toward him.

The U-boat was a strange, savage weapon, one that was used to deadly effect by the Imperial German Navy. Before the war, such vessels were seen as little more than interesting novelties. Then, on September 22, 1914, a single German U-boat in the North Sea sank three aging British armoured cruisers in under an hour. Nearly 1,500 British sailors were lost in this one-sided encounter. The world was shocked; Germany was delighted and made more U-boats.

Approximately 230 feet long and less than twenty-one feet at its widest, U-*86* was built in Kiel, Germany, in 1915 and entered service a year later. The sub was grey in colour; its top was flat, save for a jutting conning tower and its deck gun. U-*86* had two hulls — a round outer hull gave the vessel its cigar-like shape, and an inner pressure hull prevented the sides from collapsing when the sub went underwater. Fuel and ballast tanks were positioned between the hulls, while horizontal rudders on the sides helped guide and steer the sub during dives.

Like other U-boats, however, U-86 spent most of its time on the surface. Generally, it only submerged to fire a torpedo, escape attack, or give the crew a rest. Engine technology was the issue. On the surface, using a pair of six-cylinder, four-stroke diesel engines, it could reach 16.8 knots — faster than the *Llandovery Castle* had been going when it was hit.

Its diesel engines could only be used on the surface, however. They required oxygen to function, and so they couldn't be used underwater. Operating them underwater would have consumed the sub's limited supply of fresh air and emitted dangerous fumes, asphyxiating the crew. Submerged, U-86 had to switch to an electric battery engine that didn't rely on oxygen, but it only offered enough power to propel the sub at half the speed and a fraction of the diesel's range. U-86 would travel nearly five thousand nautical miles while on patrol from June 20 to July 12, 1918 — almost all of it on the surface. Less than two hundred nautical miles were logged underwater.

Prior to submerging, U-86, like other subs, had to disconnect its diesel engines, seal hatches, and ready the electric motors. Once all openings were fastened shut, "sea water is admitted into big open tanks. Powerful suction engines, in the central control of the boat, draw out the air from these tanks, so as to increase the rapid inrush of the water. The chief engineer notifies the captain as soon as the tanks are sufficiently filled, and an even weight is established so as to steer the boat to the proper depth for attack," explains the *Journal of Submarine Commander von Forstner*, a First World War memoir.

During a dive, U-boats had to keep moving forward, while the rudders guided it beneath the waves. Complete submersion might take ninety seconds with an experienced crew, or several minutes with a new crew. Regardless, the U-boat was helpless during the process, unable to use its deck gun or torpedoes and vulnerable to being shelled or rammed. Under the waves, U-86 had to move continuously, like a shark, or it would sink. If U-86 went deeper than fifty metres (164 feet), water pressure would crush its hulls.

While underwater, maintaining oxygen for the crew was as imperative as maintaining power in the electric batteries. "It is essential before a U-boat submerges to drive out the exhausted air through powerful ventilating machines and to suck in the purest air obtainable," writes von Forstner.

Underwater, this air was augmented by oxygen cylinders and a chemical-based air purification system that reduced carbon-dioxide levels. The goal was to prevent cerebral hypoxia among the crew (caused when the brain doesn't get enough oxygen). "Preparations of potassium" were the main chemicals used for the air-purification process, according to von Forstner.

This set-up provided temporary relief, however; at most, a U-boat could only spend a few days underwater. Beyond that, the sub needed to surface, take in fresh air, and recharge the electric batteries — as this involved the sub's main engines, the process could not be done underwater. The recharging process took several hours.

Beneath the surface, the crew avoided moving around or talking too much to preserve oxygen. If the water was shallow and familiar to the captain, subs sometimes rested on the ocean bottom — briefly. True submarines that could spend weeks underwater were still many years away.

Surface travel could be dangerous too, with waves crashing over the top of the U-boat. Everyone up top would be exposed to wind and rain, and sometimes they had to be secured to the sub with ropes so they wouldn't be washed overboard.

The interior of these submarines is described in the book *U-Boat Stories: Narratives of German U-boat Sailors*, a collection of German maritime memories from the Great War:

> [I]magine a steel cylinder … terminating in a point at either end. In the centre of it on the upper side is a tower. Aft — that is, at the back end — there are two torpedo tubes on the underside. Next to them is the electric kitchen, then the electric motors, and then the Diesel engine room. Then the control room, with the compass, the horizontal rudder-wheel, and the valves. In front of that is the officers' and warrant officers' room. Right in front, in the bow, are two more torpedo tubes. Between every compartment is a bulkhead, and a hatchway leads from the conning tower to the body of the vessel. The control room is the most important part of the boat — as indeed,

its name implies. The periscopes are in the conning tower. Built against the exterior of the boat are the diving tanks which give the boat its shape. To them are attached the horizontal rudders, two on each side, one in front and one behind.

U-boat conning towers sometimes contained tiny windows that offered a glimpse of the undersea world. Most crew members, however, were not allowed to access the conning tower lookout or use the periscope. As a result, the majority of sailors in a sub were never able to see their surroundings.

Powerful as they were, U-boats were finicky and fragile. A single shell could rupture their hulls. U-boats could be rammed and sunk by ships, and they sometimes struck sea mines and exploded. In a sinking submarine, the crew had almost no chance of escape.

Subs in U-86's class typically carried a crew of thirty-five. Some of these men stood on the submarine deck and conning tower, gaping at the destruction they had wrought. Petty Officer Walter Popitz of U-86 observed three or four lifeboats in the water and many people trying to swim. The U-boat made no attempt to rescue anyone but eased near Sergeant Knight.

"It was then pitch dark and I heard an order in good but slightly accented English to go alongside of what proved to be a submarine.... I scrambled aboard the submarine and seven or eight Germans gathered around me asking 'What do you want?'" Knight later recounted to reporters.

Before Knight could respond, four German sailors grabbed him and tossed him back into the freezing water. Knight kept sinking and rising. He grabbed more wreckage to remain afloat and didn't try to climb onto the sub again.

Major Thomas Lyon had been playing cards with some nurses when the torpedo hit. Five feet eleven inches tall, with grey eyes, brown hair, and a moustache, Lyon was thirty-six years old. Scottish by birth, he had graduated from Edinburgh University's medical school then trained as a

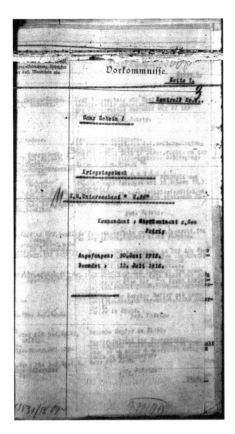

The *Kriegstagebuch*, or war diary, of
U-*86* Commander Helmut Patzig
contains some serious omissions.

physician and surgeon before moving to Canada in 1912. He headed to
British Columbia, where he worked as a doctor serving remote communities
among other positions. At the outbreak of the war, Lyon joined a militia unit
as a medical officer then volunteered for the CAMC.

On April 10, 1915, Lyon signed an attestation paper — the document
marking his introduction into the military. He promised to "be faithful and
bear true Allegiance to His Majesty King George the Fifth, His Heirs and
Successors" and to "faithfully defend His Majesty, His Heirs and Successors,
in Person, Crown, and Dignity, against all enemies and will observe and
obey all orders of His Majesty, His Heirs and Successors and of all the
Generals and Officers set over me. So, help me God."

The form also noted Lyon was unmarried and Presbyterian.

Lyon worked at various hospitals during his military service and suffered from serious illnesses himself. He had narrowly avoided being torpedoed on a previous hospital ship. After the *Llandovery Castle* was hit, Lyon realized he didn't have his glasses with him. "I am some what short sighted and had not my glasses," Major Lyon would later explain.

Lyon managed to make it back to his room, where he grabbed a flashlight and a lifebelt. He noticed that all the other cabins were empty. On the deck, Lyon encountered several crew members and medical personnel, and observed three lifeboats in the water. Lyon approached Captain Sylvester and another officer on the bridge, only to receive some bad news.

"The Captain said the ship would sink in a minute and there were no boats left," recalled Major Lyon.

No seaworthy boats, that is. Then, a ship's officer announced that there was in fact a serviceable lifeboat left — Lifeboat No. 4, which was dangling over the side, partly in the water, partly in the air. Accompanied by Captain Sylvester and others, Major Lyon raced to untangle the ropes affixed to the lifeboat. The boat was lowered onto the water, and a few people scrambled on board, including Lyon and Sylvester. There were slightly under a dozen occupants in the lifeboat, and they rowed furiously to get away from the ship, which was now standing almost straight up, bow facing the sky as it sank. The men in the lifeboat had only travelled about forty feet when the *Llandovery Castle* completely disappeared under the surface. It had taken roughly ten minutes for the vessel to sink after being torpedoed.

People were screaming and struggling in the water. Major Lyon and Captain Sylvester shone their flashlights on the scene, and the occupants of Lifeboat No. 4 began plucking people from the ocean. They soon rescued nearly a dozen men, including privates Cooper, Taylor, and Pilot, and some crew members.

Rescue efforts were abruptly halted, however, when U-*86* motored beside the lifeboat. A German sailor shone a light on the lifeboat.

"Come alongside," barked someone on the sub, speaking in English.

"We are picking up men from the water," responded an indignant occupant of Lifeboat No. 4.

"Come alongside at once," repeated the English-speaker.

To emphasize the point, a sailor on the U-boat fired a pistol in the air twice. A threat was issued in English, either from the same speaker or from Commander Patzig himself (witness accounts differ). The men in the lifeboat were warned that the sub would fire its "big gun" next if they didn't comply. The big gun was a 10.5 cm deck cannon, used to blast holes in the sides of ships. The guns were aimed to hit the ships below the waterline. With holes in their hulls below the waterline, the ships would fill with water and sink, sparing the need for a torpedo. On June 21, Patzig had sunk a 339 ton Norwegian merchant ship called the *Eglantine* with 56 cannon shots.

The torpedo was the submarine's most powerful weapon, but U-*86* carried only twelve of them, which meant Patzig had to be selective in their use. Roughly twenty feet long, torpedoes were large, bulky, and expensive. Once in attack position, the U-boat's torpedoes could be readied in tubes that were situated in the bow or stern of the vessel. Eyeing a ship through a periscope, Commander Patzig would have to make complicated calculations involving distance, speed, water conditions, wind, and potential impact. Even if everything went to plan, the failure rate for torpedoes ran high. Torpedoes frequently went off-course, failed to detonate, or simply sank to the bottom. U-*86* had actually fired two torpedoes at the *Llandovery Castle*, for example — the first of them missed the ship.

Captain Sylvester decided it was best to heed the sub's command. The men in Lifeboat No. 4 used their oars to pull up next to U-*86*. The Germans wanted to speak with the highest-ranking ship officer in the lifeboat. Captain Sylvester left the lifeboat and stepped onto the submarine deck near the conning tower. An English-speaking U-boat sailor told him to identify his vessel.

"The hospital ship *Llandovery Castle*," said Captain Sylvester.

"Oh yes, but you were carrying eight American flight officers," stated the interrogator.

Taken aback, Captain Sylvester said, "I beg your pardon; we are not. We have seven Canadian medical officers on board and the ship is chartered by the Canadian government to carry sick and wounded men from England to Halifax."

The interrogator refused to budge: "You have been carrying American flight officers."

"I have been running to Canada for six months with wounded and give you my word of honour that we have carried none except patients, medical staff, crew and sisters," insisted the captain, referencing a pair of trips made before Ottawa chartered the ship.

The interrogation lasted about five to ten minutes, then Sylvester was sent back to the lifeboat. The Germans said they wanted to talk to a Canadian medical officer. Major Lyon was the senior medical officer present, so he jumped from the lifeboat onto the sub. As he landed, a German sailor grabbed his arm, causing him to fall. Lyon hit the deck hard, breaking his right foot. Wincing in pain, the major did his best to answer questions.

"You are an American flight officer," said the English-speaking interrogator.

"No. We never carried anything but patients," replied Lyon.

The Germans, the major later told reporters, "seemed obsessed with the idea that American aviators were aboard, and it took us some time to convince them otherwise."

The U-boat crew felt they had grounds for suspicion. Two years earlier, a German U-boat sank a British passenger liner, the *Lusitania*, in roughly the same area. Only a third of the 1,959 passengers and crew members on board survived. The dead included 123 Americans, which enraged the United States.

This attack was depicted as an act of German barbarism — a savage attack against a defenceless, unarmed ship carrying civilians. In truth, the *Lusitania* was transporting war supplies: 5,671 cases of ammunition and cartridges, "along with 189 containers of unspecified 'military goods,'" according to the book *German Submarine Warfare in World War I*.

That hardly justified the murder of civilians, but it fed into the belief among U-boat crews that the Allies weren't playing fair. If the Allies used civilian ships to transport war goods, it seemed reasonable to assume they used hospital ships in the same manner. There is no evidence that this was the case, but the sub crew remained obstinate in their belief. The sailors were "coolly polite" as they flung accusations at him, Lyon recalled. He would later muse about the possibility that spies had fed the Germans stories about American pilots being transported on Canadian hospital ships.

Finally, Major Lyon was told to get back to the lifeboat. As he tried to limp away, a German officer took him aside and whispered a warning in English.

"Clear off at once," said the officer.

Major Lyon relayed this warning to his fellow passengers in Lifeboat No. 4. Captain Sylvester said he had been given the same advice. The lifeboat contained a sail, and this was hoisted. As the lifeboat tried to get away, the submarine began circling through the debris.

Lifeboat No. 4 was "making good speed north" but the sub "persisted in following us, occasionally speeding across our bow or stern, missing us by inches," wrote Private Pilot in his diary.

The U-boat stopped moving, and a voice called out, demanding to speak to yet more men. The sub commander seemed determined to get the information he wanted to hear.

Two members of the ship crew — Second Officer Leslie Chapman and Fourth Officer Darley Barton — were ordered onto the sub. Was the *Llandovery Castle* carrying American pilots, demanded the U-boat crew. The officers said no. Then, the interrogator introduced a new subject.

"You had ammunition on board; there was a loud explosion," said the sailor.

Chapman and Barton realized the man was referring to the second loud blast, almost certainly caused by the boilers bursting on contact with the frigid ocean. Chapman explained this to his interrogator. The U-boat crew pondered the matter then told the officers to go back to the lifeboat.

Lifeboat No. 4 had acquired some passengers by this point. Purser Evans spotted the lifeboat, swam to it, and was plucked out of the water, exhausted, soaked, and freezing. CAMC orderly George Hickman was another new passenger.

At some point in the evening, U-*86* intercepted Lifeboat No. 7, which contained Hickman. Hickman was ordered onto the sub and told to go below decks. He was instructed to write down the name of the ship he'd been on. Hickman wrote "Llandovery Castle," and an officer checked the name against a list of known ships in a manual. Most U-boats carried these manuals, which offered the names of all known Allied ships, along with their images and other information. This guide made it easier for the sub commander to identify targets and claim gross tonnage sunk after a successful kill.

Hickman was asked if there were any American flying officers on the *Llandovery Castle*. He said no. Hickman was told he could go, but when he went up to the sub deck via a metal ladder, he discovered his original lifeboat was gone and Lifeboat No. 4 was now alongside the sub. Either the U-boat had abandoned Lifeboat No. 7, or it moved off on its own accord. In any case, Hickman became part of the contingent on Captain Sylvester's lifeboat.

As Lifeboat No. 4 fled the area, First Lieutenant Patzig issued commands. Most of the U-boat crew who were topside went below decks. Only Patzig, a pair of lieutenants named Ludwig Dithmar and John Boldt, and a fourth man named Meissner remained on top. Meissner was the sub's gunner and he set up the 10.5 cm stern cannon on the deck.

Below decks, Petty Officer Popitz was startled to hear the deck gun firing. There were no enemy ships in the vicinity, so the U-boat crew assumed the lifeboats were being shelled. No one went up top to intervene.

Sergeant Knight was still struggling in the water when the firing began. Some of the shells were being directed at the lifeboat he was attempting to approach. Knight was swept into a trough and momentarily lost sight of the lifeboat. When he crested, the lifeboat was gone. He seized another piece of wreckage and clung to it. He counted about twenty shots in total.

Lifeboat No. 4 was roughly half-a-mile from the U-boat when the shelling started. Major Lyon offered a slightly more conservative estimate regarding the barrage.

"I can recall at least twelve shots, presumably in the area where the lifeboats and survivors were supposed to be. One shell came very close to our own boat," stated Lyon.

In his diary, Pilot said the sub tried to shell Lifeboat No. 4, but "owing to the complete darkness … he did poor shooting."

If not motivated by sheer sadism, the only reason for the Germans to shell the lifeboats was to eliminate witnesses. After getting the same answers from all the people he interviewed, Patzig must have realized his mistake. The *Llandovery Castle* didn't contain any American flyers or munitions. It was an unarmed hospital ship, and U-*86* was in violation of Hague rules. As mentioned, German Admiralty directives allowed the hunting of hospital ships in designated areas, but the seas off the coast of Ireland were not included. So, Patzig was doing his best to kill all possible witnesses to his war crime.

Sergeant Knight was picked up by Lifeboat No. 4 during the barrage, becoming the last person to be rescued. There were now two dozen people in the lifeboat — six Canadian medical personnel and eighteen British crew members.

Relying on oars, the sail, and Captain Sylvester's guidance, the men steered the lifeboat as fast as possible away from the U-boat, leaving behind 234 dead colleagues. They headed in the general direction of Ireland, their presence concealed from the U-boat in the darkness. It had been about two hours since the torpedo attack.

The weather was still calm, as the North Atlantic goes, so the survivors didn't face powerful winds or towering waves. They hoped that, with luck, they might eventually land on the Irish coast and get help. In the meantime, they had to cope with hunger and cold.

"The Germans sent us afloat into the darkness without a word of farewell, suggestion, direction, or anything, but we were all thankful to get away from them. The uncertainty of our position overcame thoughts of my own injury, but above all, I could not help wondering what had become of the others. After the submarine disappeared with a swish all was stillness — a terrible stillness. There were no more cries for help heard," Major Lyon later told a newspaper.

He added, "I can emphatically state that the submarine made no attempt to rescue anyone, but on the contrary, did everything in its power to destroy every trace of the ship and its personnel and crew."

As U-*86* headed back to base, the mood below decks was sombre. "During the following days [the U-*86* crew] were extremely depressed. A subsequent collision with a mine, which placed the U-boat in the greatest danger, was regarded as a punishment for the events of the 27th of June," stated a later judicial court ruling.

Lieutenant Patzig might not have been worried about divine punishment, but he did note the incident in his *Kriegstagebuch* ("Boat was strongly shaken. Ran on a mine. Engines stopped. Battery gas, smoke, and fire in the foreship. Lights out."). He praised the "resolute calm" of the technical crew who dealt with the sea mine aftermath and said all his men demonstrated "outstanding spirit" during the voyage.

This jarring event served to heighten an already unpleasant atmosphere. Like all submarines, the interior of U-*86* was gross and uncomfortable; the air reeked of machine oil, food, dirty clothing, and body odours — to save on water, crews didn't bathe and often wore the same clothes for the entire patrol, which could last weeks. The fact that space was limited in the subs was made worse by the fact that the sub was also crammed — filled with food, fuel, deck gun shells, and other provisions. Adding to the misery, the interior remained consistently humid, regardless of the outside temperature, keeping clothes and bedding permanently moist. At one point, U-*86*'s batteries became extremely hot, resulting in "oppressive heat and a lack of air" inside the sub, wrote Patzig.

Two days after attacking the *Llandovery Castle*, Patzig gathered his crew in the cramped sub control room. "Whatever has happened, I take on my conscience before God, and I want you to say nothing about it," stated Patzig.

He said he would take full responsibility for the attack on the *Llandovery Castle*, but he told the crew that they were forbidden from talking about the incident to anyone. The sub contained a pair of prisoners from the steamship *Atlantian*, which U-*86* had sunk previously. One prisoner was a British wireless operator named J. Crosby. Patzig repeated his order to the prisoners — do not say anything about a torpedoed hospital ship. The captive men were not in a position to disagree.

Patzig was determined to leave both Allied authorities and his own superiors in the dark. His *Kriegstagebuch*, which was otherwise packed with details about weather, atmospheric conditions, ships he stalked, and mechanical issues on the sub, omits any reference to the *Llandovery Castle*. Patzig's entry for June 27, 1918, offers blasé observations such as "12.00 Noon — Atlantic WNW 3, Sea 3, cloudy — Course 190 degrees" and nothing more.

Patzig even falsified a chart depicting his route. The doctored chart made it seem like the sub was nowhere near the bit of ocean where the *Llandovery Castle* was torpedoed.

If the mood on the sub was sombre, Patzig's hunting instincts remained intact.

On July 1, U-*86* sank two more vessels — an American troopship called the USS *Covington* and a British steamer called the SS *Origen*. These attacks were detailed in Patzig's war diary, which also included a handwritten tally of successful kills. Four vessels and their estimated tonnage were mentioned in the summary: the *Eglantine*, the *Atlantian*, the *Covington*, and the *Origen*. The *Llandovery Castle* was conspicuously absent from the list.

Patzig figured if his war diary wasn't questioned and everyone kept their mouth shut, no one would find out about the war crime he had committed.

Then, having covered his tracks, "Captain Patzig and his sea wolves" continued their voyage home, wrote Toronto newspaper, the *Globe*.

This summary in the *Kriegstagebuch*, or war diary, of U-*86* Commander Helmut Patzig of ships sunk by the sub makes no mention of the *Llandovery Castle*.

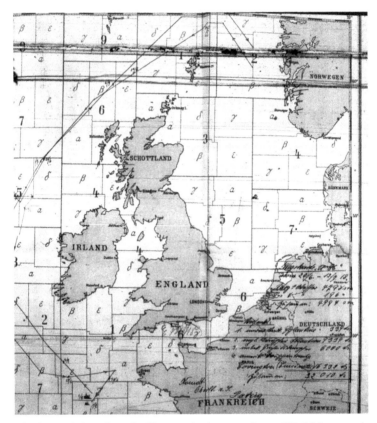

The doctored chart from the *Kriegstagebuch*, or war diary, of U-*86* Commander Helmut Patzig. The *Llandovery Castle* does not appear on the list of ships sunk during the patrol.

CHAPTER TWO

Floating Hospital

As His Majesty's Hospital Ship (HMHS) *Llandovery Castle* steamed toward Halifax for the final time, Nursing Sister Gladys Irene Sare wrote a letter to her sister, whom she called "My dear Win." In the top right corner of her note, she wrote her location ("Llandovery Castle") and the date ("June 14, 1918"). Then she mused about family, duty, and linen.

"Instead of registering your table linen, I bought it — a good idea, eh! Mother will tell you that I had only a few hours notice to leave on transport duty and here I am, not far from Halifax, expecting to get in on Monday," wrote Sare.

As well as writing more about textiles ("Everything is so awfully dear now in England, you'd never believe the price of linen"), she commented on her safety. By that point in the war, there were finally signs that the conflict was tilting in the Allies' favour. The big German offensive launched earlier that year was running out of steam, and fresh troops from America were pouring onto the battlefield. However, the outcome of the war was still far from certain and Atlantic shipping lanes still teemed with German U-boats.

"I suppose mother will be worried but I do wish she wouldn't. I did not solicit the job or try for it in any way, in fact do not want it, but they sent me so here I am. Since things have been so rotten in France, I am glad, because I hate to appear a quitter by sitting high + safe in England + Atlantic travel is active service of the most active kind," she added.

Nursing Sister Gladys Sare of the Canadian Army
Medical Corps.

That said, Sare thought she might be transferred to a different post,
"so this will probably be my only trip [and] if not well, I'll buy some more
things."

Sare was born in Bath, England, on June 6, 1889. Her family moved
to Montreal when she was still an infant. She studied at Montreal General
Hospital then signed up for overseas medical duties in January 1916. She was
shipped to Europe and assigned to Moore Barracks Hospital in Shorncliffe,
U.K. (later designated No. 11 Canadian General Hospital) in April. A few
months later, she was treated as a patient in the same hospital after contract-
ing diphtheria — a potentially fatal illness at the time. Upon recovery, she
worked in France then briefly served on the hospital ship *Letitia* in June
1917 before being transferred back to Britain. She was told to report to the
Llandovery Castle in early June 1918.

In her letter, Sare mentioned that her colleagues on board included "Fortescue of the M.G.H. '05." This was presumably a reference to Nursing Sister Margaret Fortescue, who had also worked at Montreal General Hospital.

"Perhaps mother could get to Halifax to see me. I would love to see her this time," added Sare.

She closed her missive, "Very much love, Glad."

Nurse Sare was part of a massive Canadian medical effort that was comprised of a vast network of hospitals, casualty clearing stations, field ambulances, medical depots, and mobile labs in England and France. At its Great War peak, the Canadian Army Medical Corps had the bed capacity to accommodate over thirty-six thousand patients.

Canadian soldiers wounded in battle were usually brought to safety by stretcher bearers, who also applied basic first aid to stop bleeding. The stretcher bearers took their patients to a regimental aid post, where a medical officer provided more thorough treatment. Then, the patient was shunted to a series of other facilities, including an advanced dressing station for field ambulances and casualty clearing stations. Injured soldiers would then be placed on special hospital trains, accompanied by doctors and nurses, and taken to hospitals for convalescence.

During the course of the war, the overseas CAMC boasted 1,528 medical officers, 15,624 personnel of "other ranks," and 1,901 nursing sisters, according to the *Official History of the Canadian Forces in the Great War 1914–1919*. Nicknamed "Bluebirds" on account of their blue-and-white uniforms, nurses enjoyed a unique status: they were officers, with the equivalent military rank of army lieutenant and could vote in federal elections. The Wartime Elections Act of September 1917 granted women serving in the armed forces as well as mothers, wives, and sisters of military men the right to vote. Federal voting rights for Canadian women in general wouldn't come for another year.

Nursing Sister Sare's colleagues on the voyage to Halifax included Rena McLean, who was something of a celebrity. McLean's wealthy father had interests in real estate, factories, and a fishing fleet, and was also a member of the Canadian Senate. Senator John McLean lived in an expansive home in Souris, Prince Edward Island, with his wife, Matilda.

Nursing Sister Rena McLean of the Canadian Army Medical Corps.

Nicknamed "Bird," McLean was born June 14, 1880, in P.E.I. After graduating from Halifax Ladies' College in 1896, she studied nursing at a hospital in Rhode Island. Rena was working in the operating room of a Massachusetts hospital when the war broke out. She joined the CAMC in September 1914 and was included in the first wave of Canadian nurses sent to Europe that autumn.

At a time when women were expected to be cloistered and clueless, military nurses were exposed to danger, hardship, and gore. They assisted with surgery, administered medicine, applied and changed dressings, calmed the wounded, and consoled the dying. More mundane duties included tidying wards, making beds, stocking medical supplies, and cleaning mud and blood off injured men. Nursing sisters also provided patients with hot drinks, food, and cigarettes. They were expected to be unmarried and abide by a strict code of behaviour.

Nursing Sister McLean served at No. 2 Canadian Stationary Hospital in Le Touquet, France, then in England. In the fall of 1915, she was awarded the Royal Red Cross, 2nd Class (an honour given to nurses who showed exceptional skill and dedication). In June 1916, McLean worked on the SS *Scandinavian*, which took injured Canadians from Britain back home, then was posted to a hospital in England.

McLean was later transferred to the port of Salonika, Greece. Conditions there were awful, with brackish water, extreme temperatures, swarms of insects, and rampant disease. She went back to England in autumn 1917, then the following year, she was transferred once more to hospital-ship duty. She made a single round trip between the United Kingdom and Canada on HMHS *Araguaya*, worked briefly in England, then was assigned to the *Llandovery Castle* in March 1918.

Because of her family's prominence, Rena's visit to Halifax in 1918 was considered noteworthy enough to be covered by the press. "Senator McLean, who returned home to Souris, P.E.I. this week, came to Halifax to meet his daughter, Miss Rena McLean, a Red Cross nurse, who came from overseas with a number of invalided soldiers. Miss McLean has had some thrilling experiences since her departure from Canada over three years ago," stated the *Evening Mail* in March 1918.

McLean wore a star badge on her uniform, indicating she had been serving overseas in a war theatre since 1915. Many of her nursing peers sported the same medallion. Like Nurse Sare, she wrote a letter to her family while the *Llandovery Castle* was still at sea. "Here we are once more approaching Halifax, but still as far from home as ever…. This may be my last trip over, and, if it is, that means I don't get home until dear knows when, for as soon as I get to England, I am going to put in for France and once there it will be hard enough to get away," wrote McLean, in mid-June 1918.

While McLean was eager to return to land-based medicine, working on a hospital ship was considered a lighter assignment than serving near the frontline. "Nurses were often posted to transport duty after a prolonged period of service overseas or service under unusually difficult circumstances," notes the book *Sister Soldiers of the Great War: The Nurses of the Canadian Army Medical Corps.*

———

Hospital ships were not pleasure cruisers, however, and nurses were kept busy. Such vessels were essentially "floating hospitals" to quote a historical account. The *Llandovery Castle* contained facilities for surgery, X-ray examinations, and other procedures, along with vast stores of medical supplies and a laundry to wash and sterilize bed and hospital clothing.

The ship's X-ray department was "well-equipped" and its equipment in "excellent condition," states a report after the ship was inspected in Britain before it left for Canada.

The *Llandovery Castle*'s operating room was "fully equipped to deal with ordinary surgical cases. Drums of dressings were sterilized.... All instruments were polished and greased to prevent rusting." The operating facilities were "spotlessly clean and all equipment was in good condition," added the report.

Each patient on the *Llandovery Castle* received a ticket at embarkation with details about the ward, bed number, lifeboat, and dining space that had been assigned to them. During the voyage, patients wore "hospital blues" — a uniform of sorts — while their regular khaki uniforms were put in storage. Depending on their injury or rank, patients were accommodated in cots, bunkbeds — called "double-tier berths" in reports from the era — or cabins. Many of the interior cabins and walls in the *Llandovery Castle* had been removed or rearranged to provide space for these patients.

Sadly, there was no shortage of the latter. The First World War had been a bloodbath from the very start. On August 22, 1914, during the Battle of the Frontiers, twenty-seven thousand members of the French Army were killed in battle — a single-day toll that was higher than British fatalities on the opening day of the horrific Battle of the Somme.

The advent of static trench warfare, combined with unimaginative leadership, all but guaranteed the slaughter would continue. Infantrymen were forced to slog toward enemy trenches, while navigating barbed wire and thick mud. Sluggish ground assaults were usually stopped cold by emplaced machine guns, artillery, and rifle fire. New weapons such as flamethrowers and poison gas added to the horror.

In addition to staggering numbers of dead, the war produced countless gruesome injuries. Medical technology had advanced to the point where men who previously would have died on the battlefield could now be kept alive — not always a blessing.

"Some of the new patients have dreadful dreadful wounds. One young boy with part of his face shot away both arms gone & great wounds in both legs. Surely Death were merciful. Many head cases which are heartbreaking, & many many others. The men are so good & patient, & so grateful for even the smallest attention," wrote CAMC nurse Clare Gass in her diary on June 7, 1915, while working in France.

By 1918, Canada was fielding more than one hundred thousand troops in Europe. Through a combination of courage and new tactics, Canadian troops had achieved impressive victories, but even these triumphs came at a devastating cost. During the Battle of Vimy Ridge, which took place in northern France during April 1917, the victorious Canadian Corps suffered over 10,500 casualties, including nearly 3,600 deaths. Later that same year, members of the Canadian Expeditionary Force took part in the vicious Battle of Passchendaele in Belgium. While the Allies won the battle, four thousand Canadians died and twelve thousand were wounded.

Soldiers on hospital ships had paid some of the heaviest dues in the fight against German militarism. The basic policy in the Canadian army, as in all militaries, was to return ill or injured men to active duty as soon as they recovered. Canadian soldiers were only placed on hospital ships and sent home if the army thought they were too damaged for further use, at least in a combat role. Such patients faced a long rehabilitation in Canada, their fighting days over.

Before it was sunk, the *Llandovery Castle* made five voyages between Britain and Halifax, transporting sick and wounded Canadians. Two of these voyages were made under British auspices while the remainder occurred after Canada took over the vessel in March 1918. In total, the ship brought 3,215 patients across the ocean. Other than a handful of ailing nursing sisters, all these patients were men.

The *Llandovery Castle*'s last transport contained 644 patients, plus crew members and medical personnel. Twenty-seven patients were listed as "stretcher cases," while the remainder had injuries or illnesses "of a less serious nature," as a subsequent report put it.

A stretcher case referred to a soldier who couldn't move on their own power and needed to be carried around. The term "of a less serious nature" must be qualified. Over half the patients in the *Llandovery Castle*'s final transport "had lost either an arm or leg," notes a history of the British Merchant Navy. This was corroborated in Nurse McLean's letter: "[T]his trip, more than half our patients are amputation cases and would make your heart sick, only they are so cheerful and happy themselves," she wrote.

Such men might not be stretcher cases, but they were severely disabled.

A few patients hadn't been hit by bullets or shrapnel. Fourteen men had tuberculosis (TB) — a familiar scourge for soldiers in the wet, crowded trenches. Other diseases commonly suffered by soldiers at the Front included cholera, smallpox, trench foot, and typhoid. Another thirty-seven patients were listed as "mental," in the insensitive language of the day. These soldiers were psychiatric casualties, their minds and nerves crushed by the relentless slaughter.

Patients did their best to maintain their spirits during the crossing, which usually took a week or more. "We have all looked forward with the greatest possible degree of pleasure in anticipation to our voyage home. But I venture to doubt that even the most optimistic of the [soldiers] on board hoped for such a pleasurable trip as this has proved to be," stated a daily news bulletin written by *Llandovery Castle* patients.

This bulletin had been published June 15, while the ship was still at sea. The editor was identified as "Gunner J.W. Hearn" by the *Ottawa Citizen*, which would later run excerpts of the publication. His full name was James Wilfred Hearn, and like many patients on the *Llandovery Castle*, he had been in medical care a long time.

Born November 20, 1893, in Sydney, Nova Scotia, Hearn joined the CEF on September 23, 1914. According to his attestation paper, Hearn was single, and stood five foot six, with brown hair and blue eyes. He said he was a student (other documents listed his former occupation as journalist, which would make sense, given his role as newsletter editor). Hearn was shipped to Britain in October 1914 and posted to France the following year with the 2nd Brigade, Canadian Field Artillery.

On September 26, 1916, Hearn was badly wounded when a bullet tore through his left arm and penetrated his lung. His injury was listed as "GSW. Arm + Chest. Serious" on a medical form from No. 22 General Hospital, Camiers, France (GSW stood for gunshot wound). Antibiotics didn't exist at the time, and Hearn became ill, likely because of infection. He was transferred to the United Kingdom and made the rounds of many different hospitals. In early 1917, Hearn was placed in the Canadian Convalescent Hospital in Bearwood, Wokingham, which was housed in a former mansion. A year later, at the No. 5 Canadian General Hospital in Kirkdale, Liverpool, Hearn consulted a doctor about chest pain and shortness of breath.

"Says [the pain] is not constant but shoots into his chest. The shortness of breath appears on exertion," reads a handwritten entry on Hearn's medical file, from February 1918.

The medical case sheet also contained drawings of scars on Hearn's flesh and said he had been aspirated four times (that is, had fluid withdrawn from his chest with a needle). The document included a grim diagnosis: "disability permanent."

"Large foreign body lies against Aorta, moves with respiration and beats with heart," states a follow-up report, based on a February 27, 1918, examination at No. 11 Canadian General Hospital, Moore Barracks, Shorncliffe.

The same form contained a series of questions, asking if the patient was "Fit for duty" or "Fit for base duty." In both cases, the medical examiner typed "No." Asked if they recommended the patient be "Invalid(ed) to Canada" the doctor wrote "Yes" which is how Hearn ended up on the *Llandovery Castle*.

Fortunately for Hearn, the *Llandovery Castle* "was a well appointed ship.... The arrangements for the transport and care of returned invalid soldiers were excellent, with special accommodation for various orders of cases — those capable of moving about freely, those who had been lamed or had lost a leg, the tuberculous, the insane, etc. Each voyage has seen improvements in her equipment," according to a report written after the sinking.

This doesn't appear to be an exaggeration; the *Llandovery Castle* newsletter was filled with lavish praise for the crew and medical staff.

I would like, through the medium of publicity, to voice on behalf of the patients on board our heartfelt and most sincere appreciation of the kindness shown to us by the officer commanding troops, medical officers, matron, nursing sisters and personnel, without a single exception. A naturally tiresome journey has been made very pleasant, indeed, through the efforts of staff of the Llandovery Castle.… To the captain, officers, and crew of HMHS Llandovery Castle, I also, on behalf of their passengers, wish to extend thanks for a safe and as speedy as possible voyage — J.W.H.

Hearn and his fellow patients might have been entertained by the likes of William Jackson, a talented musician and member of the *Llandovery Castle* medical staff. Born in Yorkshire, England, in 1888, Jackson moved with his family to Saskatoon in the early 1900s. His father, John Jackson, became principal of the Conservatory of Music and "organized the first orchestra" in that city, according to the *Saskatoon Daily Star*.

Son, William, was a kindred spirit who played clarinet in the Saskatoon City Band and won a gold medal at a music competition for his musical abilities. He was working as a stenographer for the Saskatoon police when the war broke out. Jackson, who was a member of the Canadian Milita at the time, signed up in September 1914 and became a CAMC orderly.

In a letter from England published December 19, 1914, in the *Saskatoon Daily Star*, Jackson explained his duties: "We have to help the doctors attend to all cases of sickness and accidents in the battalion, and on route marches we render first aid to those who fall out."

A series of postings to No. 1 General Hospital (later renamed No. 1 Canadian General Hospital) ensued, along with Jackson being promoted to corporal in 1915. While appointed acting sergeant in 1917, Jackson's service record states that he reverted "to permanent rank of corporal at own request" later that same year. Corporal Jackson was transferred to the *Llandovery Castle* in the spring of 1918 but was apparently tardy in informing his parents about this new posting.

Orderly William Jackson of the Canadian Army
Medical Corps.

"Mr. and Mrs. John Jackson had received word of their son, William
Jackson, who is in active service, through P.H. Munroe. Mr. Munroe says
Mr. Jackson is now serving on a ship and he attended two concerts at which
he played," stated a small article published in late May in the *Saskatoon
Daily Star*. While it's unknown if Jackson gave a shipboard performance
to patients during the last voyage to Canada, he clearly wasn't shy about
demonstrating his musical prowess.

———

On Monday, June 17, 1918, just as Nursing Sister Sare predicted, the *Llandovery Castle* arrived in Halifax. The weather was pleasant that day, with a high of 20° Celsius, moderate wind and no rain.

Halifax was still recovering from a devastating explosion. On December 6, 1917, a cargo ship called the SS *Imo*, and a ship called the SS *Mont-Blanc*, which was packed with explosive war munitions, collided in Halifax Harbour. The *Mont-Blanc* caught fire then exploded, killing nearly two thousand people. Almost nine thousand people were injured — often by flying glass — and nearly every structure within half-a-mile of the blast epicentre was destroyed. It was the most powerful man-made explosion on Earth prior to the atomic bomb. Medical assistance poured in, the city was rebuilt, and soon ships were using the harbour again. It was imperative to keep the port open to maintain the war effort.

A chatty column called "Along the Waterfront" in the *Evening Mail*, a local newspaper, provided details about ships entering the harbour. "Another cargo of sugar has reached Halifax safely thru the waters where the German submarines are operating on this side of the Atlantic," the columnist added on June 17.

No doubt due to wartime security regulations, the *Llandovery Castle*'s arrival went unmentioned in the column. The same edition that day featured plenty of other war news. An article with the headline "Bloodiest Defeat for Germans Since Struggle Before Verdun" gloated over developments on the battlefield: "[T]he French cannon and machine guns levelled the closely ranked, gray, green figures down like a mowing machine cuts hay," wrote the *Mail*.

After docking, the *Llandovery Castle* was boarded by Dr. Robert Harold Ker, a lieutenant colonel in the CAMC. Dr. Ker had been a physician-surgeon in Vancouver before joining the CAMC in July 1916. Having served in Europe, he was at the time working as assistant director of medical services embarkation in Halifax. Dr. Ker's visit to the ship was far from just a formality. None of the crew, medical staff, or patients were allowed to disembark as the doctor scrutinized the ship and its paperwork. He described that visit later.

> I examined the nominal rolls of all the personnel on board, except the crew of the said ship. I mustered the medical personnel, and I also inspected all the patients, issuing the necessary orders for their distribution to hospitals and institutions in Canada…. Thereafter, I caused a search to be made of said ship, and ascertained that there were on board of her, in addition to the medical personnel and patients referred to, no other persons except the crew. All the medical personnel on board her were members of the Canadian Army Medical Corps and all the patients were invalided officers and soldiers of the Canadian Expeditionary Force. There were no prisoners on board the said ship, either as patients or otherwise.

This inspection process was necessary to ensure Canada was maintaining its treaty obligations regarding hospital ships.

The original Geneva Convention of 1864, an international initiative to bring humane standards to warfare, focused only on land-battles. Provisions to extend the Geneva Convention to cover fighting at sea were introduced in 1868 but were never ratified. It took until the first Hague Peace Conference, held in the Netherlands in 1899, for hospital ships to receive protections similar to those enjoyed by land-based units. The second Hague Peace Conference in 1907 renewed these protections; under Hague X, one of the conventions to emerge from the 1907 gathering, clearly identified hospital ships were immune from attack provided they weren't armed or carrying soldiers with weapons or war supplies. The 1907 Hague Conventions remained in effect throughout the Great War.

Once Dr. Ker finished his inspection, patients disembarked from the *Llandovery Castle*, some of them carried on stretchers. Before leaving, their khaki uniforms had been returned to them, and hospital blues discarded.

Once on shore, patients were dispersed to hospitals, rehabilitation centres, and convalescent homes across the country. Their care was now in the hands of a civilian organization called the Military Hospitals Commission.

Some patients would spend the rest of their lives in treatment, too badly injured to manage basic bodily functions, much less hold down a job.

After leaving the ship, newsletter editor Hearn was granted a furlough — that is, leave from military duties. He was told to report to the Pine Hill Convalescent Hospital in Halifax on July 1, so he could be assessed to determine his future in the army. While he was in no shape for fighting in the trenches, a desk job or some other support role remained a possibility. Sisters Sare and McLean, and anyone else who had penned a letter during the voyage, posted them and then prepared for the return voyage to Britain.

As patients from the *Llandovery Castle* contemplated their new lives in Canada, CAMC orderly Private Joseph Francis Lafountaine was coping with a family crisis. Lafountaine had signed up in September 1914 and served at the No. 2 Canadian General Hospital in France, and other posts before being transferred to the *Llandovery Castle*.

When the ship docked, he received devastating news from his mother. A telegram informed him his father was sick and likely to die. Could Lafountaine return to Toronto to see his dying father, asked his mother? Private Lafountaine hastily arranged for a leave of absence and rushed to Toronto with the understanding he would immediately return to the ship if so ordered.

On April 18, 1912, shipping magnate Sir Owen Philipps officially acquired the Union-Castle Mail Steamship Company. Sir Philipps, who also owned the Royal Mail Steam Packet Company, became chairman of the Union-Castle Line (which retained its name). Sir Philipps was from Wales and, to honour his background, decided that all new ships made by Union-Castle after the corporate buyout were named after Welsh castles. The first such vessel was a five-hundred-foot, twin-screw steamer built by Barclay, Curle & Co., in the vast shipyards of Glasgow, Scotland. The ship was christened *Llandovery Castle*.

With rows of portholes on each side, two masts, and a single funnel, the *Llandovery Castle* was registered on December 12, 1913. Put into service as a passenger liner shortly after it was completed in early 1914, the *Llandovery*

Castle primarily travelled from Britain to East Africa. The sinking of the *Titanic* had not diminished the popularity of ocean cruises.

An ad published December 26, 1913, in the *Western Morning News* noted that the *Llandovery Castle* was scheduled to depart from London, England, for East Africa via the Suez Canal in late January 1914.

"The advent of the Llandovery Castle marks an interesting and important epoch in the history of ocean travel," reported the *Newcastle Daily Journal* on January 8, 1914.

The ship wasn't in the same league as superstar passenger liners such as the *Britannic, Olympic,* and the ill-fated *Titanic* (all of them owned by the White Star Line). However, photographs taken shortly after the ship was launched reveal the *Llandovery Castle* to have been luxurious in its own right. The ship contained a large, airy, first class promenade deck with wooden benches, and a first class smoking room with couches, chairs, wooden panelling, a checkerboard floor, and skylight. The second class music room was also well-furnished, with a piano, and snug chairs. Even the third class dining saloon, while spartan, featured white tablecloths, wooden chairs, and palm trees for ambiance.

HMHS *Llandovery Castle.*

Throughout the summer of 1914, the presence of the *Llandovery Castle* was routinely noted in shipping news columns. On August 5, 1914, the *Nottingham Evening Post*, for example, stated that the ship had arrived in Gibraltar, en route to Southampton, England, from South Africa.

That summer, events in what is now the nation of Bosnia and Herzegovina would completely alter the *Llandovery Castle*'s destiny. On June 28, 1914, Archduke Franz Ferdinand, heir to the Austro-Hungarian Empire, was assassinated by a terrorist in Sarajevo. The major powers of Europe had long competed for military, economic, and colonial domination, and they soon stumbled into all-out war. The fighting, which commenced in early August, pitted the Central Powers (Germany and Austria-Hungary) against the Allies (Great Britain, France, and Russia). Canada wasn't fully independent at the time and automatically went to war when the United Kingdom did. The Ottoman Empire, Italy, and the United States stayed out of the conflict, at first. A host of other countries, both in Europe and elsewhere, were also drawn into the fray: Serbia, Montenegro, Belgium, Luxembourg, Portugal, Greece, Czechoslovakia, and Armenia fought at different times with the Allies, while Bulgaria fought with the Central Powers. Countries outside of Europe, including Japan, China, Brazil, and Siam (Thailand), also participated in the war.

In early 1915, the *Llandovery Castle* began doing mail runs, transporting letters as well as passengers. Putting letters on a ship was cheaper than sending telegrams across thousands of miles. Long-distance air mail was still in its infancy. In late January of that year, the ship left South Africa on a nineteen-day voyage to Plymouth, England.

"The Llandovery Castle brought 483 bags of mails, and 93 cases of parcels post," stated the *Western Morning News* after the ship arrived in Plymouth. While there, it took on two hundred tons of coal in preparation for a new journey, added the article.

The ship couldn't entirely escape the war's reach. Days after conflict broke out, nine crew members were "charged as enemy aliens" in Britain after "attempting to land at a prohibited port without permits," reported the (London) *Evening Standard*.

The men were German, but since they boarded the ship in South Africa before hostilities erupted, British officials decided not to imprison them.

Instead, the men were forced to register as foreigners and were told by the judge to "observe the laws of this country and to lead a peaceful existence till the war is over."

The *Llandovery Castle* would soon be drawn into the fighting. The British Army, which was suffering horrendous casualties in continental Europe, needed a vast fleet to transport reinforcements and return wounded men across the English Channel. To augment its ranks, the British Admiralty began to exercise its legal right to requisition civilian vessels that flew the Union Jack flag. The *Llandovery Castle* and other Union-Castle liners were taken over by the British government for the war effort.

"By the end of 1915, thirteen out of the pre-war intermediate Union-Castle fleet of seventeen steamers had been converted into hospital ships," states *Union-Castle Chronicle 1853–1953*.

The *Llandovery Castle* briefly transported troops in early 1916, then it was converted into a hospital ship for British soldiers. This entailed a drastic retrofit to create suitable accommodation for patients, crew, and members of the Royal Army Medical Corps (RAMC). Under British management, principal medical officers (PMOs) were given starboard side cabins near the promenade deck. Nursing sisters were placed in portside cabins, while rank-and-file RAMC members were housed in double-tier berths. A first class lounge on the bridge deck became a dining room, with a separate area designated as a sitting room for nurses. The second class music room on the promenade deck became a smoking room for officers.

The ship exterior was also changed dramatically, as per Hague rules.

In her memoir, *Lights Out: A Canadian Nursing Sister's Tale*, Katherine Wilson-Simmie, offers a first-hand description of what hospital ships looked like:

> The [HMHS] Asturias was the first hospital ship that I had seen at close range. Painted white from bow to stern, the ship was encircled by a wide band of green, studded with innumerable electric light bulbs. The Crosses reached from the water's edge to the very top of the ship. When we arrived it was growing dark, and we had an idea of what

the ship must look like on the water at night, all brilliantly lighted, like a huge jewel set forth to sail.

All Allied hospital ships sported a similar appearance. The idea was to be as visible as possible, so even at a distance, no one could mistake them for anything but a vessel on a medical mission.

As part of the process to convert it to hospital use, the *Llandovery Castle*'s name was communicated to the Central Powers — another Hague regulation. Then, it began travelling to ports in the Mediterranean Sea, taking on patients and then bringing them back to Britain. The *Llandovery Castle* was part of a vast armada performing similar duties at ports across Europe.

In her book, *Our Bit: Memories of War Service by a Canadian Nursing-Sister*, CAMC Nursing Sister Mabel Clint offers a vivid description of how patients were brought on board hospital ships.

> While we awaited orders to disembark in the morning, wounded began to arrive on the dock, in long lines of ambulances, and we had our first actual contact with war-wreckage, straight from the front. The walking cases were provided for on deck, and an endless row of stretchers came up the gangway. The staff were speed and gentleness incarnate, and not a word or groan came from the victims, who had of course already received first aid during the night. A crane lifted a dozen at once on a baggage platform and Sisters set about changing blood-soaked dressings, while orderlies entered particulars from the tags attached to each uniform. In a corner, covered with the Union Jack, a rough box indicated one who needed no attention. Only a few days before perhaps he had crossed the Channel absolutely 'fit.' Two other hospital ships arrived and were told about 2,000 would be embarked before evening.

Born June 21, 1876, in Quebec City, Clint enlisted in September 1914. She based her description on the *Carisbrook Castle*, another

Union-Castle-liner/mail-ship turned hospital ship, when it docked in Boulogne Harbour, France, shortly after hostilities broke out.

In the early period of the war, U-boats generally left hospital ships alone, and even gave merchant ships fair warning before sinking them. After spotting a merchant ship, a U-boat would make its presence known via flag signals, then order the ship to halt. "If he does not obey, the warship makes his orders more imperative by firing a blank shot as a warning. If then the merchantman tries to escape, the warship is justified in hitting the runaway," explains the *Journal of Submarine Commander von Forstner*.

Given that they were lightly armed, if at all, merchant ships usually gave up without a fight. Sailors from the sub would row to the ship and check documents regarding the vessel's cargo, nationality, crew, passengers, port of departure, and final destination.

"If the ship is [from a neutral country] and her papers are satisfactory, she is allowed to proceed, whereas an enemy's ship is either captured or sunk. If a neutral ship carries contraband of war, this is either confiscated or destroyed, but if it exceeds half the total cargo, then this ship is also condemned," writes von Forstner.

Once the merchant crew got away on lifeboats, the U-boat usually sank the ship with its deck gun, to save on torpedoes.

Given this chivalrous approach, a willful naïveté prevailed on early hospital ship voyages. Nurse Clint describes a 1915 voyage in the Mediterranean Sea thus:

> Up to this late, no hospital ships had been sunk by the enemy ... and so, brightly lighted, we streamed through the moonlit evenings, all hands on deck and rigging, while sing-songs were a nightly feature in the warm dusk. The ship's Medical staff gave an excellent concert, each member among officers and sisters being talented in some way.... Our C.A.M.C. personnel held many contests and a sports' day with the R.A.M.C. and swapped many yarns doubtless below decks.

Nursing Sister Lena Davis experienced an equally easygoing journey around the same time. Born in Beamsville, Ontario, in 1885, Davis worked as superintendent of nurses at a psychiatric hospital in Toronto before enlisting in the CAMC on April 7, 1915. She was posted to Canadian hospitals in France then Salonika. In 1916 Davis contracted malaria and was moved to Malta on the *Llandovery Castle*, which was still in British service.

"We are now anchored in Malta and have had a most pleasant trip from Salonika," noted Davis in a September 15, 1916, letter written on stationery with a *Llandovery Castle* letterhead while she travelled with a handful of other ill nurses.

> Five of us have Malaria, one had typhoid, and one just worn out.... We have most comfortable quarters. Each of us has a single cabin. In each there is a white enamel bed stead, wardrobe, wash stand, chest of drawers and a large window, not a port hole. I suppose because we are patients we have such comfortable quarters.... We have no idea what is going to happen [to] us next but rather expect we will have to change boats for England.

Nurse Davis would eventually be taken to Britain, but before then, another convalescing nursing sister, named Helen Fowlds, was also brought to Malta. Born in Hastings, Ontario, in 1889, Fowlds graduated from Grace Hospital, Toronto, as a nurse then enlisted in the CEF in 1915. She worked at Canadian hospitals in France and Greece. By summer 1916, exhausted and ill with a respiratory ailment, she requested a transfer and was transported from Greece on a familiar ship.

"It took ages to load but we finally started, reaching the Llandovery Castle about 4:30.... Two Sisters from #5 are going back and two English sisters.... My cold improves slowly but I feel awfully miserable still.... We have a cabin each and are quite comfortable," noted Fowlds in her diary, on September 25, 1916.

Fowlds would also end up in England, slowly recovering in hospital.

The light-hearted days of hospital ship travel didn't last for long. In early February 1915, Berlin launched unrestricted submarine warfare to break the stalemate on the Western Front. U-boats were permitted to sink any merchant or military ship near Great Britain and Ireland without warning. As an island nation, Britain depended on imports of food. By sinking incoming merchant ships, Germany figured it could starve the United Kingdom into submission. Berlin believed this was entirely fair, given that the British Royal Navy was blockading German ports, preventing merchant ships from docking.

"If we were to starve like rats in a trap, then surely it was our sacred right to cut off the enemy's supplies as well," notes a submariner in *U-Boat Stories: Narratives of U-Boat Sailors.*

The launch of unrestricted submarine warfare was not a secret — Germany placed ads in American papers warning travellers about the new policy. However, it was still a shock when the *Lusitania* was torpedoed by a U-boat on May 7, 1915. The attack enraged the U.S. government and public, and Germany temporarily halted unrestricted submarine warfare so as not to draw a new opponent into the war.

Another danger lurked in the waterways, however. Between 1915 and 1917, seven Allied hospital ships were sunk or damaged after hitting sea mines. The *Britannic* (sister ship to the *Titanic*, before being turned into a hospital ship) was one of the victims. It struck a sea mine in the Aegean Sea in late 1916, killing approximately thirty crew members and medical staff.

As the war progressed, life got tougher for U-boats. Great Britain began sending out "Q-ships" — military vessels disguised as run-down merchant steamers. These mystery ships acquired their unusual name from Queenstown, their home port in Ireland. The idea was to lure German subs by appearing as an easy target. When the U-boat was at point-blank range, preparing to send a boarding party to search the Q-ship, hidden deck guns on the latter would open fire, blowing the sub apart. Such tactics infuriated German sailors, who regarded them as underhanded.

"The seas were full of U-boat decoys cunningly tricked out in various disguises," wrote a disgusted sailor in *U-Boat Stories.*

Undeterred, Germany massively expanded its U-boat fleet, from under forty subs at the start of the war to nearly one hundred by early 1917. With the additional vessels, Berlin was convinced it possessed the naval firepower to bring Britain to its knees. Unrestricted submarine warfare resumed in February 1917. A set of German directives issued that year took things a step further; U-boat commanders were given permission to attack hospital ships, under certain conditions, in the Mediterranean Sea and in a "maritime zone" that extended from the western reaches of the English Channel up into the North Sea. Hospital ships in the latter zone would be "considered as belligerent and [would] be attacked without further consideration," stated a German memorandum. This drastic strategy reflected German paranoia that hospital ships were illicitly transporting soldiers and war supplies.

Germany alerted the Allies to its brutal policy change regarding hospital ships through diplomatic channels. Unsurprisingly, British authorities vehemently protested and denied hospital ships were violating Hague rules in any way. However, even before the directives had been issued, hospital ships were being marked for destruction.

On March 17, 1916, a Russian hospital ship named the SS *Portugal* was torpedoed by a German sub in the Black Sea. There weren't any patients on board, but eighty-five crew and medical personnel died. The *Portugal* was flying a prominent Red Cross flag when it was hit. It became the first Allied hospital ship to be deliberately sunk by a U-boat.

Almost exactly one year later, the *Asturias* — the same vessel mentioned by Nursing Sister Wilson-Simmie in her memoir — became the first British hospital ship to be torpedoed by a German sub. The ship had been travelling at night off the Devonshire coast with its hospital lights on. It wasn't carrying any patients, but several crew members and medical personnel died in the attack. The ship was beached and later towed to Plymouth, England.

Just a few days later, the *Gloucester Castle* (another former Union-Castle liner turned hospital ship — was torpedoed near the Isle of Wight. It was transporting four hundred patients. Fortunately, the ship didn't sink, and the patients were transferred to other boats. Following the transfer, the *Gloucester Castle* was towed to a safe port.

Before he travelled on the *Llandovery Castle*, CAMC officer Thomas Lyon nearly fell victim to Germany's more aggressive submarine strategy. After enlisting, Lyon served as commanding officer of the Canadian Convalescent Hospital in Kent, England, then was transferred to No. 5 Canadian General Hospital in Salonika. Like many of his Salonika colleagues, Lyon became ill, first with dysentery then pneumonia. In May 1917 Lyon was taken to Malta on the *Dover Castle* (also a former Union-Castle steamship).

The *Dover Castle* dropped Lyon and other patients off in Malta then boarded six hundred new patients and set a course for Britain. On May 26, 1917, off Algeria, the ship was torpedoed by a U-boat. Most of the patients were transferred to other vessels before the *Dover Castle* sank, but it was still a close call for Lyon, who was later transported to France and then England without incident.

Sub attacks on hospital ships became so frequent a British company published a booklet about the topic. Released in 1917, *The War on Hospital Ships* offers first-hand survivor accounts and makes for very grim reading.

A full-page article published May 29, 1918, in the *Evening Star* in Halifax and other newspapers, offered further details about the war on hospital ships. Headlined "Nurses and Wounded as Targets for Hun Torpedoes," the piece was accompanied by a cartoon featuring drowning nurses, a sinking ship, and a gloating Kaiser-like figure on top of a surfaced submarine.

"Recently we have had another record of German barbarity in the torpedoing of the hospital ship [HMHS] Rewa, made dramatic because the missile of destruction struck her where the Red Cross of Mercy was painted on her side, as if it were a bull's eye for just such murderous shots," read the opening lines, which referenced the British hospital ship *Rewa*, torpedoed January 4, 1918, in the Bristol Channel.

If the rhetoric was over-the-top, the article offered a strange but plausible explanation for the barrage of questions thrown at *Llandovery Castle* victims about American aviators. Quoting from an unnamed German media outlet, the article said the pilot myth likely stemmed from an incorrect appraisal of documents found on captured U.S. servicemen.

"Prisoners openly admit that it is the general practice for aviators to enter American [Army] Ambulance Service for their passage to Europe and to cross on hospital ships. After they are landed in France they immediately transfer to the automobile corps and thence into the air service," states the German report cited in the *Evening Star* article.

This would seem a rather roundabout way for American pilots to join the war effort (and unnecessary, given that the United States had troop ships of its own). The *Evening Star* suggested that the Germans were confusing an earlier practice with current policy. "The aviators which Germany refers to as having crossed to France for Red Cross work crossed at their own expense on regular passenger ships before [the United States] entered the war and were driving neutral ambulances," states the feature story.

These early volunteers stuck around after the United States became involved in the war, and some might indeed have been captured. Out of ignorance or malice, their German captors conflated "passenger ships" with "hospital ships" and a propaganda legend was born.

The article also managed to be eerily prescient, despite its sloppy reporting. The writer mentioned a February 26, 1918, attack on the hospital ship HMHS *Glenart Castle*, then wrote: "Shortly after the Glenart Castle, the big Llandovery Castle, on mercy bent, was torpedoed."

Given this story appeared a month before the *Llandovery Castle* really was attacked, the journalist was either clairvoyant or mixed up the ship with the *Guildford Castle*. The latter was a hospital ship torpedoed March 10, 1918, while transporting patients in the Bristol Channel. The *Guildford Castle* had its navigation lights on and was flying a Red Cross flag. On this occasion, the torpedo didn't explode, no one was hurt or killed, and the ship safely made its way back to port.

Despite these risks, in early 1917 the Canadian government decided to establish its own fleet of hospital ships. Ottawa would charter five British-made vessels during the war to transport Canadian soldiers across the ocean. In addition to the *Llandovery Castle*, these vessels were the *Araguaya*, *Neuralia*, *Essequibo*, and *Letitia*. They made a total of forty-two voyages during the war, returning 28,238 ill and injured patients to Canada.

A sixth vessel, His Majesty's Canadian Hospital Ship (HMCHS) *Prince George*, never saw action. A former coastal steamer on the West Coast, the *Prince George* was requisitioned by the Canadian government as a hospital ship in August 1914. It quickly became clear the German military had little interest in the Pacific region. The *Prince George* was decommissioned from hospital duties in September, without having transported any wounded Canadian soldiers.

As Canada developed its own hospital ship fleet, it requested additional assistance from Great Britain. In response, British officials arranged for the *Llandovery Castle* to convey 629 Canadian patients from Liverpool to Halifax on September 19, 1917. These patients were supervised by the Royal Medical Army Corps.

Around the same time, after recovering from his illness, Thomas Lyon was posted to HMHS *Araguaya* with the rank of captain. One of his colleagues on the ship was Arthur Knight. During his time on the *Araguaya*, Lyon dutifully wrote meticulous reports. Mostly, these reports touched on medical topics, but on a voyage to Halifax, Lyon offered details about the weather. "[B]y the time we were getting into Mid Ocean the weather was warm with little sunshine and the ship was continually being stopped by small patches of fog day and night," stated Lyon on December 8, 1917.

In an era before satellite mapping, lidar (light detection and ranging — a remote sensing system that analyses the light reflected from lasers shone underwater), sonar, and radar, fog was a deadly menace that could obscure rocks, shoals, sandbars, icebergs, and other ships. When heavy fog took hold, ships slowed drastically or stopped altogether.

On February 16, 1918, the *Llandovery Castle* made another voyage from Liverpool, with 648 Canadian patients and a British medical staff. Shortly after returning to the United Kingdom, the ship was turned over to Canadian authorities, who quickly began assembling their own medical team while retaining the original crew.

In March 1918, Lyon and Knight were both transferred to the *Llandovery Castle*. Lyon was promoted to major while Knight would serve as an acting sergeant. Thomas Macdonald was appointed commander of CAMC personnel on board.

Born December 15, 1877, in Port Mulgrave, Nova Scotia, Macdonald graduated from Bellevue Hospital Medical College, New York, in 1900. He

Lieutenant Colonel Thomas Macdonald of the Canadian
Army Medical Corps.

practised medicine in Port Hawkesbury, Nova Scotia. He became active in
the Canadian Militia, then joined the CAMC on April 15, 1916.

Macdonald was shipped to the United Kingdom. A variety of postings in
England ensued: at the Canadian Convalescent Hospital in Bearwood Park;
the No. 11 Canadian General Hospital in Moore Barracks, Shorncliffe; and
the Canadian Military Hospital in Liverpool. The latter was a medical clearing centre for Canadians heading home on hospital ships.

Macdonald was transferred to France in mid-1917, serving in various
posts, then was ordered back to Britain in March 1918 to take up duties
on the *Llandovery Castle*. He travelled to Liverpool and supervised the
loading of equipment and supplies for the *Llandovery Castle*'s inaugural
cross-Atlantic voyage with a Canadian medical staff.

On March 23, 1918, while being manoeuvred to a new position by tug-
boats to accommodate another vessel at the pier, the *Llandovery Castle* was

hit by a barge. The ship's starboard propeller was damaged, and the vessel was placed in dry dock for repairs. It was an inauspicious beginning for Canada's latest hospital ship.

Within a few days, the propeller was fixed, and the *Llandovery Castle* was ready to take on patients. Embarkation began at 1:00 p.m. March 28, and was completed in two hours. The first transport included thirty-eight officers, twenty-nine troops suffering from psychological issues, seventy-six tubercular cases, twenty amputees, and thirteen stretcher cases, notes Macdonald in a report. Another 430 patients were lumped together as "various cases."

The ship left Liverpool on March 29. Once underway, staff, orderlies, and patients who were ambulatory were put through fire and emergency preparedness drills. If the worst happened and the *Llandovery Castle* had to be abandoned, every person on board knew which lifeboat they were supposed to go to.

In his detailed report, Macdonald touched on cultural differences between Canada and Great Britain. Macdonald had wanted to implement a meal plan for patients called "the Canadian Hospital Diet." He was vague on what this consisted of, but this diet was deemed too expensive by administrators. In its place, patients had to subside on the "Imperial Hospital Diet," which was apparently lacking compared to the Canadian Diet — prior to embarkation, patients were only given "tea, bread, and butter" for supper, complained Macdonald.

To improve the situation, the CAMC commander added porridge to the patients' breakfast and "fish or an equivalent" for supper. This still did not prove sufficient.

"On Tuesday, 2-4-18, there was a general complaint made at the breakfast to the orderly officer, that the patients were not getting sufficient to eat. I took the matter up with the chief [s]teward and decided to amend the diet for the remainder of the trip," wrote Macdonald.

Macdonald doesn't offer any specifics about the dietary amendments but says "there were no complaints" following the shift.

In the same report, he praises the nursing sisters on board, while making some staffing recommendations for future voyages. "The permanent Nursing Sisters carried on every day and did very efficient work, but I cannot too strongly recommend that the Total Nursing Staff be made permanent, as of the seven temporary Nursing Sisters, four were sick 4 days and one for 3 days, all suffering from mal-de-mer.... By having a permanent staff that would be free from Mal-de-mer, the work would then be fairly divided, and not as it is at present," wrote Macdonald, using a fancy term for "seasickness."

Macdonald noted that Thomas Lyon served as "Sanitary Officer" and made daily inspections of the ship's sanitation facilities. The CAMC commander also had good things to say about the onboard chaplains, who "did considerable work in providing entertainment for the patients and attending to their moral welfare."

Discipline "was satisfactory, with one exception" (that went unmentioned), and "relations between the C.A.M.C. Officers and Personnel and the Ship's Officers and Crew left nothing to be desired," added Macdonald.

One patient, in Ward G, came down with a bad case of pneumonia during the journey and was transferred to another ward. Medical staff feared the man might die, but he survived.

Following disembarkation in early April, the *Llandovery Castle* went through an elaborate process of inspection, repairs, reprovisioning, and restaffing, then headed back to Britain for more patients.

The *Llandovery Castle* continued going back and forth, delivering ill and injured men to Canada, although not everything went smoothly. In early May, as the ship was prepped in Britain, Major W. Percival Yetts of the Royal Army Medical Corps discovered something amiss. "I have the honour to report that after embarkation had been finished in H.S. 'LLANDOVERY CASTLE' yesterday evening, I happened to notice on board an orderly carrying an article of Officers baggage from which protruded the hilts of two swords.... I called the attention of the Adjutant Capt. Yates, to these and suggested that he should send them to this office before the ship sailed together with directions as to their disposal," wrote Major Yetts, in a memo dated May 7, 1918.

Major Yetts was the deputy assistant director of medical services (DADMS), embarkation in Avonmouth, U.K. He sent his memo to the director of medical services, embarkation (DMS) and the notice went up the chain of command.

The case "warrants very careful investigation.... I am directed to request that a report be forwarded as soon as possible, and that in the meantime, orders be issued to ensure that similar cases will not arise in future," stated a May 14 letter from an official at the Headquarters of the Overseas Military Forces of Canada to the DMS.

The swords probably belonged to a wounded Canadian officer who wanted to keep them as souvenirs. While they posed little threat to any Germans, their presence violated Hague Convention rules. Patients on hospital ships were not allowed to take guns, swords, or any weapons on the journey to Canada.

A few days after the sword controversy, there was a terrible reminder of the dangers facing Canadian medical staff. On the evening of May 19, 1918, the No. 1 Canadian General Hospital, No. 7 Canadian General Hospital, and No. 9 Canadian Stationary were attacked by German bombers. All three facilities were part of a vast military medical zone established near Étaples, France, which also featured British hospitals. This wasn't the first time German planes bombed Canadian medical facilities — Salonika hospitals had also been subjected to aerial attacks. It was, however, one of the worst raids of its kind. In an article published in the August 1918 *Bulletin of the Canadian Army Medical Corps*, Lieutenant Colonel J.A. Gunn, CAMC, wrote about the attack on No. 1 Canadian General Hospital:

> The first bombs that fell in our line, evidently incendiary, landed on our men's quarters, which were situated close to the railway. These were soon in flames and afforded an excellent target for the enemy, who within a short time dropped eight or ten bombs in this area. The fact that most of the men were asleep accounts for the large number of casualties. More than half of the personnel indeed were casualties, with fifty-one N.C.O. [non-commissioned officers] and O.R. killed and forty-five wounded, of whom six subsequently died.

The lieutenant colonel's account continued, "Immediately following the dropping of the bombs on the men's quarters several were dropped in the neighbourhood of the officer's and sister's quarters.... Another [bomb] fell at one end of the sister's quarters and practically destroyed one wing. Fortunately this wing was used by sisters who were on night duty, and so the rooms were empty at the time, otherwise the casualties among the nursing sisters would have been much greater. As it was, one sister was killed."

The nurse in question was Katherine Maud Macdonald, who was born in 1893 and enlisted in 1917 in London, Ontario. Two other nursing sisters — Margaret Lowe and Gladys Wake — would also die in the following days from injuries incurred during the attack. Between the three hospitals, scores of patients and staff were killed or injured.

Tragic as the raid was, it could have been much worse. No. 9 Canadian Stationary Hospital hadn't received any patients; however, some medical staff were injured or killed. Of the 1,156 patients being treated at No. 1 Canadian General Hospital, approximately 300 had femur injuries, which required that their legs be immobilized. It would have been impossible to move the men during the raid. Fortunately, the femur ward was not hit. Other patients were put under their beds or moved to safety by CAMC staff.

"The conduct of the personnel on this occasion was all that could be desired. While the raid was yet in progress stretcher parties hastened to remove the wounded from the scene of action to where they might receive first aid, and, while yet enemy aircraft circled about, nursing sisters went about their work with perfect coolness," reported a Colonel Etherington, of the raid on No. 7 Canadian General Hospital, in the *Bulletin of the Canadian Army Medical Corps*.

One of the medical personnel at this hospital was Henry Reid MacCallum, born in Turkey to Christian missionary parents in 1897. MacCallum would later become a philosophy professor at the University of Toronto, a highly regarded author, and a colleague of renowned academic Northrop Frye. At the time, he was just a very young stretcher bearer for the CAMC.

MacCallum maintained a diary throughout his service, which blends observations about fellow medical personnel and jaunts to Paris with tales of horror and violence. Regarding the air raid at No. 7 Canadian General Hospital, he wrote tersely, "Bombs among the wards. Terrible. Lasted for about two hours."

German bombers would return, attacking Canadian hospitals in Doullens, France, on May 29 and 30, and at Étaples once more, on May 31, causing more death and injury.

Against this backdrop of increased violence against medical staff, the *Llandovery Castle* underwent preparations for another voyage to Canada. On June 5, a day before the ship was supposed to leave Liverpool, it was inspected by a Captain A.F. Menzies. Captain Menzies passed his observations to his superior, and they became the basis of a report by the deputy director of medical services. Among other details, the captain noted that prep-work hadn't been completed.

"Civilian artisans who had been doing certain repairs were still at work. Charwomen were at work in the wards, and the salt water for flushing the lavatories had not been turned on. The ship, naturally, was rather dirty," noted the report by the DDMS.

The following day, Captain Menzies returned for a follow-up inspection. He found everything in order: "All beds had been made, the ship had been thoroughly cleaned and was ready to receive patients. The change in the appearance of the wards and decks was sufficient evidence that the staff were capable and keen on their work," states the report.

The same document offered details about the layout of the patient wards. Wards A, C, J, and K contained single-tier cots for "other ranks, ordinary cases." Ward H had single-tier cots for "nervous cases" for other ranks, while Wards B, E, F, and G were fitted with double-tier cots, also for other ranks. Ward L, located on the upper promenade deck, contained single-tier cots for officers while the dining room for patients was in Ward D. Other injured or ill officers were housed in cabins.

"The feeding arrangements, lavatories, etc., for these wards are quite satisfactory, with the exception of Wards J. and K. In these two wards the patients' dishes are washed and stored in what was one of the bath rooms connected with the lavatory," wrote the DDMS.

Captain Menzies had a few issues with the living quarters for medical personnel: "[T]here are no cupboards, dish racks or sinks in the pantry.... Food left over from a meal, such as bread, tins of jam, etc. is kept on a table. This must result in a waste of food and certainly makes the pantry look very untidy," sniffed the DDMS. The ship was cleared for departure, however, and patients began embarking.

In addition to taking on patients and provisions, the *Llandovery Castle* would be transporting documents back to Canada. A detailed memo from the headquarters of Canada's Ministry of Overseas Military Forces in London, dated June 4, provided strict instructions regarding these documents.

> After embarkation of Officers has been completed you will receive from the Canadian Embarkation Officer SEVEN copies of Officers Nominal Rolls which will be disposed of as follows: —
> 4 Copies to be delivered by hand, immediately on arrival in Canada to Director of Records, Ottawa
> 1 Handed to Immigration Officer at Port of Disembarkation
> 1 to Officer i/c [in charge] Disembarkation at Port of Disembarkation
> 1 to Officer i/c Clearing Depot, Quebec

The "nominals rolls" referred to were personnel lists of CAMC staff onboard the ship. The memo followed this up with further, very precise directions on passing off documents regarding pay and other administrative matters.

The *Llandovery Castle* left Liverpool on June 6, presumably with these important documents in hand. While protected under the Hague Convention, military authorities were under no illusions that the ship was invulnerable. "A hospital ship is exposed to all the dangers of the sea, and senior N.C.O.s trained to take charge in an emergency would seem to be a necessity," noted the DDMS report.

———

The *Llandovery Castle* received a high-ranking visitor on June 19, 1918, while it was in Halifax. Lieutenant Colonel McKelvey Bell, director of medical services for the Invalided Soldiers Commission, dropped by the ship to chat with CAMC personnel. He briefly conversed with Thomas Lyon and Lieutenant Colonel Macdonald, and some of the nurses, including Rena McLean. Of the ninety-four members of the CAMC making the return journey to Britain, fourteen were nursing sisters.

In addition to McLean, the nurses included Gladys Sare, Christina Campbell (born in Inverness, Scotland), Carola Josephine Douglas (born in Toronto), Alexina Dussault (born in Saint-Hyacinthe, Quebec), Minnie Follette (born in Port Grenville, Nova Scotia), Margaret Fortescue (born in York Factory, Hudson's Bay Territory, Manitoba), Minnie Katherine Gallaher (born in Kingston, Ontario), Jessie McDiarmid (born in Ashton, Ontario), Mary Agnes McKenzie (born in Toronto), Mae Belle Sampson (born in Simcoe County, Ontario), Anna Stamers (born in Saint John, New Brunswick), Jean Templeman (born in Ottawa), and Matron Margaret "Pearl" Fraser (born in New Glasgow, Nova Scotia).

While they came from varied backgrounds and birthplaces, the fourteen nursing sisters had much in common. They were all unmarried — the norm for Great War nurses — most were in their twenties or thirties, and several had been serving since the early days of the war. Nurses McLean, Sampson, Follette, Dussault, and Matron Fraser signed up in 1914, while Douglas, Fortescue, Gallaher, McDiarmid, Templeman, Stamers, and Campbell volunteered the following year.

Precarious health was something else that united them; stress, long hours, and coping with blood and pain under harsh working conditions produced a plethora of physical and mental health problems among medical staff. The Salonika front was particularly brutal in this regard.

"The patient went off duty at Salonika about June 1st. She had been on nighty duty for two months and had been suffering from insomnia and loss of appetite.… She has found the heat in Salonika very trying and has lost weight considerably … she is in need of a prolonged rest," reads a medical case sheet for Nursing Sister Campbell, from mid-1916.

Another report described her as "in a very nervous condition, frequently crying when spoken to. Col. Purvis Stewart has seen N.S. Campbell and has recommended a sea voyage, the climate being unsuitable for her."

Nursing Sister Christina Campbell of the Canadian Army Medical Corps.

Campbell was declared "unfit for any service" and "invalided" to England for treatment and rest.

A medical board report from Boulogne, France, dated January 5, 1917, concluded that Nursing Sister Fortescue was "suffering from debility" — or general physical weakness — due to "overwork" and "arduous nursing duties." The medical board recommended Fortescue be granted sick leave in England to recuperate. The following spring, Fortescue was admitted to hospital with bronchitis, a condition attributable to "climatic conditions

Nursing Sister Minnie Follette of the Canadian Army Medical Corps.

in France" and her military service, according to a May 2, 1918, medical report. The report graciously noted that Fortescue's infection was not "aggravated by the Officer's own negligence or misconduct."

After working for years in France, Nursing Sister Follette became ground down and burned out. She was diagnosed with nervous exhaustion. "This Nursing Sister is suffering from the strain of constant duty with the 1st C.E.F. for part of the time in a Casualty Clearing Station. She requires a considerable time of leave for complete recovery," stated her medical board report, from April 8, 1916.

Follette got better, then, like Fortescue, she developed bronchitis — respiratory infections being an occupational hazard in crowded medical wards.

Nursing Sister Gallaher was also treated for bronchitis and myalgia (muscle pain) during the course of her duties, while McKenzie was treated for pyorrhoea (gum disease). In 1917 Sampson was hospitalized with diphtheria. That same year, in Salonika, Douglas developed a serious infection in one of her fingers that required nearly two-weeks of medication and care. Stamers was also briefly taken off duty due to inflammation of her ear canal. This affliction put her in hospital for treatment in mid-1916 in Étaples, France.

Despite all they had been through, the nursing sisters on the *Llandovery Castle* continued to return to duty after recovering from their infirmities. Besides being devoted to medical care, many of the nurses had personal ties with each other. Nursing Sister Templeman, for example, was good friends with Nursing Sister Stamers. After training to be a nurse in Minneapolis, Templeman returned to her hometown of Ottawa to work before enlisting in the CEF. At No. 1 Canadian General Hospital in France (the same facility later bombed by German planes) she met Stamers, and the pair became close. They travelled back to Canada together on leave in 1917. Upon returning to Britain, Stamers and Templeman worked together at Ontario Military Hospital (later No. 16 Canadian General Hospital) in Orpington, Kent, then were posted to the *Llandovery Castle* in March 1918.

While docked in Halifax, Templeman wrote a letter to her father and sisters, one of whom was named Maude. "Llandovery Castle Hospital Ship, G.P.O. [General Post Office] Halifax, Dear Father: I guess Maude has told you I am in transport duty and will probably be on all summer, perhaps till Christmas. We were on duty all the way over here and will not have anything to do going back. They tell me you have moved to 330 James street again. How do you like that?" asked Templeman.

The letter continued: "How have you been all spring? I am enclosing a copy of the hospital paper. You might find it interesting. I am trying to get some letters written before the boat sails this morning so we will have to close. With love — Jean."

Templeman's letter, as well as excerpts from the hospital newspaper, were printed in the *Ottawa Citizen* after her death. While the outgoing editors of this newsletter had disembarked in Halifax, they clearly hoped a new team would keep the publication in print.

"A number of contributions received have been unavoidably held over owing to lack of space caused by paper shortage. It is intended on the next voyage out to issue another copy of this journal, in which all items held over from this issue will be published. (The Editor)," stated the last edition of the patient newsletter.

On June 20, Dr. Ker inspected the *Llandovery Castle* a second time. Later, he declared under oath:

> Upon receiving notice that she was ready to sail, I visited the said ship, and ascertained that there were no changes in the medical personnel, but that all the medical personnel which arrived in the said ship were returning with her, with the exception of one or two who had been given leave, and there were no additions to the medical personnel.... There were no persons, prisoners or otherwise, who proceeded from Halifax on the said ship on the 20th of June except the medical personnel referred to and the crew of said ship.

A series of bureaucrats, including the chief military embarkation officer, the deputy assistant director of embarkation in Halifax, and the naval transport officer, signed off on Dr. Ker's declaration. Only then was the ship allowed to leave Halifax.

As the *Llandovery Castle* steamed out of Halifax Harbour, a few people scheduled to be on the voyage were absent. Private Lafountaine was still in Toronto, keeping a vigil on his dying father. No one had ordered him to report to duty before the ship left, so he stayed with his family.

The ocean was relatively calm as the *Llandovery Castle* returned to Britain. The ship didn't have to contend with storms, winds, or rough seas. "Ideal summer weather prevailed. All went well and uneventfully until Thursday evening June 27," notes a subsequent government report.

CHAPTER THREE

"Hospital Ship Sinkings Were Foul Murder"

A fter escaping from U-*86*, Lifeboat No. 4 managed to travel about seventy miles in thirty-six hours. Flashlights provided a bit of illumination, but the men in the lifeboat were still cold and hungry. There hadn't been time to put on warmer clothes before the ship sank. Survivors who spent time in the water were forced to endure the journey in soaking wet clothing. While it was late June, the North Atlantic Ocean air was cool, and the men shivered.

The lifeboat contained emergency rations for fifty passengers, but the two-dozen occupants ate and drank sparingly, trying to make supplies last. No one knew how long they would be at sea. In a day and a half adrift, each man had eaten only a couple of biscuits, washed down with a mouthful of water. This meagre diet was augmented by tobacco. Captain Sylvester was happy to share his pipe and the tobacco he had retrieved from his cabin before the *Llandovery Castle* sank. The men took turns trying to smoke the pipe, which elevated morale even if "the tobacco was of little use because it got water-soaked," wrote the *San Francisco Examiner*.

On the morning of Saturday, June 29, a British destroyer called the *Lysander* spotted the forlorn lifeboat while returning from a patrol. Commander Francis Twigg ordered the destroyer to steer closer to the lifeboat to investigate. The commander had no idea who the occupants were, or where they came from. While most chivalric principles had been discarded by this point in the war, ships still routinely rescued lifeboats and took in survivors, regardless of their nationality.

The destroyer approached Lifeboat No. 4. "[When] we were near, we found it held five officers and 19 men, survivors of the hospital ship. We stopped engines and picked them up," reported a *Lysander* officer to the *Times* of London.

The men in Lifeboat No. 4 cheered when they realized they were about to be rescued. They were taken on board the *Lysander*, warmed, and fed. The six Canadian survivors consisted of Sergeant Knight, Major Thomas Lyon, and privates William Pilot, Shirley Taylor, Frederick Cooper, and George Hickman.

The surviving British sailors included Captain Edward Sylvester, Second Officer Leslie Chapman, Fourth Officer Darley Barton, Purser Henry Evans, Lamp Trimmer Albert Victor Record, Able Seaman Walter Scott, Assistant Steward Steven Savage, Deck Steward Archibald Heather, and ten other men.

"After enjoying a good meal, they took us to Plymouth," wrote Pilot, in his diary.

The *Lysander* crew became the first outsiders to learn about the attack on the *Llandovery Castle*. Since a distress message hadn't been sent, naval authorities knew nothing about the sinking. The *Lysander* sent messages by wireless telegraph informing U.K. officials about what happened. British naval authorities dispatched ships to the scene of the attack to search for more survivors, but only bits of wreckage and a single empty lifeboat were found.

The *Lysander* docked first in Queenstown, Ireland, then in Plymouth, England, on June 30, after which the rescued men were taken to hospital. Medical notes for five of the Canadians — Cooper, Taylor, Pilot, Hickman, and Knight — have been preserved. Written at King George Hospital in Waterloo, U.K., the notes indicate that the men were treated for exposure. This somewhat vague term alluded to the physical effects of being tossed on the ocean in an open-air lifeboat on chilly waters for thirty-six hours.

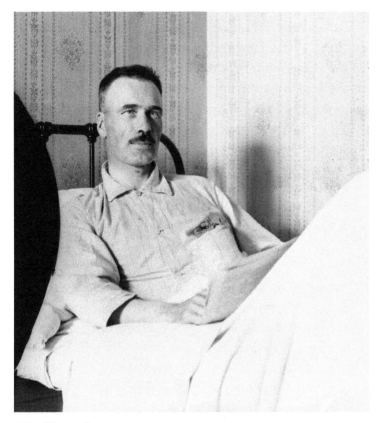

Major Thomas Lyon.

Some of the men were interviewed in hospital. A grim document titled, "Report of 4 of the Survivors of the 'Llandovery Castle'" contains their clipped remarks. While written in a dry, matter-of-fact tone, the report still alluded to the effects of trauma: "The men seemed to be fairly shaken up by their experience, and were not very communicative," states the document.

Major Lyon, who was taken to a hospital in London for treatment of his broken foot, was slightly more forthcoming. He gave a detailed statement to officials then later talked to reporters from a hospital bed. Lyon spoke at some length to the press, his comments conveying equal measures of anger and sadness.

"[H]ere I am, with every comfort and attention, but I cannot help but feel that if the Germans had not interfered, we could possibly have saved many of those poor souls in the water clinging to wreckage and crying for help that never came," stated Lyon to reporters.

Today, we might suggest Lyon was suffering from survivor's guilt, a common reaction among people who have lived through a shattering experience and wonder why they were spared while others lost their lives.

Lyon expressed sympathy for the target of the U-boat's investigation: "I dread to think what would have happened to an American flying officer, had he been in my shoes."

––––––––

Did U-86 have secret information about passengers on the *Llandovery Castle*? Some newspapers suggested that German spies were at work.

"The survivors and naval authorities here believe that the U-boat torpedoed the hospital ship deliberately on information from spies in Canada or the United States, transmitted since the ship sailed.... The commander of the German submarine accused Captain Sylvester, master of the Llandovery Castle, of carrying eight American aviators. In reality eight medical officers were booked to sail, but one cancelled his passage at the last minute," stated the *Daily Standard* from Kingston, Ontario.

The *New York Times* picked up on this theme. The paper ran an interview with an unnamed "Captain of a British steamship" who just arrived at "an Atlantic Port" from England. The captain "said that Halifax was full of spies who went there as representatives of various business firms and hung around the hotels picking up information for the enemy by listening to the conversation of the shipping men."

The anonymous source urged people not to openly discuss the "arrival or departure of steamships in Halifax over the telephone, as there were always persons listening in," continued the *Times*.

"He said there was no doubt that the information regarding the departure of the Llandovery Castle and her passengers was obtained by German spies in this way and was probably sent to the U-boat which has been lurking off the coast and relayed by her to the other side," added the *Times*.

Halifax was a major port city, so it would make sense to place spies there to glean information about outgoing ships. The *U-86*'s insistent questions about American aviators had seemed unusually precise, as if someone had provided insider information to the German crew. Or, as the *Evening Star* suggested, the obsession with American pilots might have stemmed from a misunderstanding about volunteers travelling overseas to Europe before the United States had entered the war.

Then again, the incessant questioning about American aviators might have just been a ruse on the part of the U-boat crew.

The Germans "pretended to be sure that aviators were aboard. I have my doubts about this belief being genuine, my idea being that the Germans simply used this as a pretext for the torpedoing of the Llandovery Castle," Major Lyon told the assembled journalists.

––––––––

While Lyon had to remain in treatment due to his broken foot, other Canadian survivors recovered quickly, at least physically. A July 3 memo from a CAMC lieutenant colonel stated that Cooper, Hickman, Taylor, and Pilot had been "medically examined and found free from venereal, vermin, skin, or other contagious diseases and in a fit state to travel."

Presumably, Sergeant Knight was also cleared, because the following day he had an audience with King George V at Buckingham Palace. During his visit, Knight offered an account of the sinking and rescue. He later summarized his conversation with the King for reporters. According to the *Globe*, "The King was most sympathetic and kindly, asking many questions of the young man.... Sergt. Knight's story confirms the narratives of other survivors relative to the Germans ramming and firing on the wreckage and boats from the Llandovery Castle."

News of the attack had become public knowledge, triggering outrage among the Allies and calls for revenge. Despite years of brutal fighting, some atrocities still had the power to shock.

Newspaper headlines from around the world told the story: "Germany's Latest Crime — Hospital Ship Sunk — Missing Total 234" stated the *Sydney Morning Herald* of Australia, on July 3, 1918; "Hospital Ship, Plainly Marked, Sunk by Huns; Llandovery Castle With Canadian Medicals," blared the front page of the July 2, 1918, *Globe* ("Huns" was a derogatory term for Germans). For good measure, the subhead referred to the "Brutal Conduct of German Submarine Commander."

While hospital ships had been torpedoed in the past, the *Llandovery Castle* case clearly crossed a line. There was something particularly disturbing about the notion of helpless nurses drowning and lifeboats being blown to bits by a submarine deck gun.

"Hospital Ship Willfully Sunk," stated the front page of the *San Francisco Examiner*. The same page featured a story headlined, "12 Nurses Die When Lifeboat is Shelled." The article had the wrong number of fatalities and wrong cause of death, but it underlined the global revulsion caused by the incident.

Lieutenant Colonel McKelvey Bell was sought out for comment. As one of the last people to visit the ship before it departed from Halifax, his opinion carried weight. Dr. Bell insisted only "bona-fide members of the staff and crew" were on board and "pointed out also that the British admiralty was exceedingly strict with regard to the observance of this rule," stated the *Ottawa Citizen*.

It was suggested that the *Llandovery Castle* was deliberately targeted, despite being clearly marked as a hospital ship and supposedly off-limits. "The Germans have never allowed considerations of humanity to stand in the way of their military [objectives], or they would never have begun their submarine campaign. The distinction between the sinking of the Lusitania and the sinking of a hospital ship is a purely arbitrary one, and an enemy which have never disavowed the one act will not boggle at the other," read a July 3 editorial in the *Guardian*.

"[T]here is something peculiarly infamous in a stealthy attack on a hospital ship. The vessel is not armed. It carried no fighting men. It is helpless.... The inhuman monster who commanded the submarine knew exactly what he was doing," added the *Philadelphia Inquirer*.

First Lieutenant Patzig had options, pointed out the *Inquirer*. He could have fired a shot across the bow of the *Llandovery Castle* and demanded the ship stop for an inspection. Such inspections had been common in the earlier stages of the war. Patzig rejected this more careful approach, however, and "launched his torpedo for the mere pleasure of it," concluded the *Inquirer*.

A damning statement from the British Admiralty echoed this view. "Germany's awful debt to the world continues to grow. Another hospital ship has been torpedoed.... It is to be noted in this — as in all other instances — the German submarine had a perfect right to stop and search the hospital ship under the Hague Convention[s]. She preferred, however, to torpedo the Llandovery Castle," read the statement, published in newspapers worldwide.

The *Toronto Daily News* described the sinking as "deliberate" and "devilish" — "the vessel was marked with the Red Cross. Her errand was totally unconnected with active warfare. The passengers were all in hospital work. Yet the Captain of the submarine sought to destroy passengers and ship without leaving a soul alive," stated an editorial.

Stung by this criticism, Germany issued a mealy-mouthed statement of its own. A "semi-official note from Berlin" as the *Victoria Daily Times* put it, tried to blame the sinking on Great Britain. "Like all similar assertions of the British Admiralty, the assertion in this case that a German submarine was responsible for the fate of the Llandovery Castle also is probably incorrect. It appears from the later news that no one on board the steamship observed a U-boat or a torpedo. In all probability the cause of the loss will be found to be attributable to a British mine," read the German statement.

Left unexplained was why, if the ship had hit a sea mine, a U-boat suddenly appeared in the wreckage, interrogated survivors, and then tried to kill them. No matter: few people believed the German account. If anyone did, those thoughts would later be dispelled when the *U-86* crew openly admitted to torpedoing the ship.

In Britain, Sir Edward Kemp, KCMG (Knight Commander of the Order of St. Michael and St. George), and the minister of overseas military forces of Canada, spearheaded an inquiry into the sinking. Survivors were interviewed, information corroborated, and the findings released in a report entitled, "The Sinking of the H.M.H.S. Llandovery Castle. Issued by authority of Director of Public Information OTTAWA," as the cover page put it, the document heaped praise on medical staff and crew on board the *Llandovery Castle*:

> Official verification of the facts surrounding the sinking of H.M.H.S. Llandovery Castle confirm two main points — the supreme devotion and valiant sacrifice of the medical personnel and the ship's company, whose courage and resignation were in keeping with the proudest traditions of the British Army and Merchant Marine Service; and the utter blackness and dastardly character of the enemy outrage on this defenseless institution of mercy — a crime surpassing in savagery the already formidable array of murders of non-combatants by the Germans.

It's unclear if the document was referring to Canadian medical staff or the ship's crew ("the Merchant Marine service") in terms of upholding British Army traditions. Certainly, describing Canadian military personnel as British was in keeping with the quasi-colonial mindset in Canada at the time. The report leaned heavily on testimony from Arthur Knight, who stressed the stoic heroism of the doomed nursing sisters, some of whom were selected for special praise.

"To hundreds of officers and men of the Canadian Overseas Forces the name of Nursing Sister Miss Margaret Marjorie ("Pearl") Fraser will recall a record of unselfish effort, a fitting tribute to this nation's womanhood," states "The Sinking of the H.M.H.S. Llandovery Castle."

It was noted that Fraser volunteered at the very start of the war and was kind to everyone, even wounded German prisoners: "Many times had she been the first to give a drink of water to these parched enemy casualties. Many a time she had written down the dying statements of enemy officers and men, transmitting them to their relatives through the Red Cross organization."

The report offers a detailed account of the torpedo attack, with statements from Thomas Lyon, and a list of all the CAMC personnel on board.

Matron Margaret "Pearl" Fraser of the Canadian
Army Medical Corps.

Large segments of it were republished in the August 1918 *Bulletin of the
Canadian Army Medical Corps*. A feature story in the *Bulletin* condemned
the aerial bombing of Canadian hospitals in France and the sinking of the
Llandovery Castle.

The article extolled the "stirring record of perfect discipline" shown by
medical personnel while loading and launching lifeboats. The nursing sisters
also came in for praise: "[E]very one of whom was lost, and whose sacrifice
under the conditions about to be described will serve to inspire throughout
the whole Empire a yet fuller sense of appreciation of the deep debt of grati-
tude this nation owes to the nursing service," notes the *Bulletin*.

Sadly, "with the exception of six survivors … the list of casualties includes the entire medical personnel," added the article.

Beneath these words were the names of all CAMC staff who died on the
Llandovery Castle. Accompanying the list of the dead were mini-biographies

of Lieutenant Colonel Thomas Macdonald, some officers, and all the nursing sisters. The *Bulletin* also printed the names of CAMC victims of the hospital bombings in France.

Throughout July, Captain Sylvester, Chapman, Barton, and Lyon also gave statements about the torpedo attack and its aftermath to a commissioner of oaths (a British official who takes affidavits) in the City of Westminster. Their comments echoed previous remarks they had made. That September, Dr. Robert Ker, E.C. Dean (lieutenant colonel, chief embarkation officer at the Port of Halifax), Charles Archibald (deputy assistant director medical services embarkation at the Port of Halifax), and other authorities gave statements before a notary public in Canada. The Halifax port officers all said the same thing: no one, other than authorized ship or medical personnel boarded the *Llandovery Castle* before it left Canada on June 20.

Nursing Sister Clare Gass was working in Boulogne, France, when she found out about the sinking. She expressed her shock in short, simple diary entries. "News of the sinking of our Canadian Hospital Ship Llandovery Castle has reached us today.… All the Sister[s] are lost," wrote Gass on July 6, 1918.

Three days later, referencing lost colleagues by name, she added, "Miss Pearl Fraser, Miss Fortesque & Gladys Sare were all on board the Hospital Ship Llandovery Castle."

CAMC Nursing Sister Mildred Forbes expressed similar sentiments in a letter to her friend, Cairine Reay Wilson. "Wasn't it *awful* about those fourteen girls on the Hospital ship? I knew most of them & it haunts me at night. The Canadian girls have been paying the price lately," wrote Forbes, on July 24, 1918, from No. 2 Canadian Casualty Clearing Station in France.

For Nursing Sister Helen Fowlds, the sinking represented something of a double tragedy — the loss of friends and a narrow escape for her mother. Fowlds had recovered from the respiratory illness that forced her to recuperate and was spending the summer of 1918 working at the Canadian Convalescent Officers' Hospital in Matlock Bath, England. In a peppy letter to her mother dated July 1, 1918, but mailed later, Fowlds detailed her social life and other day-to-day activities. Then, she encouraged her mother to take a ship and cross the Atlantic to visit her in Great Britain.

"You could come over and meet people.... My money is yours and you can draw every cent of it. $150 would see you through the trip with a good margin, and we can see you through once you are here.... I'll tell you what line to follow as soon as I know and in the meantime, plan your trousseau in every detail," wrote Fowlds.

A follow-up letter to her mother from July 8 struck a very different tone. "Last week I wrote you a long and enthusiastic letter about you coming over. I shall enclose it, though the sinking of the Llandovery Castle has presented another side of the situation. Fourteen of our Sisters, Fraser, Doussault, Sara, and Mary others of whom I knew more or less ... Transportation will be very much curtailed for the time being.... So you can read the enclosed for what it is worth. I wish more every day that you were here but with the submarines it is really tempting Providence to cross these days," stated Fowlds.

In her memoir, Nursing Sister Mabel Clint describes the extreme dangers facing Canadian military nurses in this period: "About a month after [the hospital bombings in France] we heard with horror and incredulity of the sinking of the Llandovery Castle hospital ship, fortunately without patients, and the drowning of fourteen Canadian Sisters and others in an open boat.... Hospital ship sinkings were foul murder," wrote Clint in *Our Bit*.

Mourning was matched by a desperate search for information. It took several days to compile a complete list of everyone on board the *Llandovery Castle* during its last voyage. There were two reasons for the delay: primitive communications and confusion about the identity of the crew. Email, electronic texts, PDFs, Excel files, and digital databases didn't exist, of course. Instant communication was possible, but problematic. Telegrams could only contain small bits of information, and long-distance radio transmissions were prone to interference and bad reception. The other issue was the multinational nature of the *Llandovery Castle*; it was chartered by the Canadian government and staffed by Canadian medical personnel looking after Canadian patients but contained a British crew.

"When a hospital ship leaves England bound for Canada, a list of invalided soldiers on her is immediately cabled to Ottawa but the procedure is not followed as regards the staff. The Llandovery Castle being on her way back after simply touching at Halifax, no names of the staff were available today," explained the *Ottawa Citizen*.

Canadian officials slowly compiled a comprehensive list of survivors and victims. The wisdom of this methodical approach was born out by premature newspaper revelations. On July 2, for example, the *Toronto Daily Star* featured a front-page story about a Staff Sergeant Knight accompanied by a photograph of a dapper-looking man with a dark moustache in a CAMC uniform.

"While a list of those on board the torpedoed hospital ship Llandovery Castle is not yet available" the *Star* said it received word that Knight was "one of the survivors."

The sergeant "joined the C.A.M.C. in Toronto about two years ago. Prior to this, he had been employed as a dispensing chemist with the T. Eaton Company.... Sergt. Knight was making his thirteenth trip on the boat, according to a friend ... this is the second sea disaster he has survived. After leaving the Exhibition Camp, Sergt. Knight was transferred to a hospital ship which about a year ago was wrecked on the Nova Scotia coast," reported the *Star*.

The problem was, the man cited in the story was Sergeant William Knight, not Sergeant Arthur Knight. As a member of the CAMC, William Knight had indeed served on hospital ships, including the *Letitia* (the vessel shipwrecked on the Nova Scotia Coast), the *Araguaya*, and the *Llandovery Castle*. However, he wasn't on the *Llandovery Castle* when it was attacked. The *Star* had confused two CAMC members with the same last name, a mistake made by other media outlets as well. The *Ottawa Citizen*, for example, listed "Staff Sergt. Wm. E. Knight, Toronto (known rescued)" on a list of "Canadians Known to be on Hospital Ship."

Government authorities clearly wanted to avoid making such misleading gaffes. The slow pace of the investigation was agonizing, however, for families awaiting confirmation about survivors and victims.

"I am writing to ask you if you can give me any information regarding my son, Pte. Hoskins, 406510, CAMC. He was attached to the Llandovery Castle Hospital Ship, from Liverpool to Halifax. I shall be glad if you are able to give me any news," said Hoskins's mother, in a letter dated July 4, 1918.

In response, a colonel, listed as an assistant director, medical services, wrote, "It is regretted that up to the present no information regarding [your son's] rescue from the "LLANDOVERY CASTLE" has been received.... So far as this Office is aware, he sailed from Halifax on board the Hospital Ship.... Should any information be received, steps will be taken to notify you."

Newspapers published a series of small, sad stories about unaccounted-for personnel. These articles sometimes turned up in unexpected places. A "Random Notes on Current Sports" column in the *Toronto Daily Star* contained items about hockey and baseball, followed by this notice: "The adjutant of the hospital ship Llandovery Castle, which was torpedoed by the Germans, was Capt. Arthur Vincent Leonard, A.M.C. of Toronto, better known in sporting circles as 'Art' Leonard, former Rugby star with Parkdale-Canoe Club and Varsity. His many friends are anxiously awaiting more definite news of him."

The same edition carried several stories about missing passengers. One piece was headlined, "Pte. G. Nash Believed Lost — No Word Received of Toronto Boy, One of the Crew of Torpedoed Llandovery Castle." A description of George Nash's short life was included: "His parents live at 453 Queen Street East, but Pte. Nash lived more of his life in Midland, where he attended high school. He was twenty-two years of age and was employed as a chauffeur. He enlisted with his county battalion but was transferred to the C.A.M.C."

In similar fashion, an article about "Nursing Sister Mary Agnes ('Nan') McKenzie, daughter of Mr. and Mrs. Thomas C. McKenzie," included her latest status update and background about her nursing career.

McKenzie "is known definitely to have sailed on the Llandovery Castle, and as no cable of her having been rescued has been received her relatives have given up all hope and now believe her to be a victim of this latest exhibition of hun deviltry," wrote the *Star*.

A graduate of Rochester General Hospital's nursing school in New York State, McKenzie worked in Toronto prior to the war. She joined the CAMC in early 1916 and was assigned to the Ontario Military Hospital in Orpington, England, and No. 11 Canadian General Hospital at the Moore

Barracks, in Shorncliffe, among other postings. She was transferred to the *Llandovery Castle* in March 1918.

Another July 4 *Star* story headlined, "Three Toronto Men on Torpedoed Ship," cited two men who were still missing, Private Andrew Wilson and Corporal Frederick Sayyae. The third man in the trio was Private William Pilot, who was described as "among the survivors" of the sinking.

Pilot's relatives were among the lucky few to receive positive news in the days after the sinking. On July 4, a Canadian Pacific telegram from an authority identified as "Director, records" was sent to Pilot's mother in Montreal. The message stated that her son "has landed safely from S.S. Llandovery Castle."

Newspapers took a parochial approach, focusing on local residents who were on the ship: "It now seems probable that at least one Kingston man has gone down in the outrageous sinking [of the] hospital ship Llandovery Castle, in the person of [Wilfred] James, son of Mr. and Mrs. Richard James.... Pte. James was a former member of Queen's Hospital Corps and had served with that unit in France for over a year. He has a host of friends in this city and was prominent in sporting circles," read the *Daily Standard* of Kingston, Ontario.

The same paper mentioned one nursing sister, Minnie Gallaher, who was "born in Kingston thirty-nine years ago but moved to Ottawa with her parents twenty years ago." Nurse Gallaher graduated from a training school at the Protestant General Hospital in Ottawa and was a nursing superintendent at Moose Jaw General Hospital before joining the CAMC. She had chatted with Lieutenant Colonel McKelvey Bell during his visit to the *Llandovery Castle* the last time it was docked in Halifax. Now, she was among the missing.

Gallaher was also mentioned in a piece titled, "The Probable Ottawa Victims" in the *Ottawa Citizen*. Nurse Gallaher, noted the paper, had been a resident of Canada's capital city prior to going overseas. The article mentioned another Ottawa resident, Private L.H. McDonald. Photographs of Gallaher and McDonald were published side-by-side, along with text that described the pair as "missing victims of fiendish German sea murder."

This same edition of the *Citizen* featured a series of tiny notices about unaccounted-for people who lived outside of Ottawa. Headlines for these brief articles read, "Toronto Sgt. Survives," "A Toronto Nurse," "Kingston Chaplain Aboard," "Two From Winnipeg," and "One From Vancouver." The first headline referred to the misidentified Sergeant William Knight. The other subjects were, respectively, Sister Mary Agnes McKenzie, Reverend Donald MacPhail, Lewis Arthur Shipman, George Harvey, and John Eaton.

The *Saskatoon Daily Star* ran a photograph and a small article about orderly William Jackson. "Lost At Sea?" read the headline to the piece published July 3, which cited Jackson's medical corps background and talent on the clarinet.

A handful of happy stories focused on people who missed the voyage, for one reason or another, and lived.

"It is now known that Nursing Sisters M.H. Taylor and Gladys Dennis, who were yesterday feared to have gone down with the Llandovery Castle, did not sail on that vessel. Nurse Taylor was for some time in charge of the Longwood R.A.F. Hospital, North Yonge Street, but word has been received by friends that she left on the 'Ionic' and not on the 'Llandovery Castle,'" reported the *Star*.

Sister Dennis's father received a telegram informing him his daughter was safe "thus relieving the anxiety that was felt for her," continued the article.

Another piece that same day concerned a different pair of missing nursing sisters who were alive and well. The nurses were Mae King and Gertrude Wright. The pair had left Toronto to embark on the *Llandovery Castle* but were delayed and didn't arrive in time to board.

Private Joseph Francis Lafountaine also made the news. The family emergency that took him home to Toronto kept him off the *Llandovery Castle* when it left port. As mentioned previously, the orderly's father, Alfred Lafountaine, died shortly after the ship departed — a tragedy that saved his son's life.

On July 4, the *Toronto Daily Star* ran a photograph of Lafountaine in uniform sitting on a chair in front of a tent. In the picture, Lafountaine is striking a pose with a *Pickelhaube* (a German army spiked helmet) on his head. "Illness Probably Saves Soldier's Life" read the text beneath the photograph. The article incorrectly calls him "Frank Lafontaine."

The same day the *Star* story about Private Lafountaine appeared, a list of all known persons who were on board the *Llandovery Castle* on its last voyage was finally issued. Released by Martin Burrell, acting militia minister, the list was published in newspapers across Canada.

"The following names of Canadian officers, N.C.O.s, and men who sailed from England on the last voyage of the hospital ship the Llandovery Castle, has been received from overseas by the militia department.... This list is subject to revisions, as it is possible that some of the staff obtained leave of absence when the ship docked at Halifax and did not return with her to England," noted the *Calgary Herald*.

Indeed, Private Lafountaine's name appeared on the list published in the *Herald*, even as the *Toronto Daily Star* remarked on his close call. The *London Free Press*, meanwhile, ran a picture of Sergeant Arthur Knight on July 4, under the headline "Londoner Saved." Unlike the earlier report in the *Toronto Star*, the *Free Press* identified the correct sergeant. In his photograph, clean-shaven Arthur Knight looks absolutely nothing like the misidentified, moustachioed William Knight.

The *Herald* list included the names of dozens of CAMC staff, along with regimental numbers (an identification number used by the Canadian military). While the article didn't explicitly state that almost everyone named was presumed dead, it strongly hinted at this sad reality. Under the heading, "Survivors reported," a segment at the end of the piece listed the six Canadian medical personnel who had been rescued. The list of survivors and presumed victims did not include the names of any crew members from the *Llandovery Castle*.

Publication of this list didn't stop the flood of correspondence regarding the fate of people on the ship. Some of this correspondence came from government offices. Bureaucrats in Canada and the United Kingdom, who clearly hadn't read recent coverage of his survival, engaged in a back-and-forth round of messages regarding Private Lafountaine.

"Your attention is invited to D.M.S. [director of medical services] Corps Orders No. 131 dated 24th July 1918., and Sub Section 678 & 680.... Your attention is invited to the fact that 43650 Pte. Lafountaine JF is not shown in these orders. A Cablegram has been sent to the D.G.M.S. [director-general of medical services] Ottawa with a view to ascertaining whether he was left in Canada or proceeded on the 'Llandovery Castle' on her last trip," read a memo dated July 27.

Interestingly, this memo spelled Lafountaine's last name correctly but got his regimental number wrong (his actual number was 34630).

More memos and telegrams ensued, before the matter was finally sorted out.

"Private Lafontaine was given leave to visit his parents in Toronto and he did not embark on the 'Llandovery Castle.' He is safe in Canada," stated an August 14 note from the Department of Militia and Defense in Ottawa to the director of medical services, Canadian Contingent in the United Kingdom.

This note used the correct regimental number but wrong spelling of Lafountaine.

People continued to hold out hope for a miracle. Maybe other lifeboats were found, or more survivors were plucked from the sea by passing ships.

"Could you kindly give me any information regarding two members of the Canadian Army Medical Corps who were on H.M.H.S. Llandovery Castle when she was torpedoed as to whether there is any possible hope of them having been picked up. Their names are Private H. Sutherland and Russell O'Neil," read a neatly handwritten letter dated July 12 sent to the "Director of Transports."

A few days later, the ADMS (assistant director of medical services) responded. The two men "are not shown among the survivors, and have been reported missing, believed drowned," he wrote.

The same colonel sent a similar response that day to a letter inquiring about Private Sidney Isaac. Isaac was "a stretcher bearer, wounded in France — and subsequently employed in hospital ships," stated the letter. The colonel confirmed that Isaac was on the *Llandovery Castle* and believed to have drowned.

Some letter writers acknowledged that the odds of finding their loved ones safe were remote: "I am writing on behalf of my sister to enquire if you could please give me any information regarding the safety or otherwise of J.A. Spittal 536315 who was a member of the Canadian Army Medical

Corps on board the torpedoed hospital ship, Llandovery Castle, and as his name was amongst the list of those believed to be included in the casualties, of course one fears the worst, but should there be any further information … regarding other survivors, including J.A. Spittal, I would be very grateful on my sister's behalf if you would kindly let me know," read an August 15 letter addressed to "The General Officer Commanding Canadian Army Medical Corps, late H.M.H.S. Llandovery Castle."

John Albert Spittal was included on the list released the previous month of people on board the *Llandovery Castle*. Like everyone beyond the occupants of Lifeboat No. 4, Spittal was presumed dead by the military.

Occasionally, letter writers received a reprieve, of sorts. A note was sent to the British-Canadian Recruiting Mission Headquarters in Chicago, Illinois, on August 31 regarding "one Angus McKenzie of the C.A.M.C. He was serving on H.M. Hospital Ship Llandovery Castle when it was sunk." The letter indicated that the person inquiring about Mr. McKenzie was an elderly man in Illinois who "is most anxious to get some information about Angus McKenzie."

The Canadian Red Cross Society, Wounded and Missing Enquiry Bureau, in London, got involved and made inquiries. Files were examined, then the colonel, ADMS, on behalf of the director general, medical services, Overseas Military Forces of Canada (OMFC) sent a response to the British-Canadian Recruiting Mission. "Records have been carefully searched in this Office and there is no trace of an Angus McKenzie ever having been carried on the strength of H.M.H.S. 'LLANDOVERY CASTLE.' The only Angus McKenzie of whom we have any trace is: — 29247 Pte. Angus McKenzie, who is presently carried on the strength of No. 16 Canadian General Hospital, Orpington, Kent, England…. This is possibly the man to whom you refer," wrote the colonel.

It is also possible the elderly gentleman confused Angus McKenzie with Nursing Sister Mary Agnes McKenzie. If so, this possibility wasn't mentioned by the colonel in his response.

Another communication revealed a family fib, or maybe just the overly optimistic outpourings of a man caught up in the war. "I am writing to you for information regarding my son…. From time to time in his letters, he told me he was expecting to receive a commission, and on the second last trip to Halifax on the Llandovery Castle he said he heard it had come through. And even he did not live to attain this end, I would be glad to know if he gained it as he was working to get it. Now that he has given his life for his King and country and to promote righteousness in the earth, it would be a great source of satisfaction to know he would have received it had he lived to return to England," a mother wrote to the Canadian Record Office in London.

A commission meant a promotion to become an officer. A subsequent memorandum, presumably not sent to the grieving mother, stated, "There is nothing on record in the Office to show that the [person in question] would eventually have received a Commission."

Underlying these messages was the horror that anyone missing and presumed drowned had physically vanished. Only rarely were families able to recover the bodies of their loved ones from the *Llandovery Castle*.

In late September, a corpse washed up on the Isle of Wight in the English Channel. The man's clothing contained the tag "Moore 529605," and he wore boots with the label, "Slater Shoe Co., Montreal." In military memos, the drowned man was identified as Private J.E. Moore from the *Llandovery Castle*. His full name was Joseph Ewart Moore.

A letter in neat, cursive handwriting, dated September 29, 1918, arrived at the CAMC records office in London. It was sent by the brother of Private Moore, who said he was writing on behalf of his sister-in-law. The sister-in-law wished to intern Moore's body in Burnley, U.K., "alongside that of her mother," explained Private Moore's brother. Government officials responded and said they would do what they could to accommodate this wish.

Most families did not have the opportunity to bury an actual body, but authorities continued to gather information for months after the sinking. On October 4, the staff captain for the brigadier general, Adjutant-General of the Overseas Military Forces of Canada, wrote the Director of Medical Services, Pembroke House, London. The letter concerned an earlier inquiry from a mother seeking word about her son, Private Clifford Hoskins. "[A]ccording to Records this man was on the 27-6-18, reported missing, believed to be drowned as a result of the wrecking of the 'Llandovery Castle'.... The enclosure to your letter above quoted has this day been forwarded to Militia Headquarters, Ottawa for enquiries and report.... As soon as a reply is received, Mrs. Hoskins will be informed of the result and she has been notified to this effect and advised of the action taken," stated the letter.

Amid the outpouring of grief, there were calls for action. Vengeance scenarios ranged from economic sanctions to violent military reprisals.

"Growth of movements, both popular and official, for trade punishment of Germany after the war is stimulated by such atrocities as the sinking of the hospital ship Llandovery Castle," reported the *New York Times*.

The British Seaman's Union wanted to extend an already existing postwar boycott of German goods by several years. The Liverpool Cotton Exchange took things a step further. In a unanimous vote, Exchange members vowed not to trade with Germans or Austrians for a full decade after the war ended. This pledge also applied to companies represented by the Cotton Exchange. For its part, the British government mused about imposing a postwar prohibition on German imported chemicals and dyes.

Trade boycotts were among the more lenient punishments under discussions. Other retaliatory measures were steeped in violence.

"With every fresh atrocity [Germany] but kindles afresh the fires of hatred for her damnable kultur. The blood boils at the very thought of helpless women, on missions of mercy, slaughtered in cold blood.... The fate of the hospital ship but renews the determination of the foes of German militarism that not a vestige of the bloodthirsty cult shall be left to propagate future ferocities," wrote the *Philadelphia Inquirer*.

Kultur was a dismissive term used at the time to describe German culture. Precisely how German militarists would be prevented from propagating wasn't spelled out, though the editorial offered a few hints: "Kaiserism must be destroyed and Germany must be penned up in her own cage, there to repent of her crimes against God and humanity."

The Canadian media was equally unrestrained. An angry editorial in the *Globe* titled, "Canada and German Murderers" cited two different atrocities: the torpedoing of the *Llandovery Castle*; and the bombing of Canadian military hospitals in France.

What can we do by way of punishment? The thought that comes to the mind first is reprisals in kind. There are thousands of young Canadians in the Royal Air Service and hundreds who fly over the German lines daily. Shall we ask them to drop bombs deliberately on German hospitals? We cannot do that. There are depths of infamy into which we must not follow the murderous hun. To kill German nurses and the helpless wounded men in German hospitals would debase our lads — the young eaglets of Canada whom we love for their chivalry no less than for their daring — to the level of the moral lepers whose crimes have made the name of Germany accursed.

If bombing German medical facilities was a step too far, the editorial suggested that killing more German troops would be a worthy response. "Along the far-flung battleline of the Western front there are Canadian soldiers in thousands whose hearts will flame in indignation when they learn of the repeated slaughter of our women. Woe to the high-born German officers — the representatives of the murderer caste — whom they encounter in the day of battle. The memory of the nurses slain by the orders of Germany's militarists will give strength and purpose to the avenging arms of Canada's sons," wrote the *Globe*.

If the public was alarmed by such heated rhetoric, few people let on. If anything, civilians endorsed the most radical measures.

"Several municipal and other councils [in Great Britain] have passed resolutions calling on the Government to strip all honours from aliens born in Germany and intern them all.… There are demands for the most vigorous air reprisals against German towns," wrote the *Sydney Morning Herald*.

These statements were typical of the ferocious anti-German sentiment of the day. Posters, plays, movies, advertisements, speeches, and newspaper articles depicted German soldiers as ape-like brutes led by tyrannical leaders. This imagery would have made sense during the Second World War, a conflict underpinned by the Holocaust and Nazi mass murder of Roma, the disabled, and Slavic peoples. Such depictions in the First World War, however, come across as jarring. While life was miserable for civilians in occupied Belgium and France from 1914 to 1918 (Germany frequently requisitioned food and squashed any resistance or disobedience with extreme violence), Hitler's New Order in Europe was on a whole different scale of genocidal brutality.

Political leaders were happy to add fuel to the public wrath directed against Germany. Several speakers at an American Independence Day event in London on July 4, 1918, called for Germany's utter destruction. Such an event might seem incongruous, but with America fully committed to the war, previous conflicts between the United Kingdom and United States were played down. As it was, the Independence Day rally featured two future prime ministers.

"The war has become a conflict of Christian civilization with scientific barbarism. One system or the other must decisively prevail. Germany must be beaten, must know, must feel, she is beaten. Her defeat must be expressed in terms of facts which will deter others from emulating her crimes," stated Winston Churchill, then the U.K. minister of munitions.

When it was his turn to speak, the Canadian representative said he agreed. "In seconding Mr. Churchill's resolution, Arthur Meighen, Canadian Minister of the Interior, denounced in scathing terms the sinking of the hospital ship Llandovery Castle by a German submarine," wrote the *Times*.

Meighen was quoted as saying, "It is better that the world should perish than that those murderers should live."

Neither man was alone, however, in sounding apocalyptic warnings. Speaking before an International Parliamentary Conference in the United Kingdom, Chancellor of the Exchequer Bonar Law didn't mince words when it came to the *Llandovery Castle* attack. "A wild beast is at large, and it is no use arguing or attempting to reason with it. We must destroy it. We must set our teeth until this end is achieved," stated Law.

Far from being critical, the media applauded such rhetoric.

"The indignation which is being displayed in England in connection with Germany's latest crime is proof that Mr. Bonar Law voiced the opinions of the great majority of the people in his address before the International

Parliamentary Conference in London.... [His statement] will be almost universally supported at the present time while public feeling regarding the sinking of the Llandovery Castle is so strong.... It will be well to remember the Llandovery Castle whenever attempts are made to raise the question of peace by negotiation," wrote the *Sydney Morning Herald*.

Law returned to the subject in a U.K. House of Commons debate on July 4. The chancellor of the exchequer was asked a series of questions about the attack on the *Llandovery Castle*. Dashing off his responses in short order, Law said the ship only carried medical personnel, was not transporting munitions, and that U-*86* tried to kill all witnesses to the torpedo attack. Law dismissed Germany's claim that the ship hit a mine, noting that "the survivors were in actual communication with the submarine commander."

One of those survivors became embroiled in a mundane bureaucratic matter after recovering from his traumatic experience. The issue centred around Arthur Knight's rank with the CAMC. Knight had served as acting sergeant on the *Llandovery Castle*, even though he was never officially

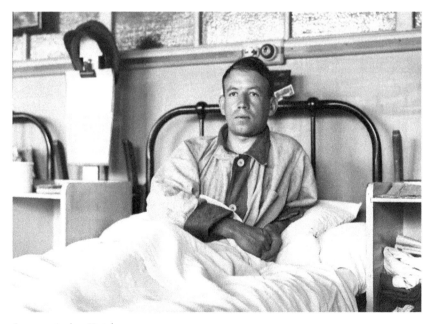

Sergeant Arthur Knight.

promoted to this post. As far as the Canadian military was concerned, Knight was still a corporal, a lower rank with less pay.

This situation annoyed Knight, who was no longer at the King George Hospital. After meeting the flesh and blood George V at Buckingham Palace, Knight requested a transfer to the Massey-Harris Convalescent Home for Canadian Soldiers. A facility in Dulwich, U.K., the convalescent home was founded by the Massey-Harris Company, a major Canadian manufacturer of agricultural equipment. The transfer was granted and at the Convalescent Home, Knight poured out his frustration in letters, some on hospital stationery, to military and medical authorities.

"I was made Sergt. on the 12th March and Major Macdonald who was our O.C. on the ship told me that I would be paid for my third stripe and that it would be confirmed, and it was on the second trip that I told Major Macdonald that I had no pay then. He told me that he would be sure that I got it on the last trip when we got torpedoed. He showed me the papers and I saw it with my own eyes that I was to be confirmed, but the papers got lost with the boat. Major Lyons [*sic*] can speak for me on that question," wrote Knight, in one letter.

Major Lyon, who was recuperating at the Prince of Wales Hospital in London, received one of Knight's missives and sought to help his former ship colleague. Lyon dashed off a note of his own to Lieutenant Colonel Chisholm, the assistant director general of medical services, Overseas Military Forces Canada. "Sir, I beg to enclose a letter received from Srgt. Knight CAMC of the Llandovery Castle. His statement that he has been acting as a srgt. Since March 12, 1918, is quite correct. During the last two trips he acted as orderly sergeant and carried out his duties in an extremely efficient manner. I am quite sure his name could have been down on the list for promotion and think the loss of part II orders is an undeserved misfortune in his case," stated Major Lyon.

Lyon received a very bureaucratic response:

> Please be advised that it is not considered desirable to show his promotion to the rank of Sgt., in Part II Orders the recommendation never having been received

from the late Officer Commanding Troops, H.M.H.S. Llandovery Castle.... The promotion of Other Ranks on the Llandovery Castle was taken up several times verbally with the late Major MacDonald, who refused on these occasions to forward any recommendations.... As soon as A/ Cpl. Knight is available for duty an effort will be made to place him in a position where he may receive appointment to A/Sgt., or such Rank as he is suitable.

Lacking verbal or written confirmation from Macdonald, the deceased CAMC commander on the *Llandovery Castle*, Knight's promotion story couldn't be corroborated. The issue was eventually resolved the following year in Knight's favour, with a promotion to acting sergeant and appropriate backpay.

Orderly William Pilot also had to cope with some bureaucratic matters following his rescue. He was issued a new Active Service Pay Book, good for July 1, 1918, onwards ("Old pay book lost on Llandovery Castle, June 27th, 1918" reads a handwritten entry in the new Pay Book). The page with the latter comment contains Pilot's signature, regimental number (69), and a series of entries detailing "CASH PAYMENTS, REMITTANCES AND OTHER CHARGES."

"If this book is found not in the possession of the owner and it cannot be returned immediately to the Paymaster of the Officer's or soldier's unit, it is to be forwarded immediately to any of the following, as the case may be," reads a typed notice in the new pay book. Lost pay books could be forward to paymaster authorities serving in Canada, England, France, or with the "Canadian Siberian Expeditionary Force, Vladivostok," continued the notice. The latter was a reference to the Allied intervention in Bolshevik Russia.

Pilot also used his time to chronicle his experiences in the Canadian Expeditionary Force, including the *Llandovery Castle* sinking, in a new notebook that served as a diary.

Petty as these administrative matters seem, they reminded survivors of their day-to-day duty in service of the Canadian military. Paperwork needed to be finalized even as survivors grappled with their awful memories.

While Canadian administrators filed memos, reports, and documents, an anonymous clerk for insurance giant Lloyd's of London made an entry in a financial ledger in Great Britain. This handwritten note eventually appeared in a book called *Lloyd's War Losses*, which listed ships sunk by enemy action in the First World War.

The pertinent citation, written in pen, reads: "Date (1918) — June 27. Vessel: Llandovery Castle. Flag: British, Tons Gross 11,423. How Sunk: S. Position: 116 miles S.W. of Fastnet." *S* stands for "submarine" — one of the many ledger letter codes that signified how ships were lost.

Lloyd's War Losses offers very little additional information about the sinking of the *Llandovery Castle*, or any other ships that were registered to the Allies or neutral nations. It was just an entry in a ledger filled with thousands of similar entries bearing evidence of the brutal struggle on the seas and oceans during the Great War.

————

Likewise, the military careers of the *Llandovery Castle*'s last patients were also coming to an official end. On July 31, 1918, for example, James Hearn, formerly of the Canadian Artillery and *Llandovery Castle* patient newsletter underwent a medical examination. The exam would determine what future, if any, he had in the military. Hearn wasn't returning to the frontlines but might be useful in a support staff capacity.

"Physical examination reveals a well developed and well-nourished individual. Patient gets very much out of breath after walking half a mile at moderate gait and after such a walk is obliged to rest. Expansion [of chest] is slightly limited on the left side," read Hearn's medical file.

The examining physician recommended that Hearn be discharged from the military ("further treatment being useless" wrote the doctor). As a result of this prognosis, Hearn received a Canadian Expeditionary Force discharge certificate ("medically unfit for further service" states the form). He was officially discharged from the CEF on August 2, 1918 — a reprieve from future combat duties, but also an acknowledgement that the army was finished with him.

CHAPTER FOUR

"An Intensity of Feeling"

Mourners filled the pews at St. Andrew's (Presbyterian) Church in downtown Toronto. Nursing sisters, some wearing a small button indicating overseas service, took pride of place in the front three pews. Behind them and on side pews sat medical and military personnel, friends, family, and colleagues.

The memorial service held Sunday evening July 14, 1918, in the Romanesque Revival church began with the processional hymn, "How Bright These Glorious Spirits Shine." Psalms followed, along with this wartime prayer:

> We remember with gratitude at this hour all those who have been faithful unto death and who have now received the crown of life. We give Thee thanks for the courage, the fidelity and the Christ-like sacrifice of our medical officers and nurses who have braved the dangers of the battlefield and sea that they might carry their gracious ministrations to the wounded, the sick, and the dying: into Thy holy keeping we commit the souls of our brothers and sisters who have given their lives for the cause of liberty and justice.

The choir sang a hymn, then everyone joined in a rendition of "God Save the King," (The song "O Canada" existed at the time but wouldn't be enshrined as the official national anthem for decades to come).

In his sermon, Reverend John Walker MacMillan of the University of Manitoba leaned heavily on the Book of Revelation. Reverend MacMillan drew a comparison between the supernatural sufferings in the biblical account with the ongoing war. It was not a precise comparison admitted the reverend; while the unsaved faced eternal torment in hell, on Earth "the candle of hope still burns."

Reverend MacMillan assailed the attack on the *Llandovery Castle* at length. Even though the service was dedicated to CAMC staff, the reverend included the often-overlooked crew of the ship in his remarks.

> There were on that vessel three classes. The sailors are men who have shown themselves most gallant souls. The torpedoes would not have frightened them from the ocean as the Germans foresaw. We would remember them tonight.... The medical officers were in a profession which exemplifies what is worthiest in life today, the spirit of science, the spirit of obedience to law, the spirit of ministry. We would remember them tonight.... And there stood besides these sailors and these doctors and went down with them into the black water, nurses.

The reverend tossed out more anti-German barbs, then said, "As God is the God of those sailors, they shall live. As God is the God of those doctors they shall live; as God is the God of those nurses, they shall live, for He will pay them their just dues, because He is a reasonable father and a tender God."

A week later, Reverend Dr. R.J. Wilson led "a very touching and appropriate memorial service" at Chalmers United Church in Kingston, Ontario, wrote the *Daily Standard*.

The service was attended by Kingston mayor John McKane Hughes and several nursing sisters. Following the offertory, the reverend had everyone stand as he read aloud a list of *Llandovery Castle* victims. Some of the dead had belonged to the church, which "added to the pathos of the service," reported the *Standard*.

The attack on the *Llandovery Castle* had "caused the name of Germany to stink in the nostrils of all devout people.... The highest Christian virtues are attacked by the sinking of the hospital ship, which is the rejection of Christianity, an attempt to dethrone Christianity, the calculated repudiation of the Christian way as the way of the truth and the light, the reversion to the pre-Christian and diabolical views of man's nature," sermonized Reverend Wilson.

The Kingston service concluded with the "Dead March" by Handel.

Across the ocean, a requiem mass for *Llandovery Castle* victims was held at St. Etheldreda's Church, a thirteenth-century chapel in London. The July 23 service was "distinctly Canadian," with a large number of CAMC personnel, an honour guard, and high-ranking officials, noted the *Canadian Daily Record*. Officials included Sir George Perley, high commissioner for Canada, and his wife, Lady Perley, Margaret Macdonald, matron-in-chief for Canadian Army Medical Corps Nursing Sisters and Surgeon-General Sir William Donovan, director of medical services for the Royal Army Medical Corps.

The service "was marked by an intensity of feeling which accentuated its deep significance and gripped the hearts of the congregation," reported the *Globe*.

At the front of the church, a catafalque was draped with the Canadian Red Ensign flag and the Union Jack of the United Kingdom, swords, a CAMC cap, and the nursing sisters' insignia. Father Ivor Daniel, chaplain of Edmonton, Alberta, led the service.

> We have gathered together to plead before God for the souls of our brothers and sisters, the personnel and crew of the Llandovery Castle, victims of a shameless outrage, which has made us realize more than ever the nature of the struggle in which we are engaged; and which has made us more than ever determined to carry on the combat of

which they were the noble victims. At this moment, when we offer for these souls the merits of the atonement ascribed upon the Cross, their voices seem to call out of the depths of many waters to the high throne of a just and avenging God.

The service concluded with the playing of "The Last Post" on trumpets — the familiar funeral refrain for British and Canadian soldiers.

———

While the dead were mourned, the sinking of the *Llandovery Castle* became a rallying cry to spur the Canadian public and military to greater efforts to win the war. The attack was featured on a striking poster published by the Montreal Lithographing Company that urged Canadians to buy war bonds (a prime source of government revenue to fund the military effort). In the poster, a young couple flounders in ocean waves. A dark-haired woman in a white uniform bearing a Red Cross is supported by a young man in a brown uniform and a lifebelt. The woman looks unconscious or dead, her head lying parallel with the water, face blank and beautiful. The young man waves his fist at a surfaced U-boat. A pair of sailors on the sub appear to be shooting at the couple. In case anyone missed the point, a life preserver labelled "Llandovery Castle" floats in the foreground.

"Victory Bonds Will Help Stop This" reads a caption at the top of the poster. Text at the bottom proclaims, "Kultur vs. Humanity."

Anger over the *Llandovery Castle* was so widespread the attack was depicted in an American propaganda poster that also promoted war bonds. Created by the United States Department of the Treasury, War Loan Organization, the poster features a sinking ship, a menacing U-boat firing a cannon, and a lifeboat packed with male and female survivors. The copy reads "*Spurlos Versenkt*" (supposedly a German naval policy, it was usually translated as "sunk without trace").

"On June 27, 1918, the Llandovery Castle — a British hospital ship plainly marked with the Red Cross — was torpedoed by the Hun.... Determined

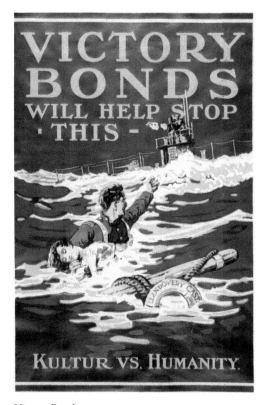

Victory Bonds poster.

to "sink without a trace" the U-boat commander shelled the lifeboats and shot nurses as they struggled in the water," reads the overheated text.

The copy continues: "Wipe out this THING that strikes in the dark, this assassin of helpless men and defenseless women.... Buy MORE Bonds. Buy with all the money you have and pledge all you can save in the months to come."

At the bottom, the poster references the "Liberty Loan Committee, Third Federal Reserve District, Lincoln Building, Philadelphia." This poster, which wrongly described the *Llandovery Castle* as a British hospital ship when it was torpedoed, was published in American magazines and newspapers. Like its Canadian equivalent, the poster placed heavy stress on the death of the female nursing sisters.

Spurlos Versenkt poster.

"Nurses were largely beyond reproach in public opinion, and aggression against them provided the Allies with some of its most potent propaganda opportunities," notes the book, *Agnes Warner and the Nursing Sisters of the Great War.*

Politicians also did their part to inflame the citizenry. While in London, England for the Imperial War Conference, Prime Minister Sir Robert Borden spoke before a luncheon of the Canadian Association and the Canadian Club of London at the Savoy Hotel. He raged against Germany's "campaign of frightfulness" — the Great War term for what today would be called terrorism.

[I]n all the annals of history there is nothing more horrible than the methods by which Germany has waged this war. Consider the systematic murder of civilian populations on land and on sea, the violation of women, the desecration of graveyards, the burning of towns and cities, the wanton destruction and annihilation of every vestige of civilization, the brutal treatment of prisoners, the bombing of hospitals, the sinking of hospital ships!.... The German militarists are possessed by devils whose name is legion.

Borden continued, "We Canadians know what it is to have our hospitals bombed.... The intent was as certain as its accomplishment was successful. If anyone should doubt, what shall he say of the sinking of our hospital ship, the murder of nurses and doctors, and the persistent attempts to destroy every survivor so that there should be no trace and no report?"

A Reuters news report about the speech published in the *Globe* quoted Borden as saying "Llandovery Castle" rather than "our hospital ship."

Borden returned to Canada and offered another inflammatory speech, at the Director's Luncheon of the Canadian National Exhibition (CNE) in Toronto, September 2.

Fiends incarnate would shrink from the nameless outrages with which [Germany] has deliberately degraded the name of humanity; they would blush for the barbarous and brutal cynicism with which she has scorned and broken every decent convention of public and international usage. Was it for nothing that the Americans went into battle shouting "Remember the Lusitania!" Was it for nothing that the Huns heard the battle cry, "Remember the Llandovery Castle" when the Canadians made their onset? The memory of these things cannot be wiped out in a day or a year, or even a century.

The war cry Borden references was allegedly uttered by members of the Canadian Expeditionary Force at the start of the Battle of Amiens on August 8.

"The primary object of the attack was to free the Amiens–Paris railway.... To Canadians, however, the battle was an opportunity to revenge the sinking of the Canadian hospital ship, 'Llandovery Castle' — and hence the official designation of the battle as the 'L.C. operations'," notes the military divisional history, *The 1st Canadian Division in the Battles of 1918*.

This was a bitterly ironic way to commemorate an unarmed ship on a medical mission to heal the wounded.

Other observers began citing the *Llandovery Castle* in discussions about postwar justice. "If we win this war (as we shall) means will be found for subjecting such outrages on law and humanity to effective punishment. Our immediate task is to make it at least as safe to travel on a hospital ship as on any other ship," stated the *Guardian* on July 3.

A follow-up editorial was published on July 8.

> The worst of these offences against international law and humanity is that the real culprits are so seldom punished as they deserve.... It is for our Government first of all to sift the facts to the utmost and then to present them to the German Government, which will be compelled then either to disprove the evidence of the crime or to repudiate the criminal. If this course were steadily pursued in detail time after time the accumulative weight of evidence would become such that the most cynical Government could not disregard it in the face of the world. In this way some check at least might be put on outrage or at the worst, if not condemned or punished by those responsible, it would be more and more deeply concerned and in the end punished by the world.

As it was, the Allies had to sift the facts on offences against law and humanity much sooner than expected. By early autumn 1918, the Allies had seized the initiative on the Western Front, backed by huge numbers of fresh troops from America. The Battle of Amiens marked the beginning of the end for the German army. More defeats and a mutiny by German sailors followed. Berlin recognized there was no path to victory and agreed to an armistice, which came into effect November 11, 1918. The CEF played a big part in the final push, a period dubbed "Canada's Hundred Days" by patriotic pundits.

While technically the Armistice was just a ceasefire, it was clear Germany had been routed (something its generals conceded in private, even as they publicly blamed everybody but themselves for the collapse). Since the Kaiser had abdicated and fled to neutral Holland, it was up to a German civilian government to negotiate the final peace terms.

As diplomats bickered, Canadians reflected. Canada was on the winning side of the war and had earned a reputation for military valour and daring. The cost, however, was appalling. In a House of Commons speech, May 27, 1919, Sir Edward Kemp — a Conservative member of Parliament for East Toronto in addition to being minister of overseas military forces — stated:

> I venture to say that few of Canada's soldiers, who enlisted so readily and with so much enthusiasm, particularly in the earliest days of the war, anticipated that they would be away from their homes so long or that they would be subjected to such privations, such hardships and such sacrifices as overtook them. Neither did we expect that we would require to send such a large force overseas. If any one had predicted in the early days of the war that we should send 50,000 or 100,000 men overseas, the estimate would have been considered a large one. Yet we have sent overseas in all 420,913 of the best blood and sinew of Canada.

In total, roughly sixty-six thousand Canadians and Newfoundlanders (Newfoundland wasn't a part of Canada at the time) died during the Great War — more fatalities than the United States suffered in the much longer Vietnam War. At the time, Canada's population stood at under nine million people.

Over 170,000 members of the Canadian Expeditionary Force were injured during the struggle. Wounds ranged from broken bones to amputated limbs and catastrophic mutilation. An unlucky few lost the ability to move, see, hear, or even venture in public without causing alarm due to their extreme disfigurement. For some veterans, military service was followed by decades of medical care.

Sixty-one officers and 528 rank-and-file personnel with the Canadian Army Medical Corps were also killed or died due to war-related causes. The *Llandovery Castle* sinking accounted for the single biggest loss of Canadian nursing sisters during the war.

During his speech, Sir Kemp praised Canada's military nurses.

> Just a word for the nursing sisters of Canada. Those of us who watched the great service they performed cannot fail to appreciate it at its full value, and in connection with the nursing sisters, whenever one talks of or refers to them in any way, one's mind irresistibly goes to the three frightful outrages perpetrated on them — the bombing of the Canadian hospitals at Etaples and Doullens, and the sinking of the Canadian hospital ship Llandovery Castle.... In the sinking of the Llandovery Castle fourteen Canadian nursing sisters were sent to a watery grave in the depths of the sea 116 miles from land, and in trying to cover up the outrage the Germans endeavoured to sink the remaining lifeboat in order thereby to obliterate all traces.

———

Even into the postwar era, the *Llandovery Castle* attack continued to claim victims. After being rescued by the destroyer the *Lysander* and returned to Great Britain, Captain Edward Sylvester was granted three months leave. He recuperated sufficiently to be given command of a ship bringing American soldiers to Europe. His health quickly deteriorated, however, requiring more rest. Captain Sylvester revived again and briefly returned to duties at sea before suffering another decline. This time, he did not regain his strength. Sylvester died of heart failure in the summer of 1920 at his home in Tonbridge, Kent. He was fifty-seven years old.

The war "had prematurely broken his career and his health gradually failed," stated an obituary in the *Kent and Sussex Courier*, published July 16. Captain Sylvester "was undoubtedly a victim to the strain of war, although he outlasted the cessation of hostilities by a year and a half. In their bereavement sincere sympathy will be felt with the widow, son and daughter and other relatives who mourn the loss of one of the most heroic figures in the naval history of the war," added his obituary.

The handful of Canadian survivors from the *Llandovery Castle* began to return home, often in a roundabout manner.

William Pilot listed his travels in his diary. He landed in Halifax on December 29, 1918, on board a ship called the *Carmania*. Early the following year, he took a hospital train to Vancouver for an eight-day trip. Promoted to corporal the previous autumn, Pilot journeyed on to Montreal, arriving January 27, 1919, then departed for Saint John, New Brunswick.

Pilot went back to England on board the RMS *Corsican*, arriving in Liverpool on February 28. He journeyed to London, went to the Canadian military base in Shorncliffe, then returned to Liverpool in mid-March. He boarded the RMS *Royal George* for another voyage to Halifax, docking on March 24. Then, he took a train to Montreal, arriving on the morning of Thursday, March 27, to officially bid the army farewell ("12 o'clock same day discharged," wrote Pilot).

Pilot's discharge certificate states that he was twenty-four years old and had served in both the Cycle Corps and the CAMC. Nothing was mentioned about the *Llandovery Castle*. Pilot received another certificate around this time from the City of Montreal, where his family lived. The text of this certificate was considerably more exuberant than the dry, bureaucratic language used in his discharge document.

"Upon your return to Montreal the Civil Authorities on behalf of all the citizens wish to extend to you a heartfelt welcome and the earnest assurance of their full appreciation of the invaluable service you have rendered to Canada, to the Empire, and to humanity.... They greet you with feelings of thankfulness and pride, realizing that you have written a glorious page in the history of the world, which will be an inspiration for future generations," states Pilot's thank-you notice from the City of Montreal.

Other survivors faced lingering effects from their ordeal, both physical and mental. In October 1918, Arthur Knight was diagnosed with "neurasthenia" at No. 16 Canadian General (Ontario Military) Hospital in Orpington, Kent. This vague term was applied to a catch-all medical condition, the symptoms of which included lack of energy, nervousness, and depression. Under the heading "Cause of Disability," the doctor wrote "Torpedoed on H.M.S. 'Llandovery Castle'" in the "Atlantic."

Knight was reexamined at No. 5 Canadian General Hospital in Liverpool: "Ever since the sinking of the Llandovery Castle patient has not felt well," stated his medical case sheet following this visit.

Knight was "invalided to Canada" shortly after the war ended, according to his service file. Back in Canada, his problems lingered. Knight met a doctor at a Toronto military hospital in early 1919, complaining of headaches and insomnia. Knight was "more easily bothered by excitement now than before, dreams a lot of the water," wrote Captain R. MacDonald, who conducted the Toronto examination. The dreams might have stemmed from the fact Knight spent "two hours floating" on the ocean, added the captain.

Knight was also assessed at Military Hospital, Wolseley Barracks, London, Ontario, in February 1919. As a result of all these examinations, Knight was discharged from the Canadian Expeditionary Force as "medically unfit" on March 21, 1919.

Knight did receive some good news around this time: shortly after his discharge, he was promoted to acting sergeant and received appropriate backpay.

For a time, the anniversary of the *Llandovery Castle* sinking was marked by memorials, plaques, speeches, and dedications. On June 27, 1919, the Canadian government changed the name of a hospital to honour Nursing Sister Rena McLean — a move that garnered a great deal of media attention.

"On the anniversary of the death on the Llandovery Castle of Nursing Sister Rena McLean, daughter of Senator John McLean, P.E.I., the Military Hospital in Charlottetown has, as a memorial to this martyred nursing sister, been re-named the Rena McLean Memorial Hospital," reported the *Weekly British Whig* in Kingston, Ontario.

In a note to P.E.I. officials, Sir James Lougheed, minister of the Department of Soldiers' Civil Re-establishment (created to guide veterans through demobilization and a return to civilian life), threw lavish praise on the deceased nurse.

> No adequate reparation can be made by Germany for the deliberate attack that they made on the Llandovery Castle, an unprotected hospital ship carrying many helpless in-valided soldiers. It seems fitting that there should be some permanent memorial of this inhuman act and of the gal-lant self-sacrifice of the nursing sisters and medical officers who lost their lives in the catastrophe while serving their country and ministering to the comfort of invalided sol-diers. I hope, by naming after her the largest hospital oper-ated by the department in the province of Prince Edward Island, her native province, there will be kept in constant remembrance in that province and throughout Canada the noble sacrifice of Nurse Rena McLean and her comrades.

There were no "invalided soldiers" on the *Llandovery Castle* when it was attacked, but the reverence for McLean's memory was still touching.

On the second anniversary of the sinking, a memorial tablet was unveiled for Nursing Sister Mary Agnes McKenzie during a ceremony at Avenue Road Presbyterian Church in Toronto. The unveiling was arranged by the graduate nurses of Toronto. As the congregation looked on, a flag covering a plaque was drawn aside, revealing the inscription: "To the glory of God and in loving memory of Nursing Sister Mary Agnes McKenzie who after three years' service lost her life by the torpedoing of the hospital ship Llandovery Castle June 27, 1918.... Their Name Liveth for Evermore."

A bagpiper played a lament, and a bugler performed the traditional mili-tary hymn, "The Last Post." This was followed by readings from scripture and more singing.

A "handsome tablet" honouring Nursing Sister Jean Templeman and thirty-nine other congregants of the Stewarton Presbyterian Church in Ottawa was unveiled November 14, 1920, wrote the *Ottawa Citizen*. The event was presided over by Reverend William McIlory.

"Those whose names appear on the tablet were dear to all and their memories would never be effaced. They, in company with others who made the supreme sacrifice, have made the Empire what it has always stood to be, the champion of religion, justice, and the defender of law and order," stated the *Ottawa Citizen*, paraphrasing the reverend.

Memorials also went up at government buildings. A brass plaque in an ebony frame was installed on the wall near the entrance to the Legislative Chamber of Queen's Park, the seat of the Ontario government, in late March 1920. The plaque featured the names of nurses who worked at the No. 16 Canadian Hospital in Orpington, Kent, who died during the war, including Nurse McKenzie. Matron-in-Chief Margaret Macdonald unveiled the tablet. The ceremony was attended by the lieutenant governor and the premier of Ontario, along with provincial Cabinet members, other dignitaries, and spouses.

The Nurses' Memorial, a white marble artwork honouring all nursing sisters who died in the war, was placed in the Hall of Honour of Centre Block (the main building on Parliament Hill in Ottawa) on August 24, 1926. Hundreds of nurses, along with acting Prime Minister Henry Drayton, former prime minister Sir Robert Borden, Ontario premier Howard Ferguson, Matron-in-Chief Macdonald, and a who's-who list of other dignitaries, attended an installation ceremony.

Matron-in-Chief Macdonald once more had the honour of unveiling the bas-relief, which consisted of sculpted likenesses of nurses set on a flat panel, making the figures appear to be coming out of the wall. On the right side of the panel, a French nursing sister from the seventeenth century holds "a suffering Iroquois baby," wrote the *Ottawa Journal*. The left side depicted nurses from the Great War era helping injured soldiers. A plaque at the bottom of the memorial reads: "Erected by the Nurses of Canada in Remembrance of their sisters, who gave their lives in the Great War, nineteen fourteen-eighteen, and to perpetuate a noble tradition in the relations of the old world and the new."

The unveiling also featured two-minutes of silence and a playing of "The Last Post" wrote the *Journal*, which described the event as "one of the most brilliant functions ever seen in Ottawa."

Out of the public eye, the *Llandovery Castle* dead were also memorialized in a very different manner by army administrators. A notice was placed in the service file of Nurse Rena McLean reading, "Reported Missing Believed Drowned Ex Llandovery Castle." Similar notices were tucked into the service files of other CAMC personnel, as the military tied up loose ends.

CHAPTER FIVE

Criminal Orders

Germany signed the Treaty of Versailles — the document that officially ended the war — on June 28, 1919.

The peace terms were harsh: Germany was forced to pay huge reparations, surrender territory, and drastically pare down its armed forces. Germany also had to take full responsibility for starting the war — an obligation that proved explosively controversial.

Under the Versailles Treaty, Kaiser Wilhelm II was to be surrendered for a trial before an Allied tribunal. The treaty also laid the groundwork for broader war crimes trials. Germany was told to track down offenders, hand them over, and provide relevant documents.

The concept of a war crimes trial fit with the common perception that the war had been a struggle for civilization against German tyranny. Less clear was how these cases would proceed. Neither history nor the Hague Conventions offered a regulatory framework for establishing a war crimes trial. At the time, there was no international criminal court and even the idea of holding military and political leaders accountable was somewhat revolutionary.

"In considering the problem of trying the War Criminals, there were no real precedents, there was no Court, and there was no generally recognized code of law," wrote British lawyer and author Claud Mullins.

Armies have long had rules of behaviour and punished violators accordingly. For severe offences, troops could face a court-martial — a legal proceeding that is the military equivalent of a criminal trial for civilians. In the First World War, members of the CEF could be court-martialed for desertion, mutiny, insubordination, cowardice, drunkenness, et cetera. The ultimate penalty was execution. Typically, a court martial dealt with individual violations of military regulations — not crimes against humanity.

One of the few cases of a military official being punished for inhumane wartime conduct involved Henry Wirz, commander of a Confederate-run prisoner of war camp in Andersonville, Georgia during the U.S. Civil War. Even by dismal Civil War POW camp standards, Andersonville stood out, being an overcrowded hellhole, where thousands of Northern prisoners died from disease, neglect, and abuse. Wirz was arrested and tried for murder following the Confederate defeat. He was something of a scapegoat, given the limited resources made available to him, but in late 1865, he was convicted and hanged, nonetheless. His case remained anomalous, however, and other Confederate leaders went unpunished for equally vile behaviour.

Despite the lack of historical examples, the Allies were determined to exact justice against German war criminals. Once the Versailles Treaty officially came into effect on January 10, 1920, concrete measures could be taken against these criminals. The Kaiser, however, could not be put on trial because the Netherlands refused to extradite him.

That said, there were plenty of other people the Allies wanted to prosecute. In February 1920, Germany was given a list compiled by the Allied nations containing the names of over 850 potential war criminals. The United States did not participate in this judicial exercise. Although it had entered the fray with great dash in 1917, following the signing of the Armistice, America had gone back to its prewar state of isolationism. President Woodrow Wilson was recovering from a stroke and consumed with an ill-fated attempt to garner support for the League of Nations, the precursor to the United Nations.

"In the end, despite America's occasional rumbles about war crimes trials, the Wilson administration did not associate itself with the war crimes provisions of the Treaty of Versailles," notes Gary Bass in *Stay the Hand of Vengeance: The Politics of War Crimes Tribunals*.

While the Kaiser wasn't on the Allies' list, plenty of other high-ranking figures were, including Field Marshal Paul von Hindenburg, Grand Admiral Alfred von Tirpitz, Admiral Reinhard Scheer, General Erich Ludendorff, and German Army Commander Helmuth von Moltke. Germany's civilian government, beset by violence from both the left and right, balked. Riots would likely ensure if all the figures on the list were rounded up.

Berlin offered a compromise: give us the evidence and the Reichsgericht (German Supreme Court) in Leipzig would conduct the trials. German judges and prosecutors would try German war criminals. Allied demands for justice would be mollified, while the German public would (hopefully) be more inclined to accept the results.

The Allies agreed to this compromise, with a caveat. If the Germans were too soft, the Allies would hold their own war criminal trials. The Allies also scaled back their demands and provided a new list to the German government in May 1920, containing the names of only forty-five potential war criminals, most of them low-ranking.

Great Britain contributed seven names to this abridged list. These included three submarine commanders: Karl Neumann, Wilhelm Werner, and Helmut Patzig. As commander of U-*67*, Neumann sank the hospital ship *Dover Castle* in the Mediterranean Sea on May 26, 1917. Werner had been commander of U-*55*, which torpedoed a British steamer called the *Torrington* near the Cornwall coast on April 8, 1917. Werner was accused of deliberately submerging his sub to drown the captured *Torrington* crew, who had been ordered to stand on the deck of the U-boat. The four other figures named by the United Kingdom were said to have mistreated prisoners.

Even this shortened list proved problematic; some of the potential defendants, including sub commander Werner, couldn't be located, and Patzig was out of reach. After the war, Patzig had moved back to his hometown of Danzig, which created a major problem for authorities. As part of the Treaty of Versailles, Germany had to yield control of Danzig, which was now categorized as a "free city" under the complicated postwar order. Danzig's affairs were administered by Poland and the League of Nations. Simply put, German and Allied officials could not legally march into Danzig and take

Patzig into custody. Germany issued an arrest warrant against Patzig but didn't carry it out.

As a show of good faith, German officials put three former soldiers on trial in Leipzig, even though they weren't on the Allies list of war criminals. The trio — Paul Niegel, Paul Sangerhausen, and Deitrich Lottmann — were accused of robbing an innkeeper in Belgium.

The Supreme Court found the three defendants guilty on January 10, 1921, and handed out sentences ranging from two to five years.

Reaction among the Allied nations was decidedly muted ("Leipzig Court Makes a Feeble Start," read a *Times* of London headline about the trial). British, French, and Belgian authorities, among others, wanted German prosecutors to focus on figures from the Allies' list of war criminals. They were also infuriated by the slow pace of German compliance with treaty obligations. Under intense pressure, a new German government led by Chancellor Josef Wirth promised to speed up the country's adherence to Versailles requirements, including trials for war criminals named by the Allies.

Holding war criminals accountable would be a unique way of achieving justice after a brutal conflict, while setting an example for future wartime conduct.

At least that was the hope as the German Supreme Court in Leipzig began to ponder a series of cases brought forward by the Allied nations.

Following the "feeble start," involving the prosecution of three low-ranking thieves, the Leipzig War Crimes Trials officially commenced on May 23, 1921. Like the trials held earlier that year, the proceedings took place in the Kaiserhalle, a large courtroom at the German Supreme Court building in Leipzig. The courtroom boasted oak-panelled walls and stained-glass windows adorned with coats of arms from various German states. Hanging on the walls were life-sized oil paintings of German monarchs, including Kaiser Wilhelm I and Frederick the Great, but not Kaiser Wilhelm II, whose likeness had been removed.

The Leipzig court featured seven justices, who wore magenta-coloured robes, "mammoth ready-made white bow ties," and "muffin-shaped bonnets of dull crimson" on their heads, reported the *New York Times*.

These legal luminaries represented "what was technically known as 'the Punishment Senate' of the Reichsgericht, Germany's supreme tribunal," added the *Times*.

The judges and a pair of state prosecutors sat on one side of a horseshoe-shaped table. The accused and their counsel sat to the right of the judicial bench, while observers from various Allied nations sat at tables to the left. The British mission was led by Sir Ernest Pollock K.C. (King's Counsel), the U.K. solicitor-general and an "eminent legal talent," according to the *Globe*. Sir Pollock (who was also a member of Parliament) and his colleagues were only there to watch, not participate.

Additional seating in the Kaiserhalle was taken up by reporters, representatives of the German government, and members of the public. Witnesses stood to give their testimony inside the horseshoe shaped table, facing the judges. The words of these witnesses were translated into German or English, so everyone could follow the proceedings. Hearings ran from nine in the morning until around eight at night, with an afternoon recess. The courtroom was typically packed with partisan German spectators, who were quick to voice their opinions.

German court procedure was decidedly different than judicial proceedings in Great Britain or Canada. Unlike in the British tradition, the German justices reviewed the available evidence and read depositions from witnesses before the trials started. They took a proactive role, with Court President Dr. Karl Ludwig Schmidt regularly questioning witnesses at length. Witnesses were rarely cross-examined, and the main prosecutor, German state attorney Dr. Ludwig Ebermayer, played something of a secondary role.

A "gaunt, able, and rather awe-inspiring man" in the words of Claud Mullins, who attended the trials, Dr. Ebermayer had the unenviable task of trying to convict his fellow citizens of war crimes. "It was for him, according to the ordinary criminal procedure in Germany, to ask for conviction or acquittal and to suggest to the Court what sentence, if any, should be passed," wrote Mullins in his sweeping account, *The Leipzig Trials: An Account of the War, Criminals Trials and a Study of German Mentality*, which was published in 1921 and remains the definitive account of the proceedings.

From the beginning, the Allies were skeptical that true justice would prevail. "All Teuton War Brutes Who Committed Atrocities Will Escape Scot-Free," read a May 24 headline in the *Globe*. As it turned out, this wasn't entirely true, although the Allies had drastically pared down their list of potential criminals. In the end, fewer than twenty defendants would appear before the German Supreme Court in Leipzig.

Some Allied nations were already backing away from the war crimes trials. "The United States, Italy and Serbia have either refused or failed to bring evidence against anyone," wrote the *Globe*. Italy, which fought on the side of the Allies in the Great War, would later join Nazi Germany to wreak havoc decades later.

The first cases heard that May concerned German soldiers accused of abusing British prisoners. Three German defendants — Karl Heynen, Emil Muller, and Robert Neumann (no relation to the submarine captain) — were convicted of mistreating their captives. Heynen was sentenced to ten months imprisonment, while Muller and Neumann each received a six-month sentence. Some of the prisoners the trio had abused had died, so the sentences were widely viewed as overly lenient ("Second Act in Leipzig Farce," read a *Globe* headline regarding Muller's sentencing).

Any remaining faith the Allies had placed in the Leipzig court evaporated on June 4, following the acquittal of U-*67* commander Karl Neumann. The case was particularly galling, because Neumann readily admitted he had fired on the *Dover Castle* hospital ship while it transported patients in the Mediterranean Sea.

Under Section 47 of the German Military Penal Code, subordinates could be punished if they obeyed an order that resulted in a civil or military crime, noted the justices. The German Admiralty, however, had given the go-ahead to stalk hospital ships in the Mediterranean and a zone from the English Channel to the North Sea. Given this, Neumann thought it was perfectly reasonable to fire on the *Dover Castle*, and the court agreed.

"It is a military principle that the subordinate is bound to obey the orders of his superiors.... The accused accordingly sank the Dover Castle in obedience to a service order of his highest superiors, an order which he considered to be binding. He cannot, therefore, be punished for his conduct," stated the German Supreme Court in the Neumann case.

The ethics of sinking a hospital ship, much less the blatant violation of the Hague Convention — orders from the German Admiralty aside — didn't enter into the equation. The Allies were seriously displeased ("German Judges Solemnly Go Through Motions of Trying War Criminal," read a *Globe* headline about Neumann).

The next series of trials focused on war criminals named by France and Belgium. One particularly shocking case involved Max Ramdohr, formerly of the German secret military police in occupied Belgium, who was accused of kidnapping and torturing young boys. The boys were imprisoned for weeks, beaten, and had their heads immersed in buckets of water. Ramdohr believed the young prisoners had information about the sabotage of rail lines used by German troop trains.

State prosecutor Dr. Ebermayer requested a sentence of two years, but even that was too much for the Supreme Court. The justices dismissed the boys' testimony on the grounds that it couldn't be corroborated. When Ramdohr was acquitted on June 11, German spectators burst into applause.

Infuriated trial observers from Belgium reported back to that country's minister of justice. The minister included these remarks in a statement to the Belgian Chamber of Representatives, who were outraged by the court's decision. The Belgian government threatened to hold its own war crimes trials, which was allowed under the Treaty of Versailles.

"The President of the Chamber, in reply to the Minister of Justice, said the Chamber was unanimous in considering the acquittal of Ramdohr a parody of justice," wrote the *Globe*.

The French cases provoked similar controversy. German general Karl Stenger was accused of issuing an order early in the war to murder wounded French prisoners. His subordinate, Major Benno Crusius, was accused of carrying out the killings. Crusius said he was just following orders. His boss denied he ever gave such gruesome instructions.

"I did nothing in the war except my duty and obligation to the leaders of the German Fatherland, to my Kaiser, the Supreme War Lord, and in the interests of the lives of fighting German soldiers," protested Stenger in court.

Upon hearing this, German spectators in the courtroom applauded again. The crowd was delighted when General Stenger was acquitted on July 6. Oddly, the unlucky Major Crusius was convicted and sentenced to two years in jail.

One day later, Lieutenant Adolf Laule was acquitted of murdering a French soldier. Next on the docket were generals Benno Kruska and Hans von Schack, both charged with criminal negligence. These generals oversaw a prisoner of war camp where thousands of French soldiers died of typhus. Had better sanitary and medical measures been taken, many of these deaths could have been prevented, argued the prosecution.

It was a strong case, but France was fed up. Just as the trial began, officials in France ordered the French mission to leave at once. The mission departed for Paris, along with all the French witnesses who were set to testify. The case collapsed and generals Kruska and von Schack were acquitted.

The outcome for future cases seemed equally bleak.

Behind the scenes, however, German authorities were scrambling to appease the increasingly furious Allied governments. Sensing the mood among their former adversaries after the opening trials, Germany decided to build a new case around the U-boat crew who sank the *Llandovery Castle*. If Commander Patzig couldn't be brought to trial, the two lieutenants who stood with him on the sub deck as lifeboats were pummelled with shells would be charged.

The German public prosecutor arranged for lieutenants Ludwig Dithmar and John Boldt to be arrested and charged with murder, even though neither man was on the Allies list of war criminals. Great Britain was invited to provide prosecution witnesses and evidence.

In late June, Boldt was arrested in Hamburg and taken to Leipzig in handcuffs — a shocking indignity as far as German right-wing parties were concerned. Dithmar's arraignment was apparently more low-key and didn't cause as much righteous indignation.

"In the Reichstag, [the Nationalists have] tabled an interpellation on the subject, demanding to know 'what steps the Government proposes to take to protect the German nation from such deep insults to its honour as are involved in the chaining of its U-boat heroes and defenders of their country,'" wrote the *New York Times*.

Hamburg police had good reason for keeping Boldt on a tight leash: "They state that Boldt, who is a daring and adroit man, is known to have declared that he would not go to Leipzig but would rather escape from the train en route. Moreover, there were unmistakable indications that a certain group of Hamburg people intended to liberate him," wrote the *Daily Telegraph*.

The decision to try Boldt and Dithmar was so last-minute, authorities had to scramble to gather witnesses. The trial date was set for mid-July 1921, which gave officials about three weeks to find enough people to testify. The Canadian government put forward a list of *Llandovery Castle* survivors from the CAMC who could act as witnesses. For unclear reasons, Sergeant Arthur Knight, then living in London, Ontario, was overlooked — a decision that displeased him greatly.

"Sergt. Arthur Knight Cannot Understand Why Actual Participants in the Greatest Tragedy of the Great War Are Not Called to Give Evidence," read the subhead to a story in Knight's hometown newspaper, the *London Advertiser*.

"Although he was one of the six Canadian survivors of the 110 who were aboard the boat, and although he was called to relate the story to the King and later was the chief witness before the court of inquiry in England, Sergt. Knight was not among those who were recommended for the trip," stated the *Advertiser*. If he wasn't able to testify, Knight did provide the newspaper with a vivid account of his ordeal on the night of the sinking, which the *Advertiser* ran on its front-page.

Testimony for the *Llandovery Castle* trial was first heard in London, England, not Leipzig. On July 4, Henry Evans, former purser on the *Llandovery Castle*, gave evidence in a Bow Street Magistrates' Court. Evans wasn't able to travel to Germany.

Evans, who was by then working on a poultry farm, was questioned by V.M. Gattie, representing the British government. Sir Chartres Biron, chief magistrate, presided. German legal counsel for the defence were also present.

The purser denied allegations that there were American flying officers on the ship and noted that the *Llandovery Castle*'s green hospital lights were on at the time of the attack. There were also highly visible Red Crosses on the sides of the ship, said Evans. He testified that "several" lifeboats and rafts were in the water, including Lifeboat No. 4, which eventually rescued him.

"Did you see the submarine again?" asked Gattie.

"Yes, she came at us at a high rate of speed, apparently to run us down," said Evans.

The sub missed the lifeboat "by inches" added the purser.

The U-boat departed and cannon fire commenced, Evans continued. Given that no other survivors turned up, he assumed the sub was shelling the other lifeboats. Evans's testimony was passed on to the German Supreme Court, along with other depositions.

While Sergeant Knight wasn't on Ottawa's witness list, Major Thomas Lyon was. Lyon had been enjoying civilian life in Vancouver, B.C., when word came that his presence was required in Leipzig. He agreed to testify, even if it meant a frantic journey half-way around the world. Speedy jet travel didn't exist at the time, so Lyon had to undertake a lengthy trip by train and ship to reach continental Europe. The former medical officer was determined to make it to Leipzig in time to testify against the men who tried to kill him.

Lyon was still in transit when the *Llandovery Castle* trial began on July 12, 1921. Reporters competed for limited seating with members of the German public and military. The British mission, led again by Sir Pollock, was present to observe.

Any hope that the defendants might show remorse was quickly dashed. Dithmar showed up in court wearing a navy uniform festooned with medals, including his Iron Cross. Boldt opted for a black suit along with his own Iron Cross medallion. Neither man made a good impression on reporters from the Allied nations.

"Both men are dark and clean shaven, with sallow complexions and a sullen and unamiable expression. Boldt's demeanour was especially truculent," wrote the *Gloucestershire Echo*.

Dr. Schmidt read out the charges against the lieutenants, which consisted of two separate offences — torpedoing the *Llandovery Castle* and massacring the survivors. Asked if they had anything to say in response to the charges, Boldt and Dithmar took the opportunity to praise their former commander.

"I gave my word to Lieutenant Patzig that I would never speak about the case, and I will keep my word," stated Dithmar.

"I obeyed my commander. His orders were law. I am not guilty. I am proud to have served under such an officer as [Patzig]," echoed Boldt.

Keeping silent also meant the lieutenants didn't have to worry about possibly incriminating themselves.

If they refused to discuss the *Llandovery Castle* ambush, Boldt and Dithmar were happy to commend their murderous commander. Boldt went on so long that at one point Dr. Schmidt cut him off. "We know that German officers are keen and brave, but what does that have to do with the case?" asked the court president.

Boldt ignored this interjection and kept ranting. He recounted an occasion where Patzig had sunk an American troop transport called the USS *Cincinnati*, despite having a bent periscope and only a single torpedo left. Destroying this ship prevented "the landing of an additional 32,000 American troops monthly. If every U-boat Commander had been as good as Patzig the war would have gone differently," testified Boldt.

The *Cincinnati*, the original name of a vessel built by a German company, was interned in a U.S. port when the war broke out. The American government seized the vessel after the United States declared war on Germany, changed its name to the *Covington*, and began using it as a troop transport. The ship was attacked after U-*86* sank the *Llandovery Castle*.

Patzig "might have have made a mistake" or devised "the wrong plans" on occasion, but that was understandable given his "passionate, holy will to break the hunger blockade and lead Germany to victory," continued Boldt.

"This is not the place to plead justification for the war," snapped the annoyed court president.

This unapologetically belligerent opening set the tone for the entire trial. Defence counsel for Boldt and Dithmar repeatedly tried to justify

German military actions, including the sinking of the *Llandovery Castle*. This defiant stance wasn't the least bit tempered when prosecution witnesses began to testify.

Leslie Chapman, second officer of the *Llandovery Castle*, spoke first on the opening day of the trial. Like all British and Canadian witnesses during the case, Chapman's words were translated into German for the court by Dr. W.E. Peters, a languages professor at Leipzig University. Dr. Peters lived in Germany but had been born in Australia and had a degree from Aberdeen University.

"Dr. Peters' interpreting left nothing to be desired. It was entirely satisfactory, and with his assistance the witnesses were enabled to give their answers fully and clearly," states the document, "German War Trials: The Report of Proceedings Before the Supreme Court in Leipzig."

Chapman "gave a thrilling account of the torpedoing and sinking of the ship and the subsequent conduct of the submarine. Chapman was an admirable witness. He was perfectly cool and collected and spoke only as to what he himself knew. His testimony appeared to make a deep impression on the court," wrote the *Western Daily Press*.

Chapman described how U-*86* pulled alongside Lifeboat No. 4 and interrupted the rescue of floundering survivors. Chapman was asked by the court president what he thought about the German crewman who ordered him onto the sub. The question would seem a rather obvious one, but Chapman responded in a dignified manner.

"Chapman replied that he would rather not say, but when pressed to answer he said he wondered what sort of man he could be who fired a torpedo against a hospital ship," reported the *Western Daily Press*.

Chapman provided detailed answers during his interrogation and said he observed seven lifeboats departing from the *Llandovery Castle*. Two capsized, but the water was calm and the remaining five could have survived had U-*86* not shelled them, said Chapman. He also testified that he saw a survivor from the ship climb aboard the sub, only to be tossed back into the ocean by sailors. Unless more than one person attempted this move, Chapman was almost certainly referring to Sergeant Knight.

Chapman's calm and steady demeamour drew praise from newspaper reporters. Even the Leipzig justices would later write that Chapman "impressed the court as a quiet, clear-headed and reliable witness."

J. Crosby, the wireless operator from the steamer the *Atlantian*, sunk previously by U-*86*, testified about conversations he overheard while below decks. Crosby gathered that the crew was aware the *Llandovery Castle* was a hospital ship but stalked the vessel anyway. On the night of the attack, Crosby heard two torpedoes launch from the sub. Roughly fifteen minutes later, he could hear the sound of the deck gun firing. He estimated the barrage lasted about twenty minutes.

Commander George Sherston of the *Snowdrop*, a Royal Navy sloop, offered poignant testimony about the search for survivors. After news of the attack on the *Llandovery Castle* came out, Sherston was ordered by British authorities to patrol the area where the ship sank. The *Snowdrop* searched the ocean for two days but found no more survivors.

Trial coverage wasn't subtle: "One by one, they pumped shells into the frail, overcrowded British lifeboats, unmindful of the cries for mercy and the groans of the dying," wrote the *Globe* on July 14, 1921.

"Yesterday, there appeared before the court two individuals who were associated with the blackest and most dastardly murder that ever befouled the pages of history," exclaimed the *Evening Mail* of Halifax that same day. The paper made a direct comparison with another notorious submarine ambush: "Not even the sinking of the Lusitania can minimize the cold-blooded cruelty and diabolical premeditation of this crime, costing as it did the lives of so many Canadians, engaged on a mission whose sacredness for centuries rendered its participants immune from attack or molestation."

On day two of the trial, it was the defence counsel's turn to put witnesses on the stand. While the witnesses acknowledged that the *Llandovery Castle* had been torpedoed (as opposed to hitting a sea mine, as earlier German propaganda tried to claim), most said the act was justified.

Gunner Meissner died before the trial started, but several of his colleagues offered testimony, including Petty Officer Walter Popitz.

Described as a "petty officer with a conscience" by the *Leicester Mercury*, Popitz was relatively forthcoming. He said U-*86* spotted the *Llandovery*

Castle in the afternoon of June 27, 1918, and tracked it for hours. The ship's hospital lights were plainly visible at dusk, making it obvious the vessel was on a medical mission, he admitted. However, Popitz insisted it was a legitimate target.

"We knew from the German newspapers that the English abused hospital ships," he testified.

That said, the ship wasn't travelling on a zig-zag course — the typical manoeuvre for surface vessels concerned about subs — indicating it felt safe from attack, said Popitz. He claimed there was some debate about whether to attack the *Llandovery Castle*. Popitz said he urged First Lieutenant Patzig to leave the ship alone, and that Dithmar agreed with this hands-off approach. Patzig was not an autocratic leader and was always open to discussing things, explained Popitz.

Petty Officer Popitz obediently went to his battle station after Patzig decided to attack the ship. The U-boat fired two torpedoes and then surfaced so the crew could look for evidence that the ship carried war supplies or soldiers, stated Popitz.

Dr. Schmidt interjected. If the U-boat crew was so convinced the *Llandovery Castle* was transporting illicit cargo or personnel, why didn't Patzig just stop the ship and search it? Such inspections were permissible under the Hague Conventions.

Popitz said that would have been impossible but didn't elaborate. The crew did feel bad about what they had done, he said. He referred to the post-ambush meeting at which Patzig took full responsibility for the attack and ordered everyone to keep quiet about it. Popitz recalled seeing three or four lifeboats filled with survivors, with other people trying to swim.

The petty officer did provide one helpful detail for the prosecution. Dr. Schmidt asked if the second explosion on the *Llandovery Castle*, which occurred when the ship was sinking, sounded like munitions igniting.

"No, it was the boilers exploding," stated Popitz.

Johannes Ney, second engineer on the *U-86*, testified next. He seemed decidedly unhappy about being in court and contradicted many previous statements he had made in a deposition. When being deposed, Ney said he saw multiple lifeboats in the water. In court, he said no, he only saw a single lifeboat. Ney mentioned shellfire in his deposition. In court, he insisted he knew nothing about any shots being fired at lifeboats. Ney corroborated Popitz's account of the all-crew meeting following the torpedo attack. While denying any first-hand knowledge, Ney admitted the crew openly discussed the shelling of the lifeboats in the days following the attack. When returning to base, the sub hit a mine, causing some damage, continued the second engineer. Some of the more superstitious members of the crew interpreted this to be a kind of divine punishment, noted Ney.

First Engineer Lieutenant Knocke also testified about the gloomy mood in the sub following the *Llandovery Castle* sinking. Even Patzig seemed contrite and upset, insisted Knocke (though the U-*86* commander was not contrite enough to record the attack in his *Kriegstagebuch*).

Several defence witnesses brought up the Royal Navy blockade of German ports; they seemed to believe that causing mass hunger among civilians justified an attack on a Canadian hospital ship. While this might have been a stretch, the defence also highlighted a harrowing incident involving a British ambush with eerie echoes of the *Llandovery Castle*.

Lieutenant Crompton, a former officer with U-*41*, told the court about an encounter with British Q-ship, the *Baralong*, on September 24, 1915. The encounter occurred in the Western Approaches — a patch of ocean west of Ireland.

The *Baralong* was a rundown civilian tramp steamer fitted with concealed 12-pounder cannons. When the *Baralong* approached U-*41*, it was flying a U.S. flag (America was neutral at the time). The German sub crew could be forgiven for assuming the vessel was just a harmless steamer from a country they weren't at war with. When the Q-ship got close, it blasted U-*41* with shells from its 12-pounders. The sub sank and Crompton, who was wounded, found himself swimming in the ocean, crying for help. He managed to get himself into an empty lifeboat, which the *Baralong* tried to ram as sailors on board laughed. A subsequent witness from U-*41* corroborated this account, adding that the *Baralong*'s name was painted over.

This wasn't the end of Crompton's testimony. He said he was rescued by a different boat, taken prisoner, and shipped to England. In late 1916, he was transported across the English Channel then taken to a prison camp in Switzerland. The vessel making the voyage was none other than the *Llandovery Castle*. While docked, Crompton said hundreds of men in brown British military uniforms boarded the vessel, which was now officially a hospital ship. If these men were soldiers, this meant the *Llandovery Castle* was guilty of breaking Hague rules. The prosecution quickly pointed out that the Royal Army Medical Corps also wore brown uniforms, which could be mistaken for soldier's garb at a distance.

While confused about the personnel he observed embarking on the *Llandovery Castle*, Lieutenant Crompton did have a valid point about Royal Navy ethics. In fact, the month before it encountered U-*41*, the *Baralong* had been involved in another potential war crime.

On August 19, 1915, U-*27* intercepted a cargo ship called the *Nicosian* off the coast of Ireland. Shells from the sub deck gun forced the *Nicosian* to a halt. Through flag signals, the U-*27* commander ordered the *Nicosian* crew to abandon ship, a command the steamer captain relayed to his men. The U-boat then proceeded to fire at the *Nicosian*, aiming to sink it without having to waste a torpedo. As the *Nicosian* crewmen frantically rowed away on lifeboats, the *Baralong* appeared on the scene, having heard reports about U-boats in the area.

Through flag signals of its own, the *Baralong* indicated it wanted to rescue the crew of the *Nicosian*. Taking note of the *Baralong*'s ramshackle appearance and American flag, the commander of U-*27* acceded to this request. The Q-ship cruised close to the sub then revealed its guns and pumped shells into U-*27*. The U-boat began to sink, and frantic submariners leapt in the water to save themselves. Royal Marines on the *Baralong* started shooting at the German sailors in the water (reportedly to avenge the recent torpedoing of the *Lusitania*). A few submariners managed to board the *Nicosian*, which was still afloat. A boarding party from the *Baralong* killed them all.

When this attack came to light, Berlin protested furiously, while British authorities tried to gloss over the incident. Testimony about the *Baralong* might have had an impact in Leipzig, except the defence counsel didn't drive the point home. Instead of focusing on Royal Navy atrocities, defence lawyers kept putting up witnesses with unlikely stories about hospital ship abuses. A defence witness named Gustav Meyer claimed to have seen a French hospital ship packed with planes, soldiers, and munitions, while he was a prisoner in Toulon, France.

U-boat commander Alfred Saalwachter perpetuated this line of argument during his testimony and insisted the Allies routinely misused hospital ships. While conceding that the *Llandovery Castle* wasn't doing anything to warrant a torpedo, Saalwachter said U-boat crews were under a lot of strain during the last year of the war. The presence of Q-ships and the possibility of an ambush left U-boat commanders in a high state of anxiety, testified Saalwachter.

A decorated submarine captain who had sunk over two dozen ships during the First World War, Saalwachter's words carried great weight. Compared to other witnesses from the German military, he came across as relatively reasonable. Saalwachter said Patzig "manifestly knew that the sinking of this vessel was unjustified" and that "there could be no justification for the shooting of helpless men in the water," wrote the *Daily Telegraph*.

Still, Saalwachter's barbs about the Royal Navy got under Dr. Ebermayer's skin. The Royal Navy wasn't on trial pointed out the state prosecutor, who also expressed annoyance with the stream of slander against Allied hospital ships. At Dr. Ebermayer's request, the court allowed a trio of previous prosecution witnesses to testify again, to rebut defence claims about hospital ship abuses.

The two final witnesses for the defence managed to introduce some of the most callous testimony heard during the trial.

Admiral Adolf von Trotha, who served as chief of the Imperial Navy from 1916 onwards, admitted that U-boat commanders behaved ruthlessly but said that was because the war had hardened their feelings. By 1918, German submarine officers felt they had to carry out their duties "regardless of considerations of humanity," stated von Trotha, according to Chicago's *Daily Herald*.

Witness Dr. Toepfer was a district medical officer who observed court-martials of German military personnel. This role apparently gave him insights into the mindset of naval officers. These officers believed hospital ships were being misused and should be put in the same category as warships, testified Dr. Toepfer. Besides, any actions that hurt the enemy were justifiable, continued the doctor.

Cruel as this view might seem, the German public was inclined to agree. German civilians and veterans alike took a dim view of the proceedings and regularly protested outside the Supreme Court building. Some of these demonstrations were organized by reactionary associations of German military officers. Newspaper articles defended Boldt and Dithmar and right-wing politicians continued to complain about how they were treated. Defence counsel was equally defiant.

Defence lawyers introduced "hatred and prejudice into their fiery speeches" and aimed their remarks at "the press and public, rather than to the Court," wrote Mullins. The justices occasionally criticized the defence lawyers when they went too far. Wishing to ensure that all witnesses had the opportunity to speak, the court took pains to accommodate Major Lyon. It extended the trial until July 15, so the former CAMC major could testify.

After travelling seven thousand miles, Lyon arrived in court "a few minutes before the hearing closed … [and he] furnished the sensation of the trial by immediately abusing the infamous and cowardly methods used by the submarine commander. He vehemently attacked Captain Patzig for the sinking of the helpless ship," reported the *Vancouver Sun*.

Described as "a tall, sunburnt man," Lyon gave "a clear account of all that happened on the night the Llandovery Castle was torpedoed," added the *Guardian*. Lyon testified that he was enjoying a card game with some nurses when the *Llandovery Castle* was torpedoed. He detailed the horror of the attack, the swift response of the crew and CAMC personnel, and his rough interrogation on the deck of U-*86*. Asked if the German sailor who manhandled him was in court, Lyon said he didn't know.

Before the court, Lyon made it very clear that the *Llandovery Castle* was an unarmed medical ship. No one on board even carried a pistol, he said. Lyon "only once saw a revolver in the possession of a patient and he took it away immediately and locked it in a safe," reported the *Daily Telegraph*.

The former medical officer told the court how a German submariner urged him to flee — "It's better for you to get away quickly" — before U-*86* tried to ram his lifeboat. Lyon's testimony clearly hit a nerve. "He speaks without a trace of emotion.... Lyon then finishes his evidence, and there is a deep silence throughout the court," wrote the *Guardian*.

After gathering his thoughts, Dr. Ebermayer launched into a tirade about the man who ordered the torpedo attack on the *Llandovery Castle*.

"Where is Captain Patzig, who boasted that he did his Fatherland a great service by sinking the American liner *Cincinnati*? Why did the brave man not appear? Why is he leaving the blame for the sinking of the hospital ship *Llandovery Castle* upon his subordinates? Why does not Captain Patzig come out of his hiding place and say, 'I sunk the *Llandovery Castle* because I was told she carried American aviators to France'?" sneered Dr. Ebermayer.

For all the barbs directed at the U-boat commander, there was a sense that "the prosecutors and judges at Leipzig were reluctant to punish fellow Germans," notes James Willis in his book, *Prologue to Nuremberg: The Politics and Diplomacy of Punishing War Criminals of the First World War*.

This became evident during Dr. Ebermayer's final address, in which he all but apologized for his role in the legal proceedings. "In my forty years as public prosecutor and judge, my office has never been so difficult as today, when I must proceed against two German officers who fought bravely and faithfully for their Fatherland," he stated.

While torpedoing the *Llandovery Castle* clearly violated Hague rules, the prosecution downplayed this aspect of the case. In fact, charges relating to the torpedo attack were dropped. The state prosecutor claimed that "the legality of the torpedoing of the *Llandovery Castle* was not a matter at issue at this trial," adding that the court was "also not concerned with the question [of] whether England had ever misused hospital ships," wrote Mullins.

"We are only concerned here with what happened after the sinking," explained Dr. Ebermayer.

This decision might have pleased German militarists, but the prosecutor wasn't done. Dr. Ebermayer said he was "fully convinced" the sub deliberately shelled the lifeboats to murder the survivors, wrote the *Daily Telegraph*.

Patzig, Boldt, and Dithmar acted together and therefore were collectively responsible for the massacre, continued Dr. Ebermayer. He insisted the lieutenants could have refused to take part in the barrage.

Dr. Ebermayer suddenly pivoted. Since no one could prove that shells from the sub hit any lifeboats — the survivors in Lifeboat No. 4 admitted they didn't see any explosions but assumed the lifeboats were under fire — Boldt and Dithmar couldn't be convicted of murder, said the prosecutor. He said a lesser charge was warranted.

"This is a case of attempted murder, the minimum penalty for which is three years imprisonment. I see no reason to go much above this and I ask for a sentence of four years," said Dr. Ebermayer.

Then, the prosecutor resumed his attack on the commander of U-*86*.

"I have no doubt, that Patzig knew and knows that his subordinates are being held responsible for these events. It would be natural and his duty for him to appear to tell the truth. If Patzig believes that he, and not the accused officers, is guilty, he should come before the court," stated Dr. Ebermayer. Patzig was a coward, and his conduct was evidence of "colossal meanness" he added.

Dithmar's defence lawyer spoke next. He said his client should be exonerated since it couldn't be proven he killed anyone.

Boldt's counsel took a different tack. He said it was unfair to convert a troopship to a hospital ship then expect U-boat crews to respect Hague naval rules. In fact, such conversions were permissible, provided the Central Powers were informed of the switch — as they were, in the case of the *Llandovery Castle*.

Firing on the *Llandovery Castle* lifeboats was fully justifiable, continued the lawyer. Letting the survivors live would enable them to fight on another day (or, more accurately, provide medical care for fighters). Perhaps sensing this wasn't a winning argument, the lawyer complained about double standards and the British naval blockade of German ports.

With that, defence counsel rested.

The court president asked Boldt and Dithmar if they wanted to say anything. Neither man did, so the justices departed to ponder their verdict.

It wasn't clear how the judges would rule. The weight of evidence suggested conviction — "It is hard to see how the German Supreme Court can avoid convicting Submarine Lieutenants Dithmar and Boldt of murder after this first trial day in Leipsic," wrote the *New York Times* on July 12, using a common alternative spelling of the city's name. Given how previous cases had been resolved, such speculation seemed unduly optimistic.

July 16 was sentencing day, and German spectators seemed giddy at the prospect of another acquittal.

"An excited crowd filled the courtroom today. Many women and numerous friends of the prisoners were present. The accused officers looked more cheerful than at any time since their trial began, but their appearance changed when the sentences were announced," wrote the *New York Times*.

The court president began to read the ruling aloud. It quickly became apparent that the justices rejected many of the defence arguments. The judges acknowledged that the *Llandovery Castle* wasn't doing anything illicit. The men in brown uniforms seen boarding the ship were clearly medical personnel, not soldiers.

"There were no combatants on board, and in particular, no American airmen. The vessel had not taken on board any munitions or other war material," stated Dr. Schmidt.

If anything, Patzig was the one who wasn't following the rules: "The German Naval Command had given orders that hospital ships were only to be sunk within the limits of a certain barred area. However, this area was a long way from the point we have now under consideration. Patzig knew this and was aware that by torpedoing the Llandovery Castle he was acting against orders," stated the court.

Like Dr. Ebermayer, the justices were mainly concerned with what happened after the ship sank. They took note of the large number of survivors who tried to get away from the sinking vessel. "[I]t may be concluded that of the boats on the starboard side, three (marked with odd numbers) were got away undamaged with two of the boats on the port side (marked with even numbers).... It is quite possible that out of these five boats which left the steamer safely, one or two may have been drawn into the vortex made by the sinking ship. But the evidence has shown that at least three of these five boats survived the sinking of the ship," stated the court president.

Regardless of the actual number, the justices agreed that the sub fired its deck gun at the remaining lifeboats, specifically to kill survivors. And this, said the court, constituted a very blatant war crime.

"The firing on the boats was an offence against the law of nations. In war on land the killing of unarmed enemies is not allowed ... similarly in war at sea, the killing of shipwrecked people who have taken refuge in lifeboats is forbidden.... The rule of international law, which is here involved, is simple and is universally known. No possible doubt can exist regarding the question of its applicability. The Court must in this instance affirm Patzig's guilt of killing contrary to international law," stated the justices.

Even though Patzig was responsible for ordering the barrage, Dithmar and Boldt were still culpable.

"Patzig's order does not free the accused from guilt ... a subordinate obeying [an] order is liable to punishment, if it was known to him that the order of the superior involved the infringement of civil or military law," continued the court.

In other words, even though obedience to authority is the norm in the military, a subordinate is not obliged to obey an order that is "universally known to everybody" as a violation of the law.

"This happens only in rare and exceptional cases. But this case was precisely one of them, for in the present instance, it was perfectly clear to the accused that killing defenseless people in the lifeboats could be nothing else but a breach of the law. As naval officers by profession they were well aware, as the naval expert Saalwachter has strikingly stated, that one is not legally authorized to kill defenseless people," read the court president.

Given this, Boldt and Dithmar "should certainly have refused to obey" Patzig's orders to take part in the shelling, continued the court.

"The killing of defenseless shipwrecked people is an act in the highest degree contrary to ethical principles. It must also not be left out of consideration that the deed throws a dark shadow on the German fleet, and specially the submarine weapon which did so much in the fight for the Fatherland," noted the justices.

Since the lieutenants refused to testify, the justices speculated about their roles. Maybe the men served as lookouts, gauging distance and shell placement as the deck gunner pummelled the lifeboats. While Commander Patzig was guilty of homicide, Boldt and Dithmar were not, said the court. "A direct act of killing, following a deliberate intention to kill, is not proved against the accused. They are, therefore, only liable to punishment as accessories," ruled the justices.

With that, the German Supreme Court passed sentence. Boldt and Dithmar would each serve four years in jail. Dithmar was also dismissed from the German Navy and Boldt was prohibited from wearing his uniform as a retired officer. The latter punishment was seen as particularly humiliating for a German war veteran.

The defendants didn't show any emotion during the sentencing, but the spectators were furious.

"When the judges had withdrawn, I saw several members of the public go up to the condemned men and sympathize with them. There was an electric atmosphere both in the Court and amid the crowd outside. The British Mission retired quietly to its private room, and then left the Court by a side door, closely guarded by German police. Thus the possibility of any unpleasant incident was avoided," wrote Mullins.

The ruling managed to antagonize all sides. Germans were outraged at the supposed severity of the sentence while Allied nations thought the punishments were ludicrously light. "The Leipzig Farces" read a headline in London's *Evening Standard*. French and Belgian officials said the trials "had been farces" wrote the *New York Times*.

In Canada, the *Globe* huffed, "If the Leipzig trials are not altogether farcical, someone must be convicted for the wholesale murder done on the night of June 27, 1918."

The ruling also sparked a great deal of confusion. How could the Supreme Court acquit U-boat commander Neumann of torpedoing a hospital ship, while Patzig was faulted for the very same act?

It all came down to the issue of "legality." The German Admiralty had expressly permitted attacks on hospital ships in the Mediterranean Sea so, therefore, Neumann didn't break any (German) laws when he sank the *Dover Castle*.

By contrast, the court decided that Commander Patzig clearly exceeded his orders. The *Llandovery Castle* wasn't anywhere near the zones where attacks on hospital ships were permitted. Further, shelling survivors in lifeboats contravened any basic sense of humanity and international law. The

German navy did not authorize the use of force against helpless people in lifeboats. Left unsaid was the notion that firing on lifeboats was a worse crime than sinking unarmed hospital ships. Had U-*86* slipped away after torpedoing the *Llandovery Castle* and left the survivors alone, it's questionable if Boldt and Dithmar would have been convicted.

Amid rage and dismay about the ruling, the German Supreme Court did earn some praise for being even-handed. "Speaking for myself and of the trials which I witnessed, I say frankly that Dr. Schmidt and his Court were fair. Fully neutral at the start, I learnt to respect them, and am convinced they performed their difficult task without fear or favour. Personally, I would be willing to be tried by Dr. Schmidt on any charge, even on one which involved my word against that of a German," wrote Mullins, whose account of the Leipzig Trials was published soon after Boldt and Dithmar were sentenced.

"The Court President, Dr. Karl Schmidt, conducted the trials with punctilious fairness and courtesy toward both the Allied witnesses and the top-level delegations from Britain, France, and Belgium, which attended the prosecution of 'their' cases," state Alan Kramer and John Horne in their book *German Atrocities, 1914: A History of Denial.*

For all that, there was a great feeling of disappointment among the Allies. Two subordinates had received relatively mild jail sentences, while the man who ordered the attack remained free.

A month after the *Llandovery Castle* trial ended, there was a hint of justice in the air. The *New York Times* reported that Commander Patzig, who had relocated to South America, was planning to turn himself in to the Leipzig court. According to the *Times*, which was simply rehashing news first reported in the German media, Patzig wanted to take full responsibility and was upset that Boldt and Dithmar were being punished for his command decision.

Patzig, however, did not surrender, and Boldt and Dithmar only spent a few months behind bars. Boldt escaped first, in late November. His departure from a Hamburg jail cell was "suspicious" reported the *New York Times*. Rumours were rampant that prison wardens had aided with the breakout. In early 1922, Dithmar also disappeared from prison.

There was speculation a shadowy, fringe right-wing group — it was identified as "the Organization Council" or Organization C or O.C. in the book, *Prologue to Nuremberg* — masterminded both escapes. There were plenty of right-wing extremist groups in Germany seeking scapegoats for defeat and outlets for their wrath. In their eyes, men like Dithmar and Boldt were national heroes, not convicts.

For all the cynicism engendered by the light court punishments, Patzig's absence, and the subsequent jail breakouts, an important fact was overlooked. In their ruling on the *Llandovery Castle* case, the German Supreme Court set a groundbreaking legal precedent.

"In the Llandovery Castle case [the Court] for the first time held that an order could not absolve a subordinate from guilt," notes an essay in *Historical Origins of International Criminal Law.*

In other words, "following orders" was no longer an acceptable defence for soldiers accused of war crimes.

It was a hugely significant ruling, one that would guide prosecutors in future war crimes trials of far greater scope than the flawed proceedings in Leipzig.

CHAPTER SIX

Disappearing from Memory

The German Supreme Court in Leipzig held two more war crimes trials after ruling on the *Llandovery Castle* case. Both trials featured figures from the Allies' abbreviated list of war criminals.

Dr. Oskar Michelsohn, accused by France of causing hundreds of deaths in a prisoner of war camp by deliberately withholding medical assistance, went on trial in June 1922. Over a dozen French witnesses were ready to testify, but they never got the chance. The French government ignored the trial, convinced it was impossible to achieve true justice at the proceedings in Leipzig. The only witnesses who testified spoke for the defence, and Dr. Michelsohn was acquitted in July.

In November 1922, the German Supreme Court met to ponder the fate of a German soldier named Karl Gruner, who was charged with theft and plunder. Gruner was acquitted of theft but convicted of plunder and sentenced to two years in jail. A month after presiding over the Gruner trial, the German Supreme Court dropped nearly one hundred additional cases from the broader Allied war-criminals list. The court claimed there wasn't enough evidence to prove these figures broke German law. It was a clear signal that Germany considered the war crimes trials to be over.

While Great Britain's response to the end of the trials was muted, authorities in France and Belgium were outraged — an understandable reaction given that most of the fighting on the Western Front took place in these countries. France and Belgium launched their own judicial proceedings against German officials, as was their right under the Treaty of Versailles. These trials took place in France and Belgium *in absentia* (that is, without a defendant present). Since the Allies didn't fully occupy Germany, defendants couldn't be tried in-person without German cooperation, which wasn't forthcoming. France conducted hundreds of symbolic prosecutions while Belgium held about eighty proceedings. Multiple convictions were obtained, but the sentencing was meaningless since none of the defendants were in the courts. This alternative system of justice petered out in 1926, as former enemy nations tried to normalize relations.

The German public remained indignant about the supposed injustice of the Leipzig War Crimes Trials. After the trials concluded, judicial authorities in Germany suspended hundreds of cases against other accused German war criminals. In July 1926, German defence lawyers asked the Supreme Court to reopen proceedings against Ludwig Dithmar and John Boldt. The two lieutenants might have escaped from jail, but both were still convicted criminals — a status their supporters wanted to rectify. A hearing was held, and in May 1928, the lieutenants were acquitted — a foregone conclusion given Germany's efforts to gloss over its recent past.

While he was never put on trial, U-*86* Commander Helmut Patzig also benefited from the push for leniency. On July 19, 1926, Patzig's arrest warrant was suspended by the Reichsgericht.

The postwar political climate in Germany "produced a groundswell of nationalist sentiment. Patzig no longer had to fear extradition or a lengthy prison sentence if he were to stand trial in Leipzig. The rescinding of his arrest warrant was proof of this," notes the *International Journal of Naval History.*

The political climate became even stormier. On March 20, 1931, the Fourth Senate of the Reichsgericht terminated all legal actions against Patzig and his case was closed. Two years later, Adolf Hitler and the Nazi Party came to power and imposed a dictatorship. In June 1933, remaining criminal proceedings against Great War criminals in Germany were halted, by order of the Nazi government. Discounting Dithmar and Boldt's brief incarceration, no one was punished for torpedoing the *Llandovery Castle* and trying to murder those who survived the initial attack.

The Rena McLean Memorial Hospital in Charlottetown, Prince Edward Island, closed in early 1920, only a few months after being re-named in her honour. The closure reflected a winding down of the war effort; fewer soldiers were returning from Europe, which meant there was less need for convalescent beds. Still, the shuttering served as an apt metaphor for the cultural amnesia that soon set in among Canadians regarding the *Llandovery Castle* and the Great War in general. As Germany strived to erase the convictions of Boldt and Dithmar and attempted prosecution of Patzig, memories of the heroism shown by those on board the *Llandovery Castle* faded in Canada.

After the Leipzig Trials concluded, media mentions about the *Llandovery Castle* became less frequent. Politicians stopped referencing the ship in speeches; through the mid to late 1920s, the *Llandovery Castle* rarely figured in parliamentary debate, except for discussions about British attempts to be reimbursed for the loss of the ship. Accounts of the tragic deaths of the nursing sisters on board the *Llandovery Castle* were often subsumed into broader tributes to wartime nurses in general.

Why did the *Llandovery Castle* disappear from memory?

The length and ferocity of the fighting in the First World War was one reason. Few people expected such a drawn-out, horrendous bloodbath. By the time of the Armistice, Canada had lost the equivalent of a small city, with most of the dead being young men and boys. There was also the legacy of countless veterans in wheelchairs, using crutches, or living in convalescent homes.

"Canada in 1919 was tired of war.... After four years of war, most people had simply had enough of tragedy, death, and misery ... the war was simply too big to be swept under the carpet. That did not mean, however, that the entire experience was suitable for discussion. First, it had to be tidied up to accommodate the desires of countless Canadians who had had enough of horror and tragedy," states Jonathan Vance in *Death So Noble: Memory, Meaning, and the First World War.*

As the German public grew increasingly belligerent and militaristic in the postwar years, the exact opposite happened in Canada. "Canadians in the 1920s chose very quickly to put the sacrifices of war behind them. An official history of the C.E.F. was commissioned soon after the end of the hostilities, but it was not felt to be important enough to complete until after the Second World War.... Soon it became the common view that the war was something one remembered ritualistically once a year and then forgot," states Eric Thompson in his essay, "Canadian Fiction of the Great War," published in the journal *Canadian Literature*.

Canadians also had new issues to contend with. The Bolshevik victory in Russia and the Winnipeg General Strike of 1919 stoked concerns about radicalism at home and abroad. Economic challenges abounded, in part because Ottawa was no longer interested in supporting a huge army or handing out lucrative war contracts. The Great War had also drastically altered gender roles. To free up personnel for the military, women had taken over many male-dominated positions in factories, farms, and corporations. This was hailed as a patriotic move while hostilities raged. Once peace was at hand, there was a strong desire, especially among men, to return to the prewar, patriarchal status quo.

War weariness was accompanied by a growing sense of cynicism. Postwar revelations made it clear that the Allied war effort had been driven in part by propaganda and lies. Like the Germans, the Allies had also engaged in morally dubious conduct — the actions of the Q-ship *Baralong* come to mind. Some well-publicized German atrocities turned out to be complete fabrications.

The 1928 book *Falsehood in War-Time*, written by Arthur Ponsonby, offers a compilation of wartime propaganda tales. A British member of Parliament, Ponsonby had been one of a handful of U.K. politicians who opposed the war. After the peace, he remained sharply critical of methods used to inflame public sentiment.

In *Falsehood in War-Time*, Ponsonby dared to challenge the common wisdom, baked into the Versailles Treaty, that Germany was solely responsible for starting the conflict. At the time, his view was seen as almost sacrilegious.

Ponsonby's book examines and dismisses many wartime atrocity stories, including allegations that German soldiers cut off the hands of Belgian children. One chapter is devoted to debunking an account of a Canadian soldier "crucified" during the Battle of Ypres in 1915. As the story went, the unfortunate soldier was pinned to either a farm wall, fence, or barn door by

German bayonets, out of sheer sadism. The story made good press, but there was no record that it ever happened, wrote Ponsonby.

The Allies also lied about the *Lusitania*, which was indeed carrying war supplies, continued Ponsonby: "From the point of view of propaganda, it was necessary to show that the Germans had blown up a defenceless, passenger ship flying the American flag and bearing only civilian passengers and an ordinary crew. This was represented as a breach of international law and an act of piracy," he noted.

Brutal as German unrestricted submarine warfare was, it's hard to say it was ethically worse than the Royal Navy blockade, wrote Ponsonby. Interestingly, his position echoed the view of countless U-boat crews, who used the blockade of German ports as justification for increased savagery at sea.

Ponsonby also scrutinized other documented atrocities. While Germany was accused of being the first to use poison gas on the battlefield, both sides eventually utilized this awful weapon, he notes. Ponsonby suggested that the aerial bombardment of Canadian hospitals in France might not have been deliberate. The German planes that bombed these facilities were flying at night, and the hospitals were situated near legitimate targets such as railroads, wrote Ponsonby. Maybe the planes missed their actual targets in the darkness and accidentally bombed the hospitals instead?

This assessment is contradicted by military reports made during the war. "It is beyond all question that the Germans made any mistake in regard to the bombing of the Hospitals at Etaples. Since the autumn of 1914, Etaples was perfectly well-known to the Germans as a great hospital area, Canadian General Hospitals No. 1, No. 7, and No. 9 being merely three Units in the colony of British hospitals which housed thousands upon thousands of beds.... The whole Area indeed must have been well marked on the enemy's map," states a document entitled, "Report of the Ministry Overseas Military Forces of Canada, 1918."

The report continues:

> No more doubt exists as to the enemy's deliberate purpose in bombing No. 3 Canadian Stationary Hospital at Doullens on the night of May 29, 1918, than the case of

the obvious open massacre among the Hospital Units at Etaples. The fort in which the hospital was situated was a landmark, and a landmark well-known to the enemy as the home of a Hospital Unit. It had been used solely for hospital purposes since the very beginning of the war; there were no ammunition dumps, stores, camps, artillery or any other military material in its neighbourhood. Giant Red Crosses were painted on its roofs; the most willfully short-sighted of enemy airmen could not have mistaken it.

Ponsonby became a member of the House of Lords in 1931. He remained a dedicated pacifist, even though this cause didn't always serve him well. During the late 1930s, British prime minister Neville Chamberlain tried to pursue peace through appeasement, i.e., giving in to Hitler's territorial demands. Ponsonby "supported Chamberlain and appeasement to the point of 'peace at any price,'" notes a 1984 article in the journal *Peace Research*.

Ponsonby "continued his anti-war efforts right up until 1939 with the hope that Britain could avoid another 'Great War,'" added his online parliamentary profile.

That year, Hitler invaded Poland and triggered the Second World War. Appeasement had failed dismally in preventing war and its advocates were perceived as hopelessly naive.

If Ponsonby was guilty of occasional overreach in his book — written years before Hitler's rise to power — his main point stands. Made-up atrocity stories might be motivational in the short-term, but once they are known to be lies, they can have long-term negative repercussions. The public might become skeptical about all atrocity stories and less inclined to believe accounts of true heroism, wrote Ponsonby.

Indeed, if the *Lusitania* had been carrying war supplies — fervent Allied denials maintained that it hadn't been — it wasn't a stretch to think that the *Llandovery Castle* was too. Certainly, Charles Yale Harrison thought as much when he wrote his notorious war novel, *Generals Die in Bed*.

Published in 1930, *Generals Die in Bed* could be described as the Canadian equivalent of the seminal German anti-war novel *All Quiet on the*

Western Front by Erich Maria Remarque. While the books were written in very different styles (Harrison is fond of short, clipped sentences and blasé observations), both reflected the wartime experience of their authors and expressed a prevailing sense of cynicism and war-weariness.

Harrison was born in the United States but moved to Montreal. He was either a student or a journalist when the war broke out — accounts vary. In early 1917, Harrison volunteered for the Canadian Expeditionary Force and was sent to France after training. *Generals Die in Bed* is based on his time on the frontline.

The novel shocked readers with its depiction of Canadian troops as little more than dumb thugs. The book features plenty of gore — "'The bayonet makes a messy job of it,' Broadbent says, 'The guts stick to the blade when you withdraw ...'" — and uses the *Llandovery Castle* as a major plot point.

In the novel, Harrison describes a visit by a brigadier general and his backup staff. Harrison's unit is getting ready for the Battle of Amiens, and the brigadier general wants to stiffen the men's resolve. To drive the soldiers to even greater rage, the general pontificates about the *Llandovery Castle*. He reads aloud a newspaper article about the attack, then volunteers some insights of his own:

> [A]fter the Llandovery Castle was torpedoed, not a helping hand was offered to our wounded comrades ... no instance of barbarism in the world's history can equal the sinking of this hospital ship ... think of it, more than three hundred wounded Canadians struggling in the choppy waters of the English channel ... the lifeboats were sprayed by machine-gun fire as the nurses appealed in vain to the laughing men on the U-boat ... the amputation cases went to the bottom instantly ... they couldn't swim, poor chaps ... the salt water added to their dying agony.

It's not clear if Harrison based this part of his novel on a real-life encounter with a bumptious general or if the scene was entirely imagined. If it did take place, either Harrison or the brigadier general badly bungled their facts.

No matter: having sufficiently enraged his listeners, the brigadier general urges them to put aside any feelings of humanity.

"[M]en, we are going into action in a few days, and we will be given an opportunity to avenge the lives of our murdered comrades ... an enemy like the German — no, I will not call him German — an enemy like the Hun does not merit humane treatment in war ... very well, if they choose to suspend the accepted rules for conducting civilized warfare, by God, two can play at that game," he states.

The staff officers chime in with similar remarks: "History will recall that the gallant Canadians did not allow this wanton act of barbarism to go unavenged," states one officer.

"[T]he battle in which we will soon be engaged will be remembered by generations still unborn as the Battle of Llandovery Castle," says another.

This inflammatory pep talk served its purpose; according to Harrison, his unit now eagerly looked forward to combat.

"Any one that did what those bastards did to the hospital ship ought to get a bayonet. It'll give me plenty of satisfaction, believe me," states a fellow soldier.

Righteously angry, Canadian troops unleash their rage as the Battle of Amiens commences. The men swarm over German positions, and don't take prisoners.

"The rifle fire drowns out their words. Doubtless they are asking for mercy. We do not heed. We are avenging the sinking of the hospital ship. We continue to fire," writes Harrison.

Following further savagery, the narrator is wounded in his right foot. The injury is serious enough to warrant his removal from the battlefield. In the final chapter, Harrison's stretcher-bound alter ego lies on a quay in Boulogne, France, waiting for orderlies to carry him onto a hospital ship. Remembering the brigadier general's remarks about sub attacks on hospital ships, the narrator is feeling uneasy. He cadges a cigarette from an orderly then asks, "Is it dangerous crossing? They say they torpedo them once in a while — like the Llandovery Castle."

"The Llandovery Castle?" snorts the orderly. "That was bloody murder, brother. Our officers oughta be shot for that. She was carryin' supplies and war material — it's a god-damned shame, that's what I say."

As the narrator ruminates on the orderly's remarks, he is taken up the gangplank and into the hospital ship. One of the final paragraphs reads: "The Llandovery Castle — carrying supplies — war material — I see the general reading us the report of the sinking just before the battle of Amiens — I see the bright sun shimmering on his brass — I hear his cold, dispassionate voice — 'couldn't swim, poor chaps — wanton act — must not go unavenged.'"

Not surprisingly, *Generals Die in Bed* stirred up a wave of anger. Arthur Currie, who commanded the Canadian Corps during the war, described the novel as "a mass of filth, lies and appeals to everything base and mean and nasty." Sir Archibald Macdonnell, another high-ranking Canadian military figure, vowed to inflict severe injury on the author. Veterans' groups demanded that the book be banned.

Critics have pointed out the rather obvious inaccuracies in the novel. "[T]here is no evidence to support two of the most contentious elements of the book: the description of the looting of Arras by Canadian troops and the accusation that the hospital ship Llandovery Castle, torpedoed in June 1918 with a full complement of medical personnel on board, was carrying military cargo in contravention of international law. These elements of the novel, it must be admitted, are completely fabricated," notes Jonathan Vance's essay, "The Soldier as Novelist: Literature, History, and the Great War," published in *Canadian Literature*.

In fairness, these historical slanders weren't the only parts of the novel that enraged readers. Many sensitive people were mortified by the depiction of Canadian soldiers as foul-mouthed simpletons who murdered prisoners of war and went on alcoholic benders with prostitutes. Even though the book was fiction, such characterizations were viewed as offensive.

Harrison's political agenda also needs to be considered. In the book, *Exiles From a Future Time: The Forging of a Mid-Twentieth Century Literary Left*, he was described as "a pro-Communist writer" who fell into disrepute with former colleagues "for alleged Trotskyist sympathies." During the early 1930s, Harrison was listed as a contributing editor on the masthead of the left-wing publication *New Masses* — the October 1931 edition also offers *Generals Die in Bed* for sale. His radical political worldview undoubtedly influenced his skepticism about the integrity of Allied military authorities and the noble intentions they espoused.

Beyond its anti-war ambitions, *Generals Die in Bed* highlighted a sad, significant point — memories of the *Llandovery Castle* were becoming increasingly cloudy in the postwar era. This dimming of memory was also an unintended after-effect of a campaign to fight growing postwar cynicism.

In the 1920s and 1930s, politicians and veterans' groups embarked on two different strategies to commemorate the Great War. Part of this strategy was to ignore specifics about the war while emphasizing admirable, but vague, principles. In his online essay "Commemoration and the Cult of the Fallen" Jonathan Vance states:

> But if the sacrifice of four years of war had not built a better country, what had it been for? Because there were so few tangible gains from the Great War that people could point to — daylight savings time hardly seemed a sufficient gain — commemoration focused on intangibles, on the timeless values that had been at the heart of Allied propaganda since 1914. For civilians, this meant liberty, democracy, Christianity, freedom, justice, western civilization — in a word, Right.

The other part of the strategy was to focus on a handful of clearcut triumphs, such as the Battle of Vimy Ridge and "Canada's Hundred Days" at the war's end. Bloody as these struggles were, Canadian troops had emerged as winners.

"In the Canadian context of what is remembered and what is forgotten, the victory at Vimy dominates the national memory of the war, while the sinking of the HS Llandovery Castle — with the greatest collective loss of life of medical personnel in the war — receives much less attention, perhaps because it fits less easily into the story of victory, and because, as already noted, it is the story of those whose work placed them officially outside combat," states Carol Acton's essay "Kitchener's Tourists" in *The Great War: From Memory to History*.

Indeed, beyond the remarkable survival of twenty-four men in a single lifeboat, "victory" is conspicuously absent from the *Llandovery Castle* story. The main villain escaped punishment, and two of his comrades received lenient sentences, escaped from jail, and were eventually acquitted.

Timing and tragedy overload are the final two factors that pushed events related to the *Llandovery Castle* to the margins of public memory.

Humans are only capable of processing so much shock and grief. People remember Hiroshima and Nagasaki, but not the equally devastating fire-bombing of Tokyo by conventional planes in March 1945. In Canada, the disastrous Dieppe Raid in the Second World War has been widely commemorated as a doomed but heroic test that provided crucial lessons for the successful D-Day landings later in the war. Canada's catastrophic military mission to Hong Kong, meanwhile, is barely remembered.

In similar fashion, the Halifax Explosion, not the sinking of the *Llandovery Castle*, dominates historical accounts of Canadian Great War catastrophes. *The Halifax Explosion: Canada's Worst Disaster* notes:

> The explosion that devastated Halifax on December 6, 1917, is one of the few Canadian historical events that the world — and, indeed, Canadians themselves — remember.... Over the years, countless articles, stories, and books — both fictional and non-fictional — have chronicled aspects of the great Halifax harbour explosion of 1917 and its tragic aftermath. There is even a play about the disaster, as well as a 2003 television miniseries called Shattered City: The Halifax Explosion, and, of course, that memorable Heritage Minute.

Produced by Historica Canada, the Heritage Minutes are a series of television spots depicting notable events in Canadian history. A 1991 Heritage Minute highlighted the heroism of a Halifax telegraph operator trying to warn a train about a potential explosion in the harbour. To date, no one has developed a Heritage Minute or a TV miniseries about the *Llandovery Castle*.

"Despite the prominence the Llandovery Castle massacre held during the war, memory of the tragic event quickly faded, in contrast to the memory of the Halifax Explosion," notes an article in the June 2018 edition of the *Canadian Journal of Surgery.*

In addition to the Halifax Explosion, the *Llandovery Castle* also competes for memory with the *Lusitania*. Both ships were British-made, stalked by a German U-boat off Ireland, and sunk with a single torpedo. There were American civilian passengers on the *Lusitania*, however, and the attack on that ship has been immortalized by the huge U.S. media industry.

The timing of the sinkings is also to be noted. The *Lusitania* was torpedoed relatively early in the war, giving the Allies years to turn the ambush into a propaganda cause célèbre. Anger about U-boat attacks influenced the decision by the United States to enter the Great War. Even today, the torpedoing of the *Lusitania* is treated as a Great War milestone.

"The sinking of the Lusitania caused the greatest sensation at the time and became history's most shocking example of unrestricted submarine warfare. Along with the coinciding first use of poison gas on the battlefield and the first air raids on cities, it signalled that the First World War would break new ground in man's inhumanity to man," states *German Submarine Warfare in World War I: The Onset of Total War at Sea.*

Barely four months after the *Llandovery Castle* sank, fighting ceased. Beyond a few speeches and posters encouraging patriotic citizens to buy war bonds, there wasn't enough time to use the attack for propaganda purposes.

———

An article about the *Llandovery Castle* in the *Canadian Journal of Surgery* contains a sad anecdote that neatly illustrates how the sinking went from global sensation to forgotten incident. While the piece mostly focuses on the murder of medical staff in the *Llandovery Castle* ambush, and the ensuing war crimes trials, it also offers a bit of personal history.

In 1924 photographic portraits of Lieutenant Colonel Thomas Macdonald and Matron Margaret Fraser were put up in the entrance hall of a new medical research facility at Dalhousie University, in Halifax. These photographs of senior CAMC personnel from the *Llandovery Castle* weren't labelled, and over the decades, the identity of the subjects was lost to memory.

Seventy years after they went up, the portraits were taken down when the medical research building was refurbished. Propelled by curiosity, two individuals — they went on to write the *Journal* article, with a third colleague — set out to determine the names of the people in the images. In the course of their research, these future medical writers learned about the *Llandovery Castle* for the first time.

"It was only when we searched out the identity of the portraits sitters that we became aware of the tragedy," they wrote.

On September 3, 1939, a passenger liner named the *Athenia* became the first British ship sunk by a U-boat during the Second World War. The ship was torpedoed off the Scottish coast, just days after the war began. Given that some of the passengers were Americans, media pundits drew historical parallels with other sub attacks.

"'Remember the Llandovery Castle!' That was the cry of the Canadian Corps as it went into action in its famous surprise attack at Amiens, August 8, 1918.... For the hospital ship just before had been torpedoed with a heavy loss of Canadian medical officers and nursing sisters. So strong was the indignation that in preparing for this battle the Canadian Corps staff named it the 'LC Operation'.... No less is the indignation as the sinking last night of the liner Athenia," wrote the *Globe and Mail*.

The *Globe* speculated that the sinking would bring America into the war. This turned out to be wishful thinking, as the United States didn't join the Allied war effort until late 1941, following the Japanese bombing of Pearl Harbor.

The article was, however, prescient in its own way. The advent of a new world war in Europe revived memories of the sinking of the *Llandovery Castle* in the previous conflict. The ship did in fact play a role in the Second World War, or at least, a new version of it did. The Union-Castle Mail Steamship Company launched a ship bearing the *Llandovery Castle* moniker in 1925. Slightly smaller than its namesake (*Llandovery Castle 2* weighed 10,639 tons, 784 tons less than its predecessor), it was also used for round-trip service between Europe and Africa.

In early 1937, the *Llandovery Castle 2* left the island of Gibraltar and headed toward Marseilles, France. Off the coast of Spain, the ship hit a sea mine, one of the countless bits of military debris left over from the Great War. The explosion damaged the ship, but it managed to reach port.

"Divers were sent down to inspect the hull and reported a hole 4.5 meters (15 feet) high and 4.5 meters (15 feet) wide below the ship's waterline. After repairs, the ship was able to return to London in June," notes a history of the Union-Castle company.

When the Second World War began, many Union-Castle ships, including the *Llandovery Castle 2*, were again converted to medical use. Fitted with 450 beds, the new *Llandovery Castle* was commissioned in May 1941. Serving in multiple war theatres, the *Llandovery Castle 2* evacuated roughly thirty-eight thousand patients during its time as a hospital ship.

The first *Llandovery Castle*, meanwhile, became top-of-mind among some pundits as the Second World War drew to a close. Discussions about putting leading Nazi officials on trial inevitably circled back to the perceived failures of the Leipzig War Crimes Trials.

"Of the twelve men tried only six were found guilty. Their punishment was light: two were sentenced to six months imprisonment, one to ten months and all were released after a week or two in prison.... Dithmar and Boldt were set free after serving four and six months respectively. The farce had been played to its ridiculous conclusion. Britain, disgusted and bored, lost all interest in the punishment of war criminals, and so the remaining 34 cases were allowed to drop on the ground of 'insufficient evidence,'" stated London's *Evening Standard* on October 10, 1944.

The article had several details wrong — for a start, the Leipzig Court handed down stiffer sentences than just ten months, and Dithmar and Boldt weren't set free but escaped from prison. That said, the piece reinforced the consensus that German war criminals got off lightly in Leipzig and that this should not be allowed to happen again. Writer I.F. Stone expressed this view in a piece titled "Will They Escape?" — the fourth article in a series devoted to the question of how to deal with Nazi war criminals. Appearing February 24, 1945, in the *Gazette and Daily* in York, Pennsylvania, among other newspapers, Stone's article used the *Llandovery Castle* case as a cautionary tale.

"The two condemned U-boat officers were treated as national heroes and permitted to escape. They never served a day of their sentence.... This is the kind of 'justice' the Supreme Court of Germany meted out after the last war to Germany's war criminals. It is the kind they will mete out again if the trial of crimes against German nationals for their race, religion or politics is to be left after this war, as the British government seems to suggest, to German courts," wrote Stone.

Again, the piece contained errors — Boldt and Dithmar did serve time, even if their sentences were truncated. However, Stone's words highlighted a growing demand for justice and an intriguing paradigm. As details about the *Llandovery Castle* sinking began to dim in popular memory, a handful of people recognized that the Leipzig Court had made history in its ruling about the ship.

Claud Mullins, author of *The Leipzig Trials*, was quick to grasp this point. "Disappointing as the War Criminals' Trials may well be from the purely legal point of view, there can be little doubt of their value from other standpoints.... Certainly the number of convictions in the Leipzig War Trials was a very small fraction of the number of men originally accused. But great principles are often established by minor events," wrote Mullins.

As Mullins observes, the German Supreme Court had established a major precedent regarding compliance with military orders. "In my view, the object of the War Criminals' Trials at Leipzig was to establish a principle, to put on record before history that might is not right, and that men, whose sole conception of the duty they owe to their country is to inflict torture upon others, may be put on their trial," notes Mullins.

With the benefit of hindsight, this point seems extremely profound.

"The Leipzig War Crimes Trials mark a significant step in the history of international criminal law.... In Leipzig, several accused persons attempted to defend and thereby absolve themselves from criminal responsibility by seeking recourse to superior orders. The Reichsgericht's rulings on this defense constitute landmark decisions," states *Historical Origins of International Law*.

There was also the novel notion that people committing obvious wartime atrocities, such as shelling defenceless people in lifeboats, violated universal legal norms.

"The real significance of the trial was that in the future, individuals would be held accountable for their actions in wartime by the standards of international law," notes an essay in the *International Journal of Naval History*.

Striking a prophetic note, Mullins suggested the Leipzig ruling about the *Llandovery Castle* might impact future court decisions. "When the time comes to build up a wider and more complete code of International Law than exists at present, and to interpret these rules of humanity into definite laws, it will probably be found that the War Criminals' Trials have given material assistance," he wrote.

Few Canadians, eager as they were to move on after the devastation of the First World War, would have shared this optimistic take on what were widely derided as farcical legal proceedings in far-off Leipzig.

CHAPTER SEVEN

In the Wake of the *Llandovery Castle*

The interior of the Kharkov Dramatic Theater was brilliantly lit with klieg lights on the morning of December 15, 1943, as the first war crimes trial against Nazi defendants began. The accused — three Germans and a collaborator — faced the death penalty for their involvement in atrocities when the Nazis occupied Kharkov (Kharkiv, in Ukrainian — this spelling will be used henceforth), Ukraine. Cameramen adjusted their lenses as they prepared to film the military tribunal for posterity and propaganda.

The accused, who were defended in court by Soviet legal counsel, represented different facets of the Nazi war machine. Captain Wilhelm Langheld had been an officer with the Abwehr (the German army's military intelligence department) and commander of a prisoner of war camp. Lieutenant Hans Ritz was a member of the SS (the frontline gang of Nazi mass murderers) and the SD (an SS security unit), while Senior Corporal Reinhard Retzlaff belonged to the German Secret Field Police. The fourth man, Mikhail Petrovich Bulanov (who was either Russian or Ukrainian, depending on the source), allegedly collaborated with the German occupiers by working as a chauffeur for the SD. Presiding over their fate was a trio of Soviet judges wearing army uniforms.

The specific charges against the accused were detailed and horrific.

"Under the direction of their superiors, the German fascist troops asphyxiated in specially equipped gas lorries — 'murder vans' — hanged, shot, or tortured to death many tens of thousands of Soviet people; plundered the property of State, economic, cultural and public organizations; burned down and destroyed entire towns and thousands of inhabited places; and drove to slavery in Germany hundreds of thousands of the peaceful population," states *The People's Verdict*, a book published in Britain that contained verbatim reports of the proceedings.

Most of the dead were Jews, but that was kept out of the official record. Trial reports from the U.S.S.R. described the victims as simply "Soviet citizens." The Kremlin wanted to promote the view that all Soviets had suffered equally under the Nazis, which was a blatant lie. The invading Germans targeted Jews, the Roma community, and Red Army political officers (commissars) for immediate slaughter.

The Kharkiv war crimes trial lasted four days. The audience was rotated daily, so as many people could witness the proceedings as possible. Admission tickets were liberally distributed to wounded Soviet soldiers, families of victims, troops on leave, and honoured workers. The Communist leadership sent some of the U.S.S.R.'s most talented writers to attend and welcomed foreign correspondents (although administrative snafus kept foreign journalists away for almost the entire trial). The Soviet leadership wanted the proceedings to garner as much publicity as possible to highlight the suffering of their country.

All four defendants pled guilty. Collaborator Bulanov admitted that he helped the Germans commit atrocities. The three accused Germans confessed to ordering or carrying out murderous actions against civilians.

"Langheld related how gas truck death chambers worked and said he had seen them functioning, with Russians inside clawing at the windows as they met death," wrote the *Chicago Tribune*. Langheld also said he personally murdered "about 100" Soviet citizens and ran concentration camps in various locales, added the *Tribune*.

While admitting their crimes, the accused stuck to the same script: they were just following orders that originated at the top of the Nazi hierarchy. "I must say there was no question of international law. Adolf Hitler was the man responsible for the reign of cruelty in the Soviet Union," stated Ritz.

While conceding their clients committed terrible crimes, the defendants' lawyers used the same reasoning when it was their time to speak. The defence counsel faced a steep challenge but did their best to try to save the lives of the accused.

"It must not be forgotten that Retzlaff served in an army of bandits, where human feelings were considered a weakness, and ruthlessness and fanaticism a virtue. Nor must it be forgotten that the principal crimes were committed by them under the orders and directives of the fascist leaders," stated defence lawyer S.K. Kaznacheyev.

Colonel N.K. Dunayev, the state prosecutor, wasn't having any of this. Colonel Dunayev, who wore a military uniform in court, brought up the Leipzig Trials during a morning session on December 18. The trials might have been a "legal farce," but they did provide a damning judicial precedent, said the colonel.

> [O]n one particular point, in order to placate world public opinion incensed by the atrocious sinking of the British hospital ship Llandovery Castle by a German submarine, even that court was compelled to declare that, although the action of the accused followed from the direct or indirect order of their commander, that did not absolve them of responsibility, as there could be no doubt that the accused realized the dishonourable and criminal nature of their commander's intention.

He continued, "It follows from this that the contention that the orders of superiors absolve the Hitlerite fiends of responsibility for their monstrous crimes should be completely ruled out. Numerous orders of the Hitlerite Government and Hitlerite military authorities prescribe such actions as, manifestly and beyond the doubt of any person, major crimes and flagrant violations of international law."

Despite this, the defendants clung to the notion of superior orders when they gave their final statements to the court. Ritz made the following point:

An atrocity remains an atrocity. I repeat that I don't want to minimize my part in them in the least. However, I don't want you to be left with the impression that I committed murders and atrocities because I derived any satisfaction from them or felt any gratification. That is not the case. The thing is that I was acting on orders. The cause lies with the entire system of orders in the German Army, which compelled me to do what I was told.... You must believe me that if I had not obeyed orders I should have been arraigned before a German military tribunal and sentenced to death.

Retzlaff said much the same in his final statement: "Gentleman judges and Prosecutor, I admit my guilt in the crimes with which I have been charged. I should like to point out that in every single case I acted on the orders of my immediate superiors. If I had not obeyed these orders, I would have been put in the same position as my victims. All my criminal acts were the result of the criminal propaganda of the Hitlerite rulers."

The Soviet military tribunal wasn't swayed by these remarks. All four defendants were found guilty and publicly hanged on December 19, 1943, before a crowd of forty thousand people in Kharkiv. Sadly, the city was brutalized again decades later, this time by invading Russian forces.

The Kharkiv war crimes trials were not without their critics. American journalist Edmund Stevens described the accused as "small fry." The proceedings were dismissed as just another Stalinist "show trial" — a type of legal lynching common in the 1930s Soviet Union, featuring defendants who confessed to ludicrous charges under duress and were automatically convicted. Many observers, however, defended the legitimacy of the Kharkiv trials. Even critics such as Stevens thought the overall proceedings were fair.

"All legal niceties were observed to a fault. The defendants and their counsel had full latitude to speak or interpolate, and every comma of what was said was translated into German for their benefit," he wrote.

In addition to being "the first trial of Germans held by any of the Allied powers," according to *Forgotten Trials of the Holocaust*, the Kharkiv proceedings were historically significant in another way. The trials marked the first of many war crimes trials of the 1940s in which the *Llandovery Castle* ruling was cited to dismiss the "superior orders" defence.

The Leipzig verdict also firmly established the principle that sovereign nations had to heed international law when it came to war crimes. This was noted in *Prologue to Nuremberg*: "The decision established a precedent in international war crimes prosecution, even though it was based upon German civil and military penal law, and during prosecutions after the Second World War lawyers often found one passage of the Reichsgericht's judgment especially pertinent, for it clearly placed international law above national law: 'The firing on the boats was an offence against the law of nations. In war the killing of unarmed enemies is not allowed ... similarly, in war at sea, the killing of shipwrecked people, who have taken refuge in lifeboats, is forbidden.'"

———

Hitler and Nazi propaganda minister Joseph Goebbels killed themselves before Germany surrendered on May 7, 1945. Captured SS chief Heinrich Himmler committed suicide shortly after the capitulation.

Plenty of Nazi accomplices were still alive, however, and were quickly placed into custody. Their ranks included Luftwaffe chief Hermann Goring, Foreign Minister Joachim von Ribbentrop, Field Marshal Wilhelm Keitel, General Alfred Jodl, and Admiral Karl Donitz. Deputy Fuhrer Rudolf Hess, captured in 1941 after he flew solo to Scotland in a bizarre "peace" mission, was also in Allied captivity.

On August 8, 1945, France, the United Kingdom, the United States, and the U.S.S.R. signed the London Agreement, which authorized the establishment of the International Military Tribunal (IMT) to put the Nazi elite on trial. A series of other Allied nations soon joined the effort to prosecute German war criminals. Unlike the Kharkiv Trials, the IMT proceedings would be a multi-nation effort aimed at the very top of the German military and political leadership.

Anticipating a common defence, Article 8 of the Constitution of the International Military Tribunal directly addressed the issue of superior orders. This provision read: "The fact that the defendant acted pursuant to [an] order of his Government or of a superior shall not free him from responsibility but may be considered in mitigation of punishment if the Tribunal determines that justice so requires."

The same tenet would later be enshrined in the Charter of the International Military Tribunal for the Far East, which was used to prosecute Japanese military and political leaders at the Tokyo War Crimes Trials. Article 6 of this charter read: "Responsibility of the Accused — Neither the official position, at any time, of an accused, nor the fact that an accused acted pursuant to [an] order of his government or of a superior shall, of itself, be sufficient to free such accused from responsibility for any crime with which he is charged, but such circumstances may be considered in mitigation of punishment if the Tribunal determines that justice so requires."

The *Llandovery Castle* ruling aside, it was widely acknowledged that letting German judges try German defendants at Leipzig had been a mistake. Given this, it was decided that the International Military Tribunal would be comprised of judges from the leading Allied nations. The trials would be held in Nuremberg, Germany, scene of many prewar Nazi rallies.

As preparations for the IMT got underway, a British military court convened in Hamburg on October 17, 1945, to preside over a case with strange parallels to the *Llandovery Castle*. The Peleus Trial, as it was called, also involved a U-boat, a torpedoed ship, and an attempt to murder shipwrecked survivors.

The *Peleus* was a Greek steamship that had been chartered by the British Ministry of War Transport. While travelling in the middle of the Atlantic Ocean, the *Peleus* was torpedoed by U-*852* on March 13, 1944. Most of the multinational crew escaped the sinking ship; they either boarded life rafts or clung to floating wreckage. U-*852* surfaced and cruised near survivors. Sailors on the sub barked questions at the shipwrecked crew, asking about the name of the vessel and its destination.

Once this information was obtained, U-*852* commander Heinz-Wilhelm Eck ordered his men to kill the survivors. Machine gun fire and hand grenades were directed at the helpless sailors. The sub remained on the scene for hours and occasionally riddled floating wreckage with bullets to break it up into tiny pieces. In addition to murdering survivors, Eck didn't want to leave behind any sizeable debris that might be spotted by a plane, revealing the presence of a U-boat in the area.

A Greek officer, a Greek sailor, and a British sailor from the *Peleus* somehow managed to escape the slaughter. After spending two weeks in the water, the trio were rescued by a Portuguese steamer and brought into port, and safety.

While Commander Eck was the main defendant, four of his crew members were also charged. Their cases were heard before a panel of British and Greek navy officers and Judge Advocate Major Melford Stevenson.

In court, Eck took full responsibility for ordering the massacre, which was carried out to eliminate all traces of the sunken steamship. While Eck didn't cite "superior orders" in his own defence, he absolved his crew of blame, saying they were merely following his command. The crewmen, for their part, echoed this statement and said they were under orders to murder survivors.

Professor A. Wegner, a German academic and legal expert, defended all the accused on matters of international law. Wegner brought up the *Llandovery Castle* ruling but said it didn't have much relevance in this trial. Not only was Hitler's regime far harsher than the Kaiser's, the *Peleus* defendants were being judged by a British military tribunal, not German justices, he explained. Wegner went on to say that the German public regarded the *Llandovery Castle* ruling as treasonous and considered the Leipzig prosecutors to be traitors.

Other defence lawyers tried a different tack, making the dubious claim that the rulings in Leipzig were based on municipal law and therefore had no bearing on international law. To buttress this weak argument, defence counsel said the *Llandovery Castle* precedent only counted when military personnel knew they were committing an illegal act. In other words, ignorance of the law was a legitimate defence.

Prosecutor Colonel R.C. Halse, Military Department, Judge Advocate General's Office, also brought up the *Llandovery Castle*, albeit in a considerably different light. Quoting the German Supreme Court ruling, the prosecutor said shooting people in lifeboats was an offense against the law of nations and clearly illegal.

Major Stevenson agreed, and stated witheringly, "The duty to obey is limited to the observance of orders which are lawful. There can be no duty to obey that which is not a lawful order ... is it not fairly obvious to you that if in fact the carrying out of Eck's command involved the killing of these helpless survivors, it was not a lawful command, and that it must have been obvious to the most rudimentary intelligence that it was not a lawful command, and that those who did that shooting are not to be excused for doing it upon the ground of superior orders?"

All five defendants were found guilty. Commander Eck and two subordinates were sentenced to death, one was sentenced to life imprisonment, and the fifth accused received fifteen years in prison. Executions took place in Hamburg, November 30, 1945, before a firing squad.

A United Nations War Crimes Commission report commented on the Peleus Trial.

> [M]uch reliance was placed in the "Peleus" case, both by the Prosecutor and by the Judge Advocate, on the decision of the German Supreme Court in the case of the hospital ship, Llandovery Castle, delivered in 1921. The case of the Llandovery Castle was treated not only as an authority for the rejection of the pleas of superior order in the case of an order manifestly illegal, but it was treated as an authority also, as it were, on a special rule applicable to the particular facts of the case, namely, the question whether or not firing on lifeboats is an offence against the Law of Nations.

The UN report also notes how alike the *Peleus* and *Llandovery Castle* proceedings were: "The facts in both cases were indeed very similar."

A day after the Peleus Trial began, an indictment was filed in Berlin by the main IMT prosecutors against the top Nazi leadership. On November 20, 1945, the Nuremberg Trials opened in a heavily guarded courtroom at the Palace of Justice.

German Labour Front leader Robert Ley committed suicide before the trial could begin. That left twenty-one defendants to face charges of Crimes Against Peace, War Crimes, and Crimes Against Humanity (an additional defendant — Martin Bormann, Secretary to Hitler — was tried *in absentia*). A fourth charge involved participating in a conspiracy to commit these crimes. Behind these charges was a litany of horrors, including the extermination of millions of Jews, Roma, and the disabled, as well as the use of slave labour, mass deportations, reprisals against civilians, and extreme mistreatment of prisoners of war.

The Nuremberg defendants all pled not guilty (although Reich Minister for Armaments and Munitions Albert Speer would modify his stance and accept some responsibility for his actions). Many of the accused fell back on the superior orders defence, even though the IMT Charter specifically dismissed such claims.

"It was also submitted on behalf of most of these defendants that in doing what they did they were acting under the orders of Hitler, and therefore cannot be held responsible for the acts committed by them in carrying out these orders.... The provisions of [Article 8] are in conformity with the law of all nations. That a soldier was ordered to kill or torture in violation of the international law of war [has] never been recognized as a defense to such acts of brutality," the International Military Tribunal later wrote.

On the stand, Field Marshal Keitel, commander of the German armed forces, admitted that his orders could be vicious. Among other measures, Keitel had authorized the use of forced labour to build German fortifications, the execution of political commissars, and the killing of hostages.

"It is correct that there are a large number of orders, instructions, and directives with which my name is connected, and it must be admitted that such orders often contain deviations from existing international law," testified Keitel.

Like other army leaders, Keitel cited the tradition of military obedience. Orders were orders, and cruel as his commands might be, Keitel felt he had to fulfill the wish of the Fuhrer. "I took the stand that a soldier has a right to have confidence in his state leadership, and accordingly, he is obliged to do his duty and to obey," testified the field marshal.

During his testimony, General Jodl, chief of the Operations Staff of the German High Command of the Armed Forces, was asked about a particularly brutal military order. The directive, issued to German army units on the Eastern front, permitted "suitable Draconian measures" to crush civilian resistance movements. These measures usually entailed mass slaughter.

Jodl said he agreed with the order and disputed the prosecution's description of it as "terrible."

"No, it is not at all terrible, for it is established by international law that the inhabitants of an occupied territory must follow the orders and instructions of the occupying power and that any uprising, any resistance against the army occupying the country is forbidden," he stated, insisting that he was carrying out policies that originated at the top of the Nazi hierarchy.

On the first day of October 1946, the Nuremberg judges announced their verdict. Nineteen defendants (including the absent Bormann) were found guilty. Keitel and Jodl were convicted on all counts of the indictment. Sentences for the convicted men ranged from execution to jailtime. Three defendants were acquitted.

In its sentencing report, the tribunal wrote, "Keitel does not deny his connection with these acts. Rather, his defense relies on the fact that he is a soldier and on the doctrine of 'superior orders' prohibited by Article 8 of the Charter as a defense."

Jodl, wrote the tribunal, also relied on "the doctrine of 'superior orders' prohibited by Article 8 of the Charter as a defense. There is nothing in mitigation. Participation in such crimes as these has never been required of any soldier and he cannot now shield himself behind a mythical requirement of soldierly obedience at all costs as his excuse for the commission of these crimes."

On October 16, 1946, ten defendants, including Keitel and Jodl, were hanged, a grim repudiation of the "superior orders" defence.

"Many of these men have made a mockery of the soldier's oath of obedience to military orders.... Political loyalty, military obedience are excellent things, but they neither require nor do they justify the commission of patently wicked acts," notes the IMT ruling.

While the Nuremberg Trials of the Nazi elite attracted the most attention, several other war crimes trials followed, many of which explicitly raised the *Llandovery Castle* precedent: "Between 1946 and 1948 there were 12 trials held at Nuremberg after the IMT proceedings. The ninth of these was called the Einsatzgruppen trial," states *Forgotten Trials of the Holocaust.*

Einsatzgruppen can be roughly translated as "special task force." Einsatzgruppen units were comprised of thugs from the SS, SD, Gestapo, police, and other organizations. There were four Einsatzgruppen units in total, each of which contained about eight hundred to twelve hundred personnel. They served behind the lines in the German-occupied Soviet Union, tasked with murdering Jews, Roma, the disabled, and Communist officials.

In addition to being efficient killers, the Einsatzgruppen kept meticulous records. A unit called Einsatzgruppen A issued a report stating it had killed 121,817 individuals in the U.S.S.R. during the summer and fall of 1941, including women, children, and the elderly. If extra victims (including "748 lunatics executed") were added to this sum, the death toll reached even higher, noted the Einsatzgruppen document. In total, Einsatzgruppen units murdered over a million people, using bullets and other means. Victims were never charged with anything, much less convicted, before being summarily executed.

Twenty-four former Einsatzgruppen members were indicted by the United States in late July 1947, and charged with war crimes, crimes against humanity, and membership in a criminal organization. The accused would be tried before an American military tribunal. The prosecution was led by Brigadier General Telford Taylor, who served as chief legal counsel for the prosecution at the IMT trials of the Nazi leadership.

"Although the indictment accuses the defendants of the commission of atrocities, persecutions, extermination, imprisonment, and other inhumane acts, the principal charge in this case is murder," wrote the U.S. military tribunal hearing the case.

One defendant committed suicide, and another was eventually severed from the trial on medical grounds. Proceedings against the remaining defendants began on September 15, 1947, at the Palace of Justice, the same location where the Nazi leadership had faced justice a year before.

Accused Einsatzgruppen members fell back on shopworn justifications. "The defendants, individually and collectively, raised five broad defenses," one of which was that they were "simply following orders," states *Forgotten Trials of the Holocaust*.

Many defendants cited adherence to a so-called Fuhrer Order — a written or verbal command directly from Hitler — that permitted summary executions of anyone perceived as an enemy of the Third Reich on the Eastern front. SS Colonel Walter Blume said he was personally revolted by the Fuhrer Order but willingly carried it out when he served in Einsatzgruppen B.

On the stand, Blume was questioned about an incident in which he told his men to shoot three people accused of telling farmers not to assist the Germans. Asked if he was familiar with the rules of war, Blume said, "In this case, I acted by carrying out the Fuhrer Order, which decreed that saboteurs and functionaries were to be shot."

When the question was put to him again, he replied, "I already stated that for me the directive was the Fuhrer Order. That was my war law."

Some of the defendants, by their own words, contradicted the widely expressed opinion that members of German murder squads faced punishment or death if they refused to carry out their duties.

General Otto Ohlendorf, who led Einsatzgruppen D, stated, "In two-and-a-half years I had sufficient occasion to see how many of my Gruppe [group] did not agree to this order in their inner opinion. Thus, I forbade the participation in these executions on the part of some of these men, and I sent some back to Germany."

A defence witness named Albert Hartel said that General Max Thomas, head of Einsatzgruppen C — he wasn't on trial — announced that any members of the unit who didn't want to commit atrocities could ask to be reassigned or sent back to Germany. Hartel claimed several people took advantage of this proclamation and returned to Germany, without sanction. As the military tribunal noted, the Nazis permitted such actions to improve the efficiency of their killing units, not from any sense of mercy.

In his closing remarks, Taylor focused on the concept of military obedience. "The general principles of international penal law with respect to the effect of superior orders on criminal responsibility are by now well-established. Normally, a subordinate is entitled to assume that orders issued to him by his superiors are lawful and do not require him to commit crimes in execution thereof," he stated.

Subordinates can't be expected to conduct a comprehensive legal review of everything they are ordered to do, said Taylor. However, a command that is "palpably criminal" should not be obeyed, a dictum "concisely set forth in the decision of the Supreme Court at Leipzig in the Llandovery Castle case," he continued.

Lieutenants Dithmar and Boldt were "well aware ... that one is not legally authorized to kill defenseless people," said Taylor, directly quoting from the Leipzig judgment.

"The language of this decision is precisely applicable to the present case; here we are dealing with even more obviously criminal orders to kill 'defenseless people' on the sole ground that they were Jews, Gypsies, or government or party officials," he added.

The tribunal agreed, and noted, "The subordinate is bound only to obey the lawful orders of his superior and if he accepts a criminal order and executes it with a malice of his own, he may not plead superior orders in mitigation of his offence."

Judgment was rendered and all twenty-two remaining defendants were found guilty. On April 10, 1948, they received sentences ranging from execution to imprisonment. In its ruling, the tribunal cited the *Llandovery Castle* decision.

> The defense of superior orders has already been passed upon by a German court. In 1921, two officers of the German U-boat 68 [*sic*] were charged with violation of the laws of war in that they fired at and killed unarmed enemy citizens seeking to escape from the sinking Hospital Ship H.M.S. Llandovery Castle. The defendants pleaded lack of guilt in that they had merely carried into effect the order given them by their commander, First Lieutenant Patzig. The German Court did find as a fact that Patzig ordered

his subordinates Dithmar and Boldt to fire at the lifeboats but it adjudicated them guilty nonetheless.

The *Llandovery Castle* ruling was also cited at the Stalag Luft III and the Hostages Trial, both of which opened in mid-1947. The former was adjudicated by a British military court in Hamburg while the latter was adjudicated by an American military tribunal in Nuremberg.

Stalag Luft III was a prisoner of war camp in Silesia, Poland, from which eighty officers of the Royal Air Force and other nations escaped on the night of March 24–25, 1944. The breakout — it became the basis of the 1963 war movie *The Great Escape* — involved meticulous planning and an underground tunnel. Prisoners assembled forged documents and civilian outfits so they could travel around occupied Europe once they broke out.

After exiting from the camp, the officers "fanned out in all directions in an effort to reach the borders of the Reich, mainly France and Belgium in the west, Czechoslovakia in the south and Denmark in the north," explained a United Nations War Crimes Commission trial summary.

Of the officers who escaped Stalag Luft III, four were captured almost immediately, while seventy-three others were captured soon after the breakout. Some officers were taken back to Stalag Luft III, some were placed in other forms of custody, and fifty were executed by the Gestapo. Only three men in the entire group managed to get out of occupied Europe.

On July 1, 1947, proceedings began against eighteen German defendants involved in the murder of the escaped prisoners. A major general presided over the British military court, which featured three Royal Air Force representatives and three British Army officers. The accused all pled not guilty and once again the issue of obedience to superior orders was raised as a defence. A United Nations report discusses the case.

> In this trial, as well as many other war crimes trials, the decision in the [Llandovery Castle] case was quoted, both by the Prosecutor and by the defense. The case was cited by the prosecution to support the proposition that the plea of superior orders provides no excuse in international law, but

only goes to mitigation of punishment. The defense tried
to distinguish the Llandovery Castle Case by saying that in
that case the court found 'as a fact' that the accused were
fully aware that the firing on survivors by a U-boat was a
crime.... If, however, the accused, as in the Stalag Luft III
case, had no such positive knowledge of the criminality of
their action, they must be acquitted.

The British military court didn't accept the defence's reasoning and
found all eighteen defendants guilty. On September 3, 1947, death sentences were passed against fifteen of the accused, with the remainder receiving
prison terms. Two death sentences were commuted, so in the end, thirteen
of the convicted men were hanged on February 28, 1948.

The Hostages Trial — also known as the Trial of Wilhelm List and
Others — featured "former high-ranking German army officers ... charged
with responsibility for offences committed by troops under their command
during the occupation of Greece, Yugoslavia, Albania and Norway," states a
United Nations War Crimes Commission trial summary.

Most of the offences consisted of reprisal killings in response to resistance activity: the defendants "issued, distributed, and executed orders for
the execution of one hundred 'hostages' in retaliation for each German soldier killed and fifty 'hostages' in retaliation for each German soldier wounded," read the charges. The defendants were accused of murdering thousands
of civilians, plundering, looting, and "wanton destruction of cities, towns,
and villages," continued the charges.

The trial opened July 8, 1947, with the indefatigable Telford Taylor serving as chief of counsel for the prosecution. The defendants uniformly pled
"not guilty." The superior orders defence was introduced in court and fared
as poorly as it did in other post-Nazi era war crimes trials.

"The defendants invoke the defensive plea that the acts charged as crimes
were carried out pursuant to orders of superior officers whom they were obliged to obey.... The rule that a superior order is not a defense to a criminal
act is a rule of fundamental criminal justice that has been adopted by civilized
nations extensively," read the United States Military Tribunal judgment.

> Implicit obedience to orders of superior officers is almost indispensable to every military system. But this implies obedience to lawful orders only ... the general rule is that members of the armed forces are bound to obey only the lawful orders of their commanding officers and they cannot escape criminal liability by obeying a command which violates International Law and outrages fundamental concepts of justice. In the German War Trials (1921), the German Supreme Court of Leipzig in the Llandovery Castle case said: "Patzig's order does not free the accused from guilt."

One defendant in the Hostages Trial committed suicide before they were arraigned while another was dropped from the proceedings due to illness. When the trial ended February 19, 1948, two of the remaining defendants were acquitted, two received life imprisonment, and six others received jail terms ranging from seven to twenty years.

As to why more severe penalties were not applied, the U.S. Military Tribunal cited lack of detailed information about hostages in international law: "The failure of the nations of the world to deal specifically with the problem of hostages and reprisals by convention, treaty, or otherwise, after the close of World War I, creates a situation that mitigates to some extent the seriousness of the offence," wrote the tribunal.

For all that, the tribunal in the Hostages Trial reiterated the legal concept established at Leipzig: obedience doesn't trump culpability when it comes to war crimes.

This principle came up for discussion on April 25, 1950, in the U.K. House of Lords. The Earl of Cork and Orrery expressed the view that two German sailors from the Peleus Trial (whose sentences were under review) might have been unfairly blamed for their actions.

"The point with which I wish to deal is the validity of the excuse for a war crime that the person committing the crime was acting under superior orders.... The tortures and punishments given in concentration camps are of quite a different character from the actions of these young men acting under military orders [to kill survivors of the Peleus]. Of course, if they are found guilty of exceeding orders, then they have 'had it': but these young men carried out orders when there was no alternative but to obey," stated the earl.

"My Lords, I am bound to say that I find myself in complete and absolute disagreement with the noble Earl who has just spoken. It seems to me the doctrine he enunciated is nothing less than the fuhrer prinzip," replied Sir William Jowitt, the lord chancellor.

The "Fuhrer Principle" was the notion that Hitler was always right, and his orders should be obeyed without question, even if they flouted written law. This authoritarian concept formed the bedrock of Nazi ideology.

The lord chancellor continued:

> As to the law, the rule of law is quite plain. In the year 1907 the Geneva Convention provided: "After every engagement the two belligerents shall, in so far as military interests permit, take steps to look for the sick, wounded, and shipwrecked, and to protect them, as well as the dead, against pillage and improper treatment." In the year 1921 the same question arose at the Leipzig Trials. They were trials for war crimes of the First World War, tried before German Courts, in regard to a ship called the "Llandovery Castle." In that case the U-boat attacked and sank a hospital ship and then attacked and drowned the survivors. The German Supreme Court — I stress the word "German" — convicted the two officers of homicide and in its judgement laid down as follows: "The firing on the boats was an offence against the law of nations."

The lord chancellor didn't have all his facts correct — Boldt and Dithmar were not convicted of homicide — but the point made in the *Llandovery Castle* ruling stood.

The Geneva Conventions of 1949 represented a new attempt to formulate humanitarian regulations for warfare. There were four conventions in total, introduced only a few years after the carnage of the Second World War. These treaties replaced and updated provisions from previous accords regarding the treatment of prisoners of war, the wounded and sick, civilians, and war at sea.

"Military hospital ships, that is to say, ships built or equipped by the Powers specially and solely with a view to assisting the wounded, sick and shipwrecked, to treating them and to transporting them, may in no circumstances be attacked or captured, but shall at all times be respected and protected, on conditions that their names and descriptions have been notified to the Parties to the conflict ten days before those ships are employed," states Article 22 of the Second Geneva Convention.

Under Articles 24 and 25, hospital ships utilized by the Red Cross, relief societies, or private organizations enjoyed the same protections. Interestingly enough, Article 26 pointedly notes that the Geneva Convention also applies to "[hospital ship] lifeboats, wherever they are operating."

As in decades past, hospital ships, it was stated, must be painted white and feature large red crosses to make them clearly identifiable.

While the Geneva Conventions of 1949 didn't stop countries from waging war with each other, they did reaffirm and codify international legal standards for unacceptable military conduct. The conventions were approved by almost every nation in the world, then signed and ratified.

"Thus the 1949 Conventions, a decisive step in the work of protecting war victims, are now attaining the universality which has always given the humanitarian law of Geneva its force," noted a commentary from the International Committee of the Red Cross.

———————

Almost half a century after the end of the Second World War, the *Llandovery Castle* ruling was cited in a major legal case in Canada.

The case involved Imre Finta, a former officer in the Royal Hungarian Gendarmerie. Nazi Germany occupied Hungary in March 1944 to prevent its Axis partner from switching sides as the Soviet army approached. The Royal Hungarian Gendarmerie helped the Germans detain and deport Jewish civilians. Finta commanded a unit that imprisoned 8,617 Jewish civilians in a brickyard in the city of Szeged. Valuables belonging to the prisoners were seized and the civilians were eventually transported to Nazi concentration camps.

Finta emigrated to Canada in 1951 and became a Canadian citizen five years later. He established a popular restaurant in Toronto. He successfully concealed his past until the 1970s, when he was finally exposed. In 1987 Finta became the first person to be charged under newly passed war crimes legislation in Canada. He was accused of robbery, kidnapping, unlawful confinement, and manslaughter. Following a lengthy trial in the Ontario Supreme Court, he was acquitted on May 25, 1990. Two years later, the verdict was upheld by the Ontario Court of Appeal.

The Finta case was complicated and involved decades-old offences. Many of the witnesses who might have been able to provide valuable evidence had died by the time the trial started. Nonetheless, the Crown appealed the verdict to the Supreme Court of Canada, citing errors made by the original trial judge. Finta, meanwhile, moved to have the Supreme Court strike down the war crimes law for violating the Canadian Charter of Rights and Freedoms.

On March 24, 1994, the Supreme Court unanimously agreed that the law used to prosecute Finta was constitutional but ruled 4–3 to uphold his acquittal.

In its judgment, the court referred to the Leipzig War Crimes Trials. Justice Peter Cory said the German judges in the *Llandovery Castle* case had rightly rejected the superior orders defence.

Shelling survivors in the *Llandovery Castle* lifeboats "was such an atrocious act and so adverse to all traditions and laws of the sea that it was on its face manifestly unreasonable. As a result, the defense was unacceptable, and the conviction correctly resulted," he wrote.

The superior orders argument was acceptable in the case of the *Dover Castle*, however, because the German admiralty had issued directives allowing attacks on hospital ships in certain areas, based on the belief they were being misused by the Allies, continued Justice Cory.

Given this, it was reasonable for Finta to assume the orders he received to round up Jewish civilians had an "air of reality" and were lawful, stated the judge. To support this reasoning, the judge cited anti-Semitism in Hungary, the prevailing notion that Jewish people supported the Allies, and the "imminent invasion" of the country by "Soviet forces." It was also legitimate for Finta to fear for his life if he didn't obey, claimed Cory.

"Even where the orders were manifestly unlawful, the defense of obedience to superior orders and the peace officer defense will be available in those circumstances where the accused had no moral choice as to whether to follow the orders. That is to say, there was such an air of compulsion and threat to the accused that the accused had no alternative but to obey," wrote Justice Cory.

Unsurprisingly, the court's decision proved highly controversial. The Canadian Jewish Congress denounced the ruling, while B'nai Brith Canada lawyer David Matas called it "morally unconscionable."

This contentious judgment was soon followed by a pioneering effort to bring a new generation of war criminals to justice. On July 17, 1998, for the first time, an International Criminal Court (ICC) was established to prosecute war criminals on a permanent basis. Canada was a strong advocate for the ICC and played a key role in the negotiations that helped establish the court.

The ICC received its mandate after 120 countries adopted the Rome Statute of the International Criminal Court. Also called the Rome Statute, this document outlined the purpose, functions, and powers of the ICC.

Article 33 of the statute explicitly addresses the issue of superior orders: "The fact that a crime within the jurisdiction of the Court has been committed by a person pursuant to an order of a Government or of a superior, whether military or civilian, shall not relieve that person of criminal responsibility."

The rule does not apply if the order wasn't "manifestly unlawful" or if the person who carried out the order didn't understand it was unlawful, and if the person obeyed the order out of legal obligation to the government or their superior, continued the statute.

"For the purposes of this article, orders to commit genocide or crimes against humanity are manifestly unlawful," adds Article 33.

Based appropriately enough in the Hague, Netherlands, (although the court can sit in other locales if the need arises), the ICC has jurisdiction over four main areas: genocide, crimes against humanity, war crimes (this includes attacking hospitals, and presumably hospital ships), and crimes of aggression. The ICC only intervenes when a country either can't or won't investigate war criminals within its borders. The court lacks its own police force, so it relies on international cooperation to arrest suspects.

The Rome Statute came into force on July 1, 2002, empowering the court to begin its work. As of May 11, 2023, the Court has heard thirty-one cases and issued forty arrest warrants.

"Thanks to cooperation from states, 21 people have been detained in the ICC detention centre and have appeared before the Court. 16 people remain at large. Charges have been dropped against five people due to their deaths.... The judges have issued 10 convictions and four acquittals," states the ICC website. Criminals convicted by the ICC include terrorists, warlords, and political leaders. Their crimes include murder, pillaging, and attacking civilian populations.

Convicted defendants include Germain Katanga — an alleged militia leader found guilty in 2014 as an accessory in a crime against humanity and war crimes, for his participation in attacks on civilians and property destruction and pillaging in the Democratic Republic of the Congo — and Ahmad Al Faqi Al Mahdi — an alleged member of a jihadist group, found guilty in 2016 for organizing attacks on historic and religious buildings in Mali. The ICC issued an arrest warrant against brutal Libyan dictator Muammar Gaddafi for murdering and persecuting civilians, but the case was dropped following his death in 2011. A warrant citing similar charges was also issued against his son, Saif Al-Islam Gaddafi, who remains at large. The ICC has investigated war crimes and crimes against humanity in Afghanistan and the country of Georgia as well.

Complementing these efforts, the United Nations established ad hoc international criminal tribunals in 1993 and 1994 to prosecute individuals responsible for war crimes, genocide, and other offences committed in, respectively, the former Yugoslavia and Rwanda. The Yugoslavia tribunal sat in the Hague while the Rwanda tribunal was based in Arusha, Tanzania. The tribunal presiding over civil war offences in the former Yugoslavia indicted 161 people and sentenced ninety to prison. Among the convicted was former Bosnian Serb president Radovan Karadžić, who received life for ordering the slaughter of thousands of Bosnian Muslims. The International Criminal Tribunal for Rwanda prosecuted defendants involved in the staggering genocide that swept that nation in the early 1990s, during which approximately one million Tutsi and moderate Hutu civilians were murdered by Hutu radicals. A total of ninety-three people were indicted by the Rwanda tribunal, with sixty-one sentenced for violating international humanitarian law.

On March 17, 2023, the International Criminal Court issued an arrest warrant against Russian Federation president Vladmir Putin, based on his actions during the brutal invasion of Ukraine.

Putin "is allegedly responsible for the war crime of unlawful deportation of population (children) and that of unlawful transfer of population (children) from occupied areas of Ukraine to the Russian Federation.... These crimes were allegedly committed in Ukrainian occupied territory at least from 24 February 2022," states an ICC press release.

An arrest warrant was also issued for Maria Lvova-Belova, commissioner for children's rights in the Office of the President of the Russian Federation.

Taking Putin and Lvova-Belova into custody would require action by the Russian police, which isn't likely to happen. Still, the warrants are a reminder there now exists a permanent judicial body that can try war criminals from around the world who commit offences that violate international law.

CHAPTER EIGHT

Centenary

On a visit to her parents in New Brunswick in 2003, Captain Barbara (Cuthbertson) Putnam was surprised to receive a precious family heirloom. A chaplain with the Canadian Armed Forces (CAF), Putnam made the trip to the Maritimes from the military base in Petawawa, Ontario, where she was posted. She would soon be deployed to Afghanistan, where Canadian troops were fighting the Taliban.

During the visit, Putnam's father, Clement George Cuthbertson, gave her a manila envelope containing family military mementoes. Her father served in the Canadian army at the end of the Second World War but didn't talk much about his experiences.

"I have these medals. You might be interested in having these," said her father, according to Putnam.

Putnam had been working as a chaplain since 2000. Her dedication to military service might have been the reason her father handed over the keepsakes, the existence of which Putnam had been unaware.

The envelope also contained a small, mysterious box. Putnam opened the box, which resembled a jewellery case. Inside, to her astonishment, there was a silver Memorial Cross. Also called the Silver Cross, this honour was introduced by the Canadian government in late 1919. It was given to mothers and widows of Canadian soldiers who died during active duty or succumbed to service-related ailments or injuries.

The medal was in the shape of a stylized Christian cross, with narrow arms at the centre, growing wider as they extended outwards. This design is called a *cross pattée*, and it's a common motif in military iconography. There was a crown near the border of the top arm, while the other arms sported maple leaves. In the centre of the cross were the initials GRI, which stood for Georgius Rex Imperator, the royal cypher of the then reigning monarch, King George V. There was a laurel behind the cross and the medal was attached to a purple ribbon. This military decoration had been given in honour of a relative Putnam had never heard of.

"It was still in the original box, with the original felt lining.... On the back it said '536249 Private C.G. Scribner,'" recalls Putnam.

Private Clement George Scribner was Putnam's maternal great uncle. He had served in the First World War. The six digits were his regimental number. The Memorial Cross had been awarded to Clementina Scribner, Clement's mother, then passed down in their family.

Born November 19, 1898, in Saint John, New Brunswick, Clement Scribner attested for the Canadian Expeditionary Force on July 31, 1916. He put down "machinist" as his trade or calling, said he was single, and gave his mother — her name is listed as Tina — as his next-of-kin. Private Scribner served in the Canadian Army Medical Corps as an orderly. He went overseas in January 1917, and was posted to No. 14 Canadian Field Ambulance then No. 16 Canadian Field Ambulance. Scribner's service file includes a will, in which he bequeathed his personal estate to his mother. On March 21, 1918, Scribner was transferred to His Majesty's Hospital Ship *Llandovery Castle*.

"Reported 'missing' believed drowned," reads a handwritten entry in his service file, dated July 5, 1918.

At the time of his death on the *Llandovery Castle*, Scribner was still a few months shy of his twentieth birthday.

"Though [my father] didn't know much about my great-uncle, he knew the cross was important to pass on, as I will someday do. I had not previously heard the story of my great-uncle and his sacrifice and have treasured this connection ever since," states Putnam.

Prior to receiving the gift, she confesses to having known "Zero. Nothing" about either the *Llandovery Castle* or her great-uncle's presence on the ship. She doesn't remember hearing her grandmother (Scribner's sister, Ruth) mention anything about him.

Putnam did some research and uncovered the history of the *Llandovery Castle*. She also discovered that Scribner's name was listed on the Halifax Memorial, a monument in Point Pleasant Park, near Halifax Harbour. The Memorial features a twelve-metre-high granite cross mounted on an octagonal base. There are bronze panels on the walls of the base, inscribed with the names of 3,267 sailors, soldiers, merchant crew, and other military personnel from Canada and Newfoundland who died in both world wars. Listed among the dead are medical personnel from the *Llandovery Castle*.

There are only a handful of other monuments that honour the *Llandovery Castle* victims. The Tower Hill Memorial in Trinity Square Gardens in London, England, for example, lists the names of over twelve thousand British merchant seamen killed during the Great War whose bodies were never recovered. The memorial includes the crew of the *Llandovery Castle*.

In Charlottetown, Prince Edward Island, a section of the land that once housed the Rena McLean Memorial Hospital was renamed in her honour in 2007. The area is now called the Rena McLean Veterans Garden. A plaque there reads:

> This garden commemorates the previous use of this site as a convalescent hospital for veterans returning from the Great War (1914–1918).... The hospital was named the Rena McLean Memorial Hospital in memory of a young island nurse, who served as a member of the Canadian nursing sisters. Rena McLean was the only Prince Edward Island nurse to lose her life during the Great War, when the hospital ship, Llandovery Castle was sunk in 1918.... The garden provides a quiet and scenic place to remember those who have given, and those who offer, their lives in service of their country.

Chaplain Putnam and her sister, Deborah Boyd, journeyed to Point Pleasant Park, not for peace and quiet, but to view the Halifax Memorial and examine another vestige of their great-uncle's life. "We made a trek over there and took some pictures of the monument. We found his name on the panel," states Putnam.

Finding Scribner's name on a war monument was important, given that beyond his service file, there is a dearth of information about the private in online archives. "I've seen his attestation record. There's very little there other than height, weight, eye colour — the sort of thing that's on everybody's record," states Putnam.

She feels a connection to Scribner, in part from his service in the CAMC. "He's looking after the ill and injured, which resonated with me, because that's what a chaplain does. We look after the ill and injured.... Chaplains provide spiritual and religious services to troops and their families. That could be in garrison, it could be at sea, on deployment, on overseas missions. You name it. That's what our role is," she states.

After the family visit, Captain Putnam resumed her work as an army chaplain, in Afghanistan and elsewhere, but continued to think about her great-uncle and the evening of June 27, 1918.

"He was a passenger on the ship, basically. I know he was part of the medical corps, but they didn't have any patients on board, they were making a return trip. So, they were basically ferrying themselves back to the next pickup point [when they were torpedoed]. I've often wondered what that night would have been like for them," she states.

In November 2016, Stephanie Martin, a composer, conductor, and academic, made a fortuitous discovery of her own. Martin was overseeing orchestral rehearsals for a performance of a work by French composer Hector Berlioz at Calvin Presbyterian Church. During a break, Martin wandered about the interior of this stately house of worship in midtown Toronto.

As the former director of music at Calvin Presbyterian, Martin was intimately familiar with the place. To her surprise, Martin discovered a wall plaque she'd never noticed before. The dark metallic plaque had been installed decades earlier to commemorate the death of Nursing Sister Mary Agnes McKenzie. Martin read the text on the tablet and was stopped short

The plaque commemorating Mary Agnes McKenzie that inspired the *Llandovery Castle* opera.

by the reference to "the torpedoing of the hospital ship Llandovery Castle June 27, 1918."

Martin knew her history; in 2014, on a trip to France with friends, she had visited Canadian graves from the First World War. "I had a heightened interest in World War One things, so I guess that's why it resonated with me when I saw the plaque and the dates," says Martin, currently an associate professor of music at York University's School of the Arts, Media, Performance and Design.

The plaque, however, left her stumped, Martin admits she had never heard of the *Llandovery Castle*, "let alone how to pronounce it."

Like Putnam, Martin began to research the ship's history. She was astonished to learn about the attack on the *Llandovery Castle*. She realized that the sinking had been a huge story for a while after it occurred and that it had since vanished from public memory. With the one-hundredth anniversary of the torpedo attack looming, Martin came up with a unique idea. *What if she were to write an opera about the* Llandovery Castle*?* An operatic treatment would be an excellent way to mark the centenary of the disaster and draw attention to a forgotten bit of history.

During her career, Martin had served as artistic director of Pax Christi Chorale (a leading community choir), director of music at the Church of St. Mary Magdalene in Toronto, and director of Schola Magdalena, a woman's ensemble. She had the skill and stamina to write a score for an opera, but who would handle the plot and words?

As Martin pondered, more synchronicity ensued. A classical music event called the Bach Music Festival of Canada commissioned her to write a piece celebrating Canada's 150th anniversary. Martin was one of four composers chosen for this honour. She decided to set a poem called "Be the River" by Maureen Scott Harris to music. Her composition was performed by an orchestra, choir, and soloists at the South Huron Recreation Centre in Exeter, Ontario, on July 16, 2017. She attended in person and was introduced as the composer of the piece.

Watching that night was Paul Ciufo, a board member of the Bach Festival and an award-winning playwright. Some of Ciufo's works had been staged by the well-respected Blyth Festival in Ontario. A historical drama Ciufo wrote, called *Narcisse*, won a 2011 Governor General's History Award, in the category of community programming. Another work, *Reverend Jonah*, was a finalist for a 2008 Governor General's Literary Award, in the drama category. Ciufo had also written a play about Canadian merchant ships in the Second World War called *On Convoy*, which he turned into a script for broadcast on CBC Radio.

Deeply impressed by the performance of "Be the River," Ciufo decided to approach Martin and pay her a compliment.

"I absolutely loved her composition. It was beautiful. After the concert, I went up to her and I just praised her song," he says.

The pair chatted, and when Ciufo revealed he was a playwright, Martin became excited — "I always need words!" she declared. Martin explained she was looking for someone who could provide a libretto for an opera-in-development.

Martin outlined her concept and Ciufo was intrigued, although he too was unfamiliar with the *Llandovery Castle*. However, there were some clear parallels to his work *On Convoy*. In Ciufo's story, a Canadian merchant ship is torpedoed by a U-boat, which then proceeds to machine gun the survivors in their lifeboats. While this part of his play was not based on a historic account, the similarities with the *Llandovery Castle* augured well for a collaboration. Ciufo agreed to provide a libretto, even though he'd never written for opera before.

With the creative team in place, funding and a tight deadline proved to be the next major challenges. Martin and Ciufo were determined to have the opera ready by the centenary of the sinking, which gave them less than a year to complete their project.

If anything, Martin seemed motivated by the time constraints, stating, "[T]here's nothing like a deadline to light a fire under you."

Martin provided Ciufo with historical material about the *Llandovery Castle*, which he augmented with his own research. The pair spoke with family descendants of the *Llandovery Castle* dead, and consulted Great War-era letters, diaries, and reports. Martin asked Ciufo to focus on the nursing sisters who drowned but otherwise gave him free rein on the words. The pair routinely exchanged ideas and discussed concepts and plot points as the libretto was developed.

Since the nurses were all unmarried and childless, Ciufo couldn't create any storylines about husbands and children. Many of the nursing sisters had been serving for years, however, so it was decided to build on this aspect of their lives.

"The sinking happened very late in the war, so the nurses had all these incredible wartime experiences leading up to that, including being at the Front and other very dangerous areas," says Ciufo.

A bit of artistic license was taken to develop plot arcs involving some of the nursing sisters and other CAMC staff. Ciufo highlighted the steadfast, maternal leadership of Matron Margaret "Pearl" Fraser, and the camaraderie between the medical personnel on board the *Llandovery Castle*. While there was no overt romance in the opera, Ciufo detailed passionate (but platonic) friendships among the medical personnel, sometimes between the nurses and male staff.

Performance funding was secured by Jennifer Collins, an arts administrator and manager of musical groups, who knew Martin from Pax Christi Chorale. Collins took on the role of producer and secured grant money from the Canada Council.

"As producer, I supported the creative development and workshops in any way that was required. So, all of the administrative stuff — venues and videographers, and contracts and publicity, and box office and ticket sales. All the behind-the-scenes stuff. All the stuff you don't see," says Collins.

The Bicycle Opera Project, a young, progressive Toronto company, agreed to perform the opera, which was simply titled *Llandovery Castle*. Under the guidance of director Tom Diamond, intense rehearsals were held once the words and music were in place.

Two inaugural performances were arranged to coincide with the centenary of the *Llandovery Castle* sinking. These performances would take place at Calvin Presbyterian Church, the same location where Martin first spotted the wall plaque for Mary Agnes McKenzie.

On June 17, 2018, the *Sunday Edition* on CBC Radio aired a documentary about the opera entitled, "To Prepare a Place for You." Produced by Alisa Siegel, the documentary explained the story of the *Llandovery Castle* sinking, the genesis of the opera, and featured interviews with Martin, Ciufo, Bicycle Opera, and descendants of medical personnel who were on board the ship.

"The story of the *Llandovery Castle* was a revelation to me. I'm always interested in the question of who it is that gets to be remembered, of who makes it into the history books and who gets left out — forgotten and erased. I think the *Llandovery Castle* and its nursing sisters fall into that category: an important and long-overlooked chapter in Canadian history, war history and women's history," said Siegel, in an interview. She added:

> I hoped listeners would be riveted by the dramatic story
> of the ship, torpedoed by a German U-boat. And I hoped
> they would be particularly moved and inspired by the

nursing sisters, the remarkable young women, colleagues, and intimate friends — brave, tough, hopeful and adventurous — who, in wartime, made back and forth voyages across the Atlantic and tended to the wounded soldiers. Naming them was important to me. I kept a list on my office wall with the names of the nursing sisters who perished.... Their names are a powerful reminder of each of their lives, their bravery, their sacrifices, and ultimately their deaths. I was thrilled to learn that these women were and are being rediscovered, studied, remembered, and honoured by a new generation of Canadians.

Unlike many people, Lesley Strelioff, who was born and raised in Saskatoon, Saskatchewan, knew about the *Llandovery Castle* from an early age. Her grandmother, Eveline Sutcliffe Gemmell, was the daughter of Corporal William Jackson, the CAMC orderly and musician who died on the ship. His story was top-of-mind in Strelioff's family as she grew up.

"My mother and grandmother were touched by the fact he had passed away so tragically," states Strelioff in an interview. She says her mother, F. Isabelle Strelioff, was "very interested in genealogy and in making sure our family knew what happened. I've got kids as well, so I've made sure I've passed on those stories, so they understand the significance of the Great War."

In 1978, when Strelioff was ten, her older sister, Gale, did a grade-school project about her family. After conducting research and interviewing family members, Gale compiled her findings in a neat, handwritten document that included a section about Corporal Jackson. While the report earned a top mark, Strelioff doesn't recall any mention of the *Llandovery Castle* in history class when she was in school.

In addition to family lore, Strelioff has downloaded her great-grandfather's service record and newspaper stories about him. "I read an article that he was playing on the boat, sharing his musical talents. To me, music is such a beautiful thing," she says.

Indeed, William Jackson's love of music has been inherited by his descendants.

"Our family loves to sing. I grew up taking singing lessons, as did my siblings, and piano lessons. My mother was very musical," says Strelioff.

There is a plaque commemorating William Jackson on a tree in the Next of Kin Memorial Avenue at Woodlawn Cemetery in Saskatoon. The plaque reads: "1914–1918 Cpl. Wm Jackson Amb. Corps Perished Llandovery Castle Age 29 Honored by Mother."

An initiative of the Imperial Order Daughters of the Empire, Memorial Avenue was built in the early 1920s to honour local war dead. In 1992 the Avenue was designated a National Historic Site of Canada. Similar memorials for First World War dead, created by local service organizations, were a once common sight in cemeteries across Canada.

Asked how she wants her great-grandfather William Jackson to be re-membered, Lesley Strelioff says, "The first step would be for people to become aware of the incident. Look at Vimy Ridge or Dieppe. You say one word and people know what it is. You say 'Llandovery Castle' and they don't."

To this end, Strelioff was delighted to learn about the *Llandovery Castle* opera. She hasn't seen a performance but is pleased that the historic event that took the life of a family member is receiving new attention.

Dave Sales knew the broad outlines of the wartime experience of his grandfather, Arthur Knight, but none of the specifics. After returning from the Great War, Knight lived in London, Ontario, once more. Following the end of the Second World War, he moved to British Columbia, with his wife, Alice May, son, William, and daughter, Marion. Knight's daughter was Sales's mother.

"My dad told me grandpa was in the war, that he had been on a German submarine and thrown back in [the water]. He didn't tell me what the issue was or anything about that. I didn't know about the Llandovery Castle," states Sales in an interview for this book.

He adds, "We always had a note up in our house when I was growing up. It was from King George, thanking my grandfather for his service."

Sales was born in Victoria, British Columbia, in 1955, and worked as a steamfitter then an instructor before retiring. Knight enjoyed spending time with his grandson, teaching Sales how to use hand tools and taking walks with the boy. Sales says his grandparents "were really good to me."

He remembers his grandfather "as quiet. He didn't talk a lot. We never talked about his experiences in the war. It was never brought up when I was a child."

Only recently did Sales learn about the *Llandovery Castle* and Knight's prominent role during the sinking of the ship. "I think, like all men of his era, he wanted to do something to support the war effort, but he wasn't willing to take lives. Why else would you become an orderly? To me, that's a good thing. It's doing what you can do, and we all try to do that," states Sales.

He notes proudly that his oldest son also works in the medical profession, as a paramedic.

Sales and other *Llandovery Castle* descendants were interviewed for the CBC Radio documentary and invited to attend the premiere of the opera. Knight's grandson was among hundreds of people present at Calvin Presbyterian for the debut performance of the opera *Llandovery Castle* on June 26, 2018.

Bicycle Opera singers wore period costumes for the premiere, but otherwise, sets and special effects were minimal. The opera was presented in the format of a radio play, with singers gathered around an antique stand-up microphone as live musicians played along.

"Bicycle Opera did a phenomenal job in every way — the performers were outstanding, the musicians, the lighting, everything was terrific. It was absolutely beautiful and moving, and so gratifying to see [the opera] brought to life," reports Ciufo.

A subsequent performance the following night — the same evening the *Llandovery Castle* was attacked — also drew a sellout crowd.

Opera Canada magazine praised "Ciufo's fine libretto" and described the music as "extremely well-crafted. The score, for voices and a nine-piece chamber orchestra is varied. At times it is lushly romantic, at others abrasive and atonal. There are even folky elements.... The Llandovery Castle is a fine piece both dramatically and musically. It has real emotional power and I, for one, felt slightly shell-shocked at the end. I hope to see a fully staged version at some point."

It took two years, but such a version was eventually enacted, at Wilfrid Laurier University (WLU), in Waterloo, Ontario. Directed by Liza Balkan and conducted by Associate Professor Kira Omelchenko, the singers and musicians were students with the WLU Faculty of Music. Three performances were held, on February 28 and 29, and March 1, 2020, in the Theatre Auditorium, WLU.

A full-length video of the final dress rehearsal of the WLU production was made and can be viewed online. The rehearsal performance includes elaborate sets, lighting, and staging, with music and voice provided by on-stage singers, a choir, and a chamber orchestra.

The WLU production opens with blue lighting and maritime sounds. Singing nurses in period costumes enter on a set resembling the deck of the *Llandovery Castle*. The opening number concludes and a staircase on the ship deck abruptly transforms into a perch for Helmut Patzig. Illuminated by a spotlight, the U-boat commander peers through binoculars. In song-form, Patzig boasts about his prowess sinking ships then announces he wants to torpedo the *Llandovery Castle*, even though it's on a medical mission. After this bit of foreshadowing, the scene shifts to life on board the hospital ship.

While all fourteen of the nursing sisters from the final voyage are portrayed, the opera focuses on Rena "Bird" McLean, Minnie "Kate" Gallaher, and Matron "Pearl" Fraser. There is a plot arc in which McLean pleads with Matron Fraser to authorize her return to active duty in Europe. The Gallaher character is more embittered and uses dark humour to express her war weariness. Major Thomas Lyon and Sergeant Knight, clad in brown CAMC uniforms, also play prominent roles. At one point, Fraser and Lyon share the stage and trade verses about war and duty.

Without warning, the ship is torpedoed. Stage lights flash, an emergency bell sounds, the music becomes terse, and loud voices shout in confusion. Major Lyon is plucked from a lifeboat and interrogated on the deck of the U-boat. The questioning follows the historical record, with the baffled major bombarded with inquiries about American pilots.

The tragedy of Lifeboat No. 5, containing the nurses and Sergeant Knight, is also depicted. The occupants desperately try to untangle the ropes binding the lifeboat to the sinking ship. The stage darkens, and the lifeboat is illuminated by blue lights and crisscrossing flashlight beams. The lifeboat capsizes and the nursing sisters struggle in slow-motion to mime drowning.

The nurses vanish. The stage lights go on, revealing overturned props depicting floating debris. Lyon stands on the sliding stairs, which now represent a lifeboat, and rescues Knight from the water. The pair sing a dirge about the nurses, who reappear like apparitions. The ghostly nursing sisters urge survivors to bear witness to their deaths. Patzig makes an appearance as the nurses step forward, singing in unison. The stage goes dark. Then, there are slides of the Halifax Memorial, which Chaplain Putnam and her sister visited. The opera ends.

"It was wonderful to attend that show. They did a marvelous job with it. It was more fully staged — there were more elaborate sets and costumes," states Ciufo of the WLU production.

Asked what he hopes audiences get out of the opera, Ciufo says, "Many things. One is that they become aware of a Canadian story that seems to have dropped from our collective memory. Making people aware of what happened is one goal."

He also wants to remind people "how extraordinary the nurses were," in terms of both breaking ground for women and personal bravery. Despite "seeing the worst humanity can do," the nursing sisters remained committed and "tried to make a positive difference, despite the ugliness confronting them, and to me, that was very inspiring," says Ciufo.

He adds, "If you just look at the negative in World War One, you would despair of the human race. We used chemical weapons on each other. Millions died and were maimed. So, if you want to find some hope somewhere in that story, look at the nurses."

"The women were officers, they could vote. They had status that other Canadian women didn't have. And that's also a fundamental piece of Canadian history that is lost, and it is incredibly interesting," adds Collins.

While equally inspired by the nurses' bravery, Martin expresses dismay over the way their deaths were used to incite soldiers in battle.

"The troops were all fired up in the name of the women who were murdered, and their image was used as propaganda. My take, and Paul's take, is that they would have been outraged by that. That prisoners were killed in the names of the nurses, whose role was to heal people," says Martin.

———————

Sadly, the nursing sisters and CAMC doctors weren't able to heal all wounds. Sales, for one, is convinced his grandfather suffered his entire life from wartime trauma, even if he wouldn't openly discuss it.

"I think, at the end of his life, he had some form of what I think was dementia. I'm only guessing. I was eleven. No one said it was dementia, but he was in a hospital and the man in the bed next to him spoke German, and he was having a lot of flashbacks to when he was in the military," recalls Sales.

Arthur Knight died in Essondale, British Columbia, on December 1, 1966. He was eighty years old.

"I remember him as a gentle man who never lost his temper and was willing to accept what life gave him," states his grandson.

Knight outlived his colleague, Thomas Lyon, who returned to Canada after testifying in Leipzig. The former CAMC major opened a medical practice in Victoria, B.C. He retired prior to the Second World War and returned to Great Britain. He resided in Deal, Kent, and died on May 24, 1948.

"He had never married, and he left the entire residue of his estate to the Edinburgh Merchant Company 'to be used for the educational benefit of orphans of members of His Majesty's Armed Forces and of the Mercantile Marine,'" states a profile of Lyon written by the Royal Canadian Medical Service.

William Pilot died April 16, 1973, in Pembroke, Ontario. He was the husband of Margaret Pilot (*née* Sheffield), and father of William, Barbara, Elizabeth, and Robert. He had ten grandchildren.

U-boat *86* Commander Helmut Patzig — he changed his name to Brummer-Patzig after the First World War — was never prosecuted for the *Llandovery Castle* atrocity. He rejoined the German navy when the Second World War broke out and commanded a captured Dutch submarine. He also helped train a new generation of U-boat warriors. Patzig died in Germany in 1984, having outlived almost all his victims by several decades.

In early 2018, Chaplain Putnam was having coffee with a friend, Lieutenant Colonel Rhonda Crew, a military nurse. Crew mentioned there was going to be a 100th Anniversary Commemoration Ceremony for the *Llandovery Castle* at the Carling Campus of the National Defence Headquarters in Ottawa. Then she asked Putnam if she knew about the *Llandovery Castle*.

"I most certainly do!" responded Putnam, by then a lieutenant colonel.

Chaplain Putnam told Crew about her great-uncle who died on the *Llandovery Castle*. Crew asked Putnam if she wanted to take part in the ceremony. Upon getting an affirmative response, Crew contacted the surgeon-general, the event host, and Putnam was invited to participate.

Approximately one hundred past and present members of Canada's military medical staff attended the commemoration ceremony, which was held June 27, 2018. Guests sat in chairs around tables as a series of speakers in full-dress uniform addressed them from a podium.

As the only person present who was a descendant of a *Llandovery Castle* victim, Lieutenant Colonel Putnam was invited to lead the prayers. She offered the following, the lines of which were repeated in French:

> On this significant occasion, we pause for a moment in memory of those men and women who died that terrible night in 1918. I invite you to spend these next minutes in personal reflection, or in prayer according to your own tradition.... I will use the refrain from the Naval Hymn, feel welcome to say it with me: O hear us when we cry to Thee, for those in peril on the sea.
>
> Gracious God, from the security of a nation at peace, from the safety of solid land beneath our feet, we turn our thoughts to a dark night 100 years ago.... We listen to the sounds of the ship sinking beneath the waves. We listen to the calls across the water of those who abandoned ship.
>
> *O hear us when we cry to Thee, for those in peril on the sea.*

Mariners and Healers together were called to care for the wounded, and to ferry them safely home. Mariners and healers, now having to save themselves, crying out to God in their distress.

O hear us when we cry to Thee, for those in peril on the sea.

Loving and Compassionate God, we, the Healers and Mariners of our day, stand here in remembrance, not only of the horror of that night, but in remembrance of the brave and beautiful souls who paid the ultimate sacrifice.... We vow to remember their sacrifice. Let their legacy be one of love and peace.

O hear us when we cry to Thee, for those in peril on the sea.

As we, the members of Health Services, with our partners and friends, mark this moment of history, let us carry with us the bravery, the sense of duty, and the call to serve of each member of the *Llandovery Castle*'s company, who went down to the sea that night.

Amen.

Putnam then struck a ship's bell, which had been brought to the commemoration. She was asked to sound the bell on behalf of the family members of the *Llandovery Castle* victims. The bell was also struck to honour the nursing sisters and other medical staff, respectively.

"It was a little overwhelming to be part of that. You do Remembrance Day ceremonies, and those are very meaningful and poignant. We do commemorations for things all the time, but this had such a family connection for me, even though I did not know [Clement Scribner]. It was quite an honour to be there and be asked to ring the bell," says Putnam.

The event also featured "tables of information about the sinking and the Nursing Sisters" and "some beautiful artwork," courtesy of Silvia Pecota, continues Putnam.

A professional photographer and artist, Pecota spent years photographing athletes for media outlets such as the *Toronto Sun*. She later broadened her subject matter to include Canadian soldiers and began augmenting photographs with original art. Much of her current portfolio follows a military theme. At the Carling Campus event, Pecota presented a print of her digital artwork, *Sacrifice*, which depicts the aftermath of the attack on the *Llandovery Castle*.

Sacrifice contains a series of stark images, with a surfaced submarine on the right, a lifeboat on the left, the sinking *Llandovery Castle* in the background, and a female figure engulfed in waves in the foreground. The female figure is actually a real-life model. "I photographed the model decades ago, as I wanted to create an allegorical image representing 'Sacrifice' and finally found the opportunity with this composition," states Pecota.

She utilized a high-tech computer system called Wacom Cintiq to create this artwork. "Honouring a part of our history — that is one of the functions of art," says Pecota.

Sacrifice also appeared in *Asleep in the Deep*, a biography of Anna Stamers, one of the doomed nursing sisters on the *Llandovery Castle*.

Closing remarks at the 100th Anniversary Commemoration were given by Major General Andrew Downes, surgeon-general and commander Canadian Forces Health Services Group. Guests who attended the event were familiar with the *Llandovery Castle* story, or at least the main elements, says Lieutenant Colonel Putnam.

"People did know about it ... [but] I don't think the general knowledge was all that great. I think that was the beauty of the ceremony, to share some of the images that Silvia brought, to have a family representative there. To have the bell rung, to give a really solemn portrayal of the loss and sacrifice of this particular vessel and the people on board. I think it was very inspired that they chose to do this," she states.

A few weeks after the ceremony, Putnam honoured her great-uncle and his colleagues in a very different way. Chaplain Putnam and her husband were on a cruise from Copenhagen to New York City, on the *Regal Princess*, part of the Princess cruise ship line. The ship was docked in the Port of Cobh (formerly Queenstown) on the southern coast of Ireland, preparing for the transatlantic leg of the journey.

Putnam and her husband have Elite membership status with Princess — a benefit given to frequent travellers. This entitles them certain perks, such as occasional access to the cruise ship captain. While docked in Cobh, it occurred to Putnam that the wreck site of the *Llandovery Castle* must be nearby. At a cocktail party, Chaplain Putnam approached the cruise ship captain with an unusual request.

"I told him about the Llandovery Castle, the little bit of history I knew. He was very intrigued by that. I said my great-uncle was on board. [The ship] is at such a depth, they've never recovered it. I said, 'Is there any way to find out if we're going anywhere near it?'" recalls Putnam.

The captain asked Putnam to follow him.

"I thought he was going to take me out to the corridor where the big map was and tell me where we were going. But we kept walking, and all of a sudden, I'm on the bridge — which is quite a privileged thing on a mega-ship, to be invited to the bridge," continues the chaplain.

The cruise ship captain gathered his junior officers and explained that they were trying to pinpoint the approximate location of the remains of the hospital ship *Llandovery Castle*. The officers took out their smart phones and did some quick online research.

Putnam didn't watch every step of the process, but there is information on the internet that might have helped the officers in their quest. The night it was attacked, Captain Edward Sylvester had been carefully monitoring the *Llandovery Castle*'s location, speed, and direction.

Following his rescue, Captain Sylvester told officials the ship was "about 114 miles S. 74 degrees W. (true) from a position 15 miles south (true) from the Fastnet" when the torpedo struck, states a navy report. The *Llandovery Castle* was "steering a steady N. 74 degrees E. (true) course at 13.6 knots," added Captain Sylvester.

Several reports with this information can be found online.

Using this, or other sources, the officers "were able to find the longitude and latitude where it went down. They plotted our course and they plotted where [the Llandovery Castle] was," says Putnam.

According to the website Latitude and Longitude Finder, which claims it can provide Global Positioning System or GPS coordinates "for any address or location," the "HMHS Llandovery Castle" can be found at Latitude 51° 17" 60.00" N and Longitude -9° 53" 59.99" W. An accompanying digital map on the website places this location in the Atlantic Ocean, near the southwestern tip of Ireland. The webpage also includes a brief essay about the sinking of the *Llandovery Castle.*

The cruise ship couldn't alter its course to go to this precise location — such a detour would be against regulations. Instead, the captain said, "At six tomorrow morning, give or take, on the port side, we will be sailing as close as we will be to the wreck site,'" recollects Putnam.

She thanked the captain then got up early the next day, which was September 18, 2018. As instructed, she went to the port side of the ship at 0600 hours.

"It was a really grey, grey wet kind of morning — that part of the world is not known for its sunshine," and the wreck site was "probably 100 nautical miles beyond where we were.... I went up on deck and looked in the general direction [of the ship]. I had a moment of personal reflection, and said a prayer," says Putnam.

Putnam thought of her great-uncle, who died in the ocean with most of his colleagues and the crew from the *Llandovery Castle.* While still a distance from where the ship sank, the early-morning observance left her feeling comforted.

"For me, that was enough. It was the best possible way to honour the sacrifice from a family member, long removed. When he was a 19-year-old kid, he probably never thought 100 years later someone would be sailing [by] the wreck and thinking about him," says Putnam.

Afterword

On the evening of March 15, 2023, Stephanie Martin, composer of the *Llandovery Castle* opera, gave a presentation at St. Thomas's Church, an Anglican house of worship in Toronto. Her appearance was part of a lecture-recital series featuring talks by musical luminaries.

The elegant red-brick church was designed in the late 1890s by Eden Smith, a prominent Canadian architect. There are stained-glass windows, wooden beams along an arched ceiling, and an ornate altar with multiple candle holders.

Martin stands at the front of the church as the audience sits in wooden pews, listening intently. She discusses her creative process, occasionally making a musical point on a black piano. A foldup table stands next to the piano, covered in books about nursing sisters in the Great War and the libretto to the *Llandovery Castle* opera. The opera forms the core of Martin's presentation. She describes her surprise at seeing the wall plaque dedicated to Nursing Sister Mary Agnes McKenzie and learning about the *Llandovery Castle*.

"That was a story I never heard growing up," she admits.

Martin talks about music, the development of the opera, and the First World War. St. Thomas's Church is the perfect venue for her presentation, given that it contains a First World War memorial baptistry.

There is no door to the entrance of the First World War baptistry, but it forms a separate space in the southwest corner of the main church interior.

The octagonal-shaped baptistry is partially enclosed by dark wooden walls, which are topped with stunning, century-old stained-glass windows. The latter were designed by a member of the famous Bromsgrove Guild and feature images of angels, medieval knights, the Crucifixion, and a wounded soldier in a Great War uniform.

The baptistry walls are covered in plaques, each of which contains the name, rank, and date of death of a church parishioner who served and died in the Great War. These details are elaborately inscribed on the plaques in gilt lettering. A huge baptismal font has been placed in the centre of the room, with a lamp above, dangling from the ceiling. Babies are baptized in this memorial to the deceased — a reminder of the continuance of life.

At Martin's signal, a nine-member choir with male and female vocalists stands and faces the audience. The choir is going to sing a piece that was performed in the *Llandovery Castle* opera by the nursing sisters, says Martin.

"This scene in the opera takes place on deck, on a Sunday morning, when all the nurses would participate in the service of worship. The fourteen nurses came from all across Canada. They were of every religious domination. So, this is an imaginary scenario — all the nurses can sing a piece of music from their own tradition, and it's just a happy coincidence that they all fit together at the same time," she explains.

Opera librettist Paul Ciufo described the genesis of this scene in an interview conducted prior to Martin's lecture. "The church service was the easiest thing to write. I wrote a few lines then said, 'The nurses sing a medley of hymns.' What I envisioned was a medley of hymns with maritime themes. I envisioned, 'Amazing Grace' then another tune, and another tune consecutively," said Ciufo.

Martin broadened the concept considerably, by having the hymns overlap. The choir at St. Thomas's puts voice to the concept. Martin has the singers perform a snippet of "Amazing Grace" followed by a bit of the Catholic hymn "Ave Maria." Then, there is a selection from a Methodist hymn called "Stand by Me," which contains a reference to ships on the water.

Having prepared the tonal groundwork, Martin sections the choir, with each group assigned a different hymn, to be sung in unison. The choristers begin and "Amazing Grace," "Ave Maria," and "Stand by Me" weave together in a vocal mashup that is chaotic but beautiful.

A brief moment of grace on the deck of the *Llandovery Castle* before the end.

———————

It might have been some solace for those on board to know their sufferings would lead to a pair of historic precedents that have guided war crimes trials since the 1940s: international standards are the measure by which war crimes should be judged and following orders — if they are unlawful — does not absolve a military subordinate of guilt. Both principles form part of the legal foundation that empowers the International Criminal Court to prosecute those who commit offences "against the law of nations" as the Leipzig judges famously stated.

On a more personal level, descendants of the ship crew and medical staff, along with the organizers of the 100th anniversary commemorations, service groups that erected memorial plaques, and the creators of the *Llandovery Castle* opera simply want Canadians to remember the bravery of the men and women brutally attacked at sea while on a healing mission during a terrible war.

Acknowledgements

I would like to thank Dundurn Press and especially publisher Kwame Fraser for their interest in this project; my girlfriend, Jeanne, for her love, support, and research assistance; Stephanie Martin and Paul Ciufo for their brilliant opera and for taking the time to speak with me; and the administrators at Library and Archives Canada and the Canadian War Museum for making my visits so rewarding and for doing an excellent job preserving important archival material.

My thanks to Chaplain Barbara Putnam, Lesley Strelioff, and Dave Sales for their willingness to speak to me and share sometimes difficult memories. I wish to thank Paul Truster, Jeanne, and my parents, Margaret and Brian Hendley, for proofreading and offering important editorial insights on drafts of this manuscript. I also wish to thank Richard MacCallum for providing me with his grandfather's wartime diary, and Dominic Farrell for being a patient and perceptive editor. Special thanks to Jerry Mason, United States Navy veteran and host of the U-boat Archive website, for providing me with a digital copy and a translation of U-*86* Commander Helmut Patzig's war diary.

Finally, I would like to thank all writers, historians, activists, and anyone with an interest in history for doing their best to keep the memory of the attack on the *Llandovery Castle* and its aftermath alive.

Notes on Sources

Introduction

The quote, "the very worst thing that Germany has yet done at sea" appeared in the *Guardian*, July 8, 1918.

Chapter One: "Do You Think There Is Any Hope for Us?"

All Canadian military service records in this and subsequent chapters were sourced from the website of Library and Archives Canada. These records are now publicly available since they are over a century old.

For more details about the attack on the *Llandovery Castle*, I recommend *History of the Great War: The Merchant Navy*, Volume III by Sir Archibald Hurd, and *The Leipzig Trials* by Claud Mullins. The government document, "The Sinking of the H.M.H.S. Llandovery Castle" from 1918 also contains useful information.

Chapter Two: Floating Hospital

The "floating hospital" quote comes from the book, *Hospital Ships and Ambulance Trains* by Lieutenant Colonel John H. Plumridge.

For more details about the Canadian Army Medical Corps (CAMC) in the First World War, I recommend *Official History of the Canadian Forces in the Great War 1914–1919: The Medical Services* by Sir Andrew MacPhail, the government document "Report of the Ministry Overseas

Military Forces of Canada 1918," and *Lifesavers and Body Snatchers* by historian Tim Cook.

For more details about the fourteen nursing sisters who died on the *Llandovery Castle*, I recommend *Sacrifice of Angels* by Robyn-Rose May, *Those Splendid Girls* by Katherine Dewar, and *Asleep in the Deep* by Dianne Kelly.

The memoirs *Lights Out: A Canadian Nursing Sister's Tale* by Katherine Wilson-Simmie and *Our Bit* by Mabel Clint are gripping first-hand accounts of what Canadian nursing sisters endured during the Great War.

The books *U-Boat Stories: Narratives of German U-Boat Sailors* and *The Journal of Submarine Commander von Forstner* offer first-hand recollections from German U-boat crews who served in the Great War.

The 1917 booklet *The War on Hospital Ships* offers eyewitness testimony from survivors of hospital ships that were attacked by U-boats.

A translation of the 1917 German naval directives permitting U-boat attacks on Allied hospital ships can be found in the book *History of the Great War — The Merchant Navy*, Vol. III.

Photographs of the *Llandovery Castle* during its time as a passenger liner are available on the Royal Museums Greenwich website: tinyurl.com /3kn9mjjr.

Chapter Three: "Hospital Ship Sinkings Were Foul Murder"

William Pilot's diary is housed at the Canadian War Museum. The museum kindly let me examine the diary in-person.

Davies (painter), Schroeder, Goodridge, Murphy, Hunt, and Ward (able seamen), Tredgian and McVey (firemen), Abraham (ward attendant) and Mousney (trimmer) were the remaining British crew members rescued from Lifeboat No. 4. Despite a comprehensive search through ship and company records, newspaper articles, government reports, books, and other published accounts, I was unable to determine the first names of these men. As was sadly typical for the Great War era, low-ranking sailors and soldiers were often listed by last name only in paperwork.

Chapter Four: "An Intensity of Feeling"

The Commonwealth War Graves Commission states that there were 64,962 fatalities among troops from Canada and Newfoundland (which was not part of the Dominion at the time) between August 4, 1914, and August 31, 1921. The latter was the commission's end date for counting war dead (i.e., those who died in battle or succumbed to wounds or injuries, even after the Armistice of November 11, 1918).

Using a different end date (April 30, 1922), the *Books of Remembrance* at the Peace Tower in the House of Commons records 66,755 Canadian and Newfoundland Great War deaths.

Sixteen hospital ships serving the nations that would later make up the British Commonwealth struck mines or were torpedoed during the war. The last victim was HMAT *Warilda*, an Australian hospital ship sunk by a German U-boat in the English Channel on August 3, 1918. Over 120 people died in that attack. Including the *Llandovery Castle*, nine Commonwealth hospital ships were torpedoed by German subs. *The History of the Great War: Medical Services General History* by Major General Sir W.G. Macpherson offers details.

Chapter Five: Criminal Orders

For more details about the Leipzig Trials, I recommend *The Leipzig Trials* by Claud Mullins, *Prologue to Nuremberg* by James Willis, and the article "When Justice is Left to the Losers: The Leipzig War Crimes Trials" in *Historical Origins of International Criminal Law*.

"German War Trials: Report of Proceedings Before the Supreme Court in Leipzig" published in Great Britain in 1921 also offers a wealth of detail about the Leipzig War Crimes Trials.

The Avalon Project, Yale Law School, is an excellent online source for international treaties and related documents: avalon.law.yale.edu/.

Chapter Six: Disappearing From Memory

The book *Prologue to Nuremberg* and the academic article, "When Justice Is Left to the Losers: The Leipzig War Crimes Trials" offer further details about other war crimes trials in Europe following the *Llandovery Castle* verdict.

Chapter Seven: In the Wake of the *Llandovery Castle*

The city today called Kharkiv, Ukraine, was known as Kharkov during the Second World War and was part of the Soviet Union. For more details about the little-known Kharkiv war crimes trials, *The People's Verdict* offers verbatim reports from the proceedings. For a more analytical take, I recommend the academic article "The Judicialization of International Atrocity Crimes: The Kharkov Trial of 1943" in the *San Diego International Law Journal*.

United Nations War Crimes Commission summaries of various post-Second World War trials are available online.

Chapter Eight: Centenary

The memorial plaque to Mary Agnes McKenzie was originally hung at Avenue Road Presbyterian Church in Toronto. It ended up at Calvin Presbyterian Church, which opened in 1927.

"To Prepare a Place for You," the CBC Radio documentary about the *Llandovery Castle* sinking and opera can be heard here: tinyurl.com/mpdv49ra.

Silvia's Pecota's digital painting of the *Llandovery Castle* can be viewed here: tinyurl.com/mr3darxx.

A full dress rehearsal of the Wilfrid Laurier University production of the opera, *Llandovery Castle*, can be viewed here: tinyurl.com/2r9e4ecn.

Bibliography

Archival Sources

Canadian War Museum

Corporal William Robert Pilot. Certificate of Appreciation from the City of Montreal. 20070096-033. George Metcalf Archival Collection. Canadian War Museum.

Corporal William Robert Pilot. Diary. Canadian War Museum. 20070096-030. George Metcalf Archival Collection. Canadian War Museum.

Corporal William Robert Pilot. Discharge Certificate and Dispersal Certificate. 20070096-034. George Metcalf Archival Collection. Canadian War Museum.

Corporal William Robert Pilot. Note from King George V. 20070096-032. George Metcalf Archival Collection. Canadian War Museum.

Corporal William Robert Pilot. Pay Books. 20070096-031. George Metcalf Archival Collection. Canadian War Museum.

Corporal William Robert Pilot. Telegram to Mrs. Cullen in Regards to Her Son Private William Robert Pilot. 20070096-029. George Metcalf Archival Collection. Canadian War Museum.

Library and Archives Canada

General Correspondence, HMHS 'Llandovery Castle.' Library and Archives Canada. RG9-III-B-2, Volume number: 3700, File number: 30-9-79, File part 1.

Personnel, HMHS 'Llandovery Castle.' Library and Archives Canada. RG9-III-B-2, Volume number: 3677, File number: 29-9-79, File part 1.

War Diary, Papers, etc. Hospital Ships, 'Llandovery Castle.' Library and Archives Canada. RG9-III-B-2, Volume number: 3751, File part 75.

National Archives, Kew (U.K.)

National Archives, Kew — Board of Trade and Successors. Registry of Shipping and Seamen: Agreements and Crew Lists. Series II. Official number 135302. BT 99/3451.

National Archives and Records Administration (USA)

Kriegstagebuch. S.M. Underseeboot U. 86, 1917/09/08-1918/10/15, PG 61669 KTB U. 86, Roll 38. *Guides to the Microfilmed Records of the Germany Navy, 1850–1945: No 1: U-Boats and T-Boats, 1914–1918* (National Archives, 1984). National Archives Microfilm Publication M1743.

Books

Acton, Carol. "Kitchener's Tourists." In *The Great War: From Memory to History*, edited by Kellen Kurschinski, Steve Marti, Alicia Robinet, Matt Symes, and Jonathan F. Vance. Waterloo, ON: Wilfrid Laurier University Press, 2015.

Bacon, John. *The Great Halifax Explosion: A World War I Story of Treachery, Tragedy, and Extraordinary Heroism.* New York: HarperCollins, 2017.

Bass, Gary Jonathan. *Stay the Hand of Vengeance: The Politics of War Crimes Tribunals.* Princeton: Princeton University Press, 2000.

Bates, Christina, Dianne Dodd, and Nicole Rousseau, editors. *On All Frontiers: Four Centuries of Canadian Nursing.* Ottawa: Canadian Museum of Civilization and University of Ottawa Press, 2005.

Bazyler, Michael J. and Frank M. Tuerkheimer. *Forgotten Trials of the Holocaust.* New York and London: New York University Press, 2014.

Bergen, Claus, and Karl Neureuther, editors. *U-Boat Stories: Narratives of German U-Boat Sailors.* Uckfield, East Sussex, U.K.: Naval & Military Press, 2005.

Boileau, John. *6.12.17. The Halifax Explosion.* Lunenberg, NS: MacIntyre Purcell, 2017.

Bridgland, Tony. *Sea Killers in Disguise: The Story of the Q-Ships and Decoy Ships in the First World War*. Annapolis, MD: Naval Institute Press, 1999.

Brown, Malcolm. *The Imperial War Museum Book of the First World War*. London: Sidgwick & Jackson, 1991.

Bryant, Michael S. *A World History of War Crimes: From Antiquity to the Present*. London: Bloomsbury Academic, 2015.

Bunch, Adam. *The Toronto Book of the Dead*. Toronto: Dundurn Press, 2017.

Busch, Rainer, and Hans-Joachim Roll. *German U-Boat Commanders of World War II: A Biographical Dictionary*. London: Greenhill Books, 1999.

Canada in the Great World War: An Authentic Account of the Military History of Canada from the Earliest Days to the Close of the War of Nations. Vol. 1. Toronto: United Publishers of Canada, 1920.

Clint, Mabel B. *Our Bit: Memories of War Service by a Canadian Nurse*. Montreal: Alumnae Association of the Royal Victoria Hospital, 1934.

Cook, Tim. *At the Sharp End: Canadians Fighting the Great War, 1914–1916*, Volume One. Toronto: Penguin Canada, 2009.

———. *Lifesavers and Body Snatchers: Medical Care and the Struggle for Survival in the Great War*. Toronto: Penguin Canada, 2022.

———. *Shock Troops: Canadians Fighting the Great War, 1917–1918*, Volume Two. Toronto: Penguin Canada, 2008.

Craig, J.D., compiler. *The 1st Canadian Division in the Battles of 1918*. London: Barrs & Co., 1919.

Cuthbertson, Ken. *The Halifax Explosion: Canada's Worst Disaster, December 6, 1917*. Toronto: HarperCollins, 2017.

Dewar, Katherine. *Those Splendid Girls: The Heroic Service of Prince Edward Island Nurses in the Great War*. Charlottetown, P.E.I.: Island Studies Press, 2014.

Dominion Bureau of Statistics. *The Canada Year Book 1919*. Ottawa: Thomas Mulvey, 1920.

Earl, Hilary. *The Nuremberg SS-Einsatzgruppen Trial, 1945–1958: Atrocity, Law, and History*. New York: Cambridge University Press, 2009.

German Warships of World War I: The Royal Navy's Official Guide to the Capital Ships, Cruisers, Destroyers, Submarines and Small Craft, 1914–1918. London: Greenhill Books, 1992.

Gibbon, John Murray. *Three Centuries of Canadian Nursing.* Toronto: MacMillan Canada, 1947.

Gibson, R.H., and Maurice Prendergast. *The German Submarine War 1914–1918.* Cornwall, U.K.: Periscope Publishing, 2002. First published 1931 by Constable & Co.

Hallett, Christine E. *Containing Trauma: Nursing Work in the First World War.* Manchester: Manchester University Press, 2009.

Harrison, Charles Yale. *Generals Die in Bed: A Story from the Trenches.* New York: William Morrow, 1930.

Heberer, Patricia, and Jurgen Matthaus, editors. *Atrocities on Trial: Historical Perspectives on the Politics of Prosecuting War Crimes.* Lincoln: University of Nebraska Press, 2008.

Horne, John, and Alan Kramer. *German Atrocities, 1914: A History of Denial.* New Haven, CT: Yale University Press, 2001.

Hurd, Sir Archibald. *The Merchant Navy.* Vol. III of *The History of the Great War.* London: John Murray, 1929.

Kelly, Dianne. *Asleep in the Deep: Nursing Sister Anna Stamers and the First World War.* Fredericton, NB: Goose Lane, 2021.

Larson, Erik. *Dead Wake: The Last Crossing of the Lusitania.* New York: Broadway Books, 2015.

Laurinaviciute, Lina, Regina M. Paulose, and Ronald G. Rogo. "The Forgotten: The Armenian Genocide: 100 Years Later." In *Historical Origins of International Criminal Law,* Vol. 1, edited by Morten Bergsmo, Cheah Wui Ling, and YI Ping, 379–408. Brussels: Torkel Opsahl Academic EPublisher, 2014.

Livesay, J.F.B. *Canada's Hundred Days: With the Canadian Corps from Amiens to Mons, Aug. 8–Nov. 11, 1918.* Toronto: Thomas Allen, 1919.

Lloyd's. *Lloyd's War Losses: The First World War: Casualties to Shipping Through Enemy Causes, 1914–1918.* London: Lloyd's of London Press, 1990.

MacPhail, Sir Andrew. *Official History of the Canadian Forces in the Great War 1914–1919: The Medical Services.* Ottawa: F.A. Acland, 1925.

Macpherson, Major-General Sir W.G. *History of the Great War: Medical Services General History,* Vol. 1. London: His Majesty's Stationery Office, 1921.

Mann, Susan, editor. *The War Diary of Clare Gass 1915–1918.* Montreal: McGill-Queen's University Press, 2004.

May, Robyn-Rose. *Sacrifice of Angels: The Overseas Deaths of Canada's First World War Nursing Sisters*. Ottawa: CEF Books, 2016.

McGreal, Stephen. *The War on Hospital Ships 1914–1918*. Barnsley, U.K.: Pen & Sword, 2008.

McKenzie, Andrea, editor. *War-Torn Exchanges: The Lives and Letters of Nursing Sisters Laura Holland and Mildred Forbes*. Vancouver: UBC Press, 2016.

Mikaberidze, Alexander, editor. *Atrocities, Massacres, and War Crimes: An Encyclopedia*. 2 vols. Santa Barbara, CA: ABC-CLIO, 2013.

Miller, David. *Submarines of the World*. New York: Orion Books, 1991.

Moller, Eberhard, and Werner Brack. *The Encyclopedia of U-Boats from 1904 to the Present*. London: Greenhill Books, 2004.

Mullins, Claud. *The Leipzig Trials: An Account of the War Criminals' Trials and a Study of German Mentality*. London: H.F. & G. Witherby, 1921.

Murray, Marischal. *Union-Castle Chronicle 1853–1953*. London: Longmans, Green. 1953.

Neuner, Matthias. "When Justice Is Left to the Losers: The Leipzig War Crimes Trials." In *Historical Origins of International Criminal Law*, Vol. 1, edited by Morten Bergsmo, Cheah Wui Ling, and YI Ping, 333–78. Brussels: Torkel Opsahl Academic EPublisher, 2014.

Nicholson, G.W.L. *Canada's Nursing Sisters*. Toronto: Samuel Stevens Hakkert & Company, 1975.

The People's Verdict: A Full Report of the Proceedings at the Krasdonar and Kharkov German Atrocity Trials. London: Hutchinson, 1944.

Plumridge, Lieutenant Colonel John H. *Hospital Ships and Ambulance Trains*. London: Seeley, Service, 1975.

Ponsonby, Arthur. *Falsehood in War-Time: Containing an Assortment of Lies Circulated Throughout the Nations During the Great War*. London: Garland Publishing, 1928.

Quinn, Shawna. *Agnes Warner and the Nursing Sisters of the Great War*. Fredericton, NB: Goose Lane and the New Brunswick Military Heritage Project, 2010.

Roussel, Mike, and Sam Warwick. *The Union-Castle Line: Sailing Like Clockwork*. Cheltenham, U.K.: History Press, 2015.

Sondaus, Lawrence. *German Submarine Warfare in World War I: The Onset of Total War at Sea*. Lanham, MD: Rowman & Littlefield, 2017.

Taulbee, James Larry. *War Crimes and Trials: A Primary Source Guide*. Santa Barbara, CA: ABC-CLIO, 2018.

Toman, Cynthia. *Sister Soldiers of the Great War: The Nurses of the Canadian Army Medical Corps*. Vancouver: UBC Press, 2016.

Vance, Jonathan. *Death So Noble: Memory, Meaning, and the First World War*. Vancouver: UBC Press, 1997.

von Forstner, Georg-Gunther. *The Journal of Submarine Commander von Forstner*, translated by Anna Crafts Codman. Boston: Houghton Mifflin, 1917.

The War on Hospital Ships: From the Narratives of Eye-witnesses. London: T. Fisher Unwin, 1917.

Willis, James. *Prologue to Nuremberg: The Politics and Diplomacy of Punishing War Criminals of the First World War*. Westport, CT: Greenwood Press, 1982.

Wilson-Simmie, Katherine M. *Lights Out: A Canadian Nursing Sister's Tale*. Belleville, ON: Mika Publishing, 1981.

Documents, Hansard, and Reports

Borden, Sir Robert Laird. "Canada At War: Speeches Delivered by Rt. Hon. Sir Robert Laird Borden, June–September 1918." Ottawa: 1918.

Director of Public Information. "The Sinking of the H.M.H.S. Llandovery Castle." Ottawa: 1918.

"German War Trials: Report of Proceedings Before the Supreme Court in Leipzig." London: His Majesty's Stationery Office, 1921.

International Committee of the Red Cross. "The Geneva Conventions of 12 August 1949." Geneva: International Committee of the Red Cross.

International Military Tribunal. "Judgement of 1 October 1946: The Trial of German Major War Criminals." Proceedings of the International Military Tribunal sitting at Nuremberg, Germany, Part 22 (22nd August 1946 to 1st October 1946).

International Military Tribunal for the Far East. "Special Proclamation: Establishment of an International Military Tribunal for the Far East." 1946.

Jowitt, Sir William, Lord Chancellor. "The 'Peleus' Trial." U.K. Parliament, Lords Chamber. Volume 166: debated April 25, 1950. tinyurl.com/22ujadv5.

Kemp, Sir Edward, Conservative ([Toronto East], Minister of Overseas Military Forces). "Canada's Overseas Forces." House of Commons Debate, 13th Parliament, 3rd Session, May 27, 1919. tinyurl.com/2p8f54nt.

Law, Bonar. "Sinking of the 'Llandovery Castle.'" U.K. Parliament, House of Commons. Volume 107 cc1858-9: debated July 4, 1918. tinyurl.com/y3e6rb9f.

"Memorial Service for Medical Officers and Nursing Sisters Who Lost Their Lives When the S.S. Llandovery Castle Was Sunk by German Submarines on the 28th of June 1918." St. Andrew's Church, Toronto, Brochure, July 14, 1918.

Military Courts for the Trial of War Criminals. Army Form A 3688, War Crimes Court, Hamburg, Germany. (undated).

Military Tribunal No. II. "Transcript of the Opinion and Judgement" (1948). Trial 9 — Einsatzgruppen Case. 4. digitalcommons.law.uga.edu/nmt9/4.

Ministry of Overseas Military Forces of Canada. "Report of the Ministry Overseas Military Forces of Canada 1918." London: Printed by His Majesty's Stationery Office.

Miscellaneous No. 16 (1917). "Correspondence with the German Government Regarding the Alleged Misuse of British Hospital Ships." London: Published by His Majesty's Stationery Office, 1917.

Miscellaneous No. 26 (1918), "Circular Despatch Addressed to His Majesty's Diplomatic Representatives in Allied and Neutral Countries Respecting the Torpedoing by German Submarines of the British Hospital Ships 'Rewa,' 'Glenart Castle,' 'Guildford Castle,' and 'Llandovery Castle.'" London: Published by His Majesty's Stationery Office, 1918.

Nuremberg Military Tribunal. "Trials of War Criminals Before the Nuremberg Military Tribunals Under Control Council Law No. 10, Volume IV." Case No. 9: *United States of America v. Otto Ohlendorf, et al* (1947–1948). Washington, DC: U.S. Government Printing Office.

Pictet, Jean, editor. "Commentary: II Geneva Convention for the Amelioration of the Condition of Wounded, Sick and Shipwrecked Members of Armed Forces at Sea." Geneva: International Committee of the Red Cross, 1960.

R. v. Finta, 1994 CanLII 129 (SCC), [1994] 1 SCR 701, canlii.ca/t/1frvp, retrieved on 2023-05-25.

Taylor, Telford. "Closing Statement for the United States of America" (1948). Trial 9 — Einsatzgruppen Case. 3 digitalcommons.law.uga.edu/nmt9/3.

United Nations War Crimes Commission. "Law Reports of Trials of War Criminals, Volume I: Case No. 1, The Peleus Trial: Trial of Kaptitanleutnant Heinz Eck, and Four Others For the Killing of Members of the Crew of the Greek Steamship Peleus, Sunk on the High Seas (1945)." London: Published for the United Nations War Crimes Commission by His Majesty's Stationery Office, 1947.

United Nations War Crimes Commission. "Law Reports of Trials of War Criminals, Volume V: Case No. 25, Trial of Lieutenant-General Shigeru Sawada and Three Others (1946)." London: Published for the United Nations War Crimes Commission by His Majesty's Stationery Office, 1948.

United Nations War Crimes Commission. "Law Reports of Trials of War Criminals, Volume V: Case No. 30, Trial of Karl Adam Golkel and Thirteen Others (1946)." London: Published for the United Nations War Crimes Commission by His Majesty's Stationery Office, 1948.

United Nations War Crimes Commission. "Law Reports of Trials of War Criminals, Volume VIII: Case No. 47, The Hostages Trial — Trial of Wilhelm List and Others (1947–1948)." London: Published for the United Nations War Crimes Commission by His Majesty's Stationery Office, 1949.

United Nations War Crimes Commission. "Law Reports of Trials of War Criminals, Volume XI: Case No. 62, Trial of Max Wielen and 17 Others: The Stalag Luft III Case (1947)." London: Published for the United Nations War Crimes Commission by His Majesty's Stationery Office, 1949.

Lectures

Martin, Stephanie. Friends of Music series, St. Thomas's Church, Toronto, March 15, 2023.

Letters and Diaries

Davis, Lena. September 15, 1916. Lena Davis Collection, Canadian Letters and Images Project: canadianletters.ca.

Fowlds, Helen. Helen Marryat fonds, Trent University Archives. Letter dated July 1 [1918]: 72-001/007(05)154.

Fowlds, Helen. Helen Marryat fonds, Trent University Archives. Letter dated July 8, 1918: 72-001/007(05)164.

Fowlds, Helen. Helen Marryat fonds, Trent University Archives. September 25, 1916, diary entry: 69-001/001(01)b

MacCallum, Henry Reid, Canadian Army Medical Corps (CAMC). Diary of 1918. Private collection, used with permission of family.

Sare, Gladys. June 14, 1918. Letter provided by Terry Wallace.

Microform

"Memorial Service for Medical Officers and Nursing Sisters, Who Lost Their Lives When the S.S. Llandovery Castle was Sunk by German Submarines on the 28th of June 1918: St. Andrew's Church, Toronto, July 14, 1918." Toronto Reference Library.

Newspapers and Periodicals

"A. Lafontaine's Death Saves Life of His Son." *Toronto Daily Star*, July 4, 1918, 17.

"Alien Seamen Discharged." *Evening Standard* [London], August 18, 1914, 13.

"Along the Waterfront." *Evening Mail* [Halifax], June 17, 1918, 12.

"Ambulance Training Is Most Useful." *Star-Phoenix* [Saskatoon], December 19, 1914, 3.

"Anger in Britain." *The Press* [Christchurch, NZ], July 5, 1918.

"Asks 4-Year Sentences for U-Boat Officers." *New York Times*, July 16, 1921, 2.

"Band Officers Elected." *Star-Phoenix* [Saskatoon], June 18, 1912, 7.

Bazyler, Michael J., and Kellyanne R. Gold. "The Judicialization of International Atrocity Crimes: The Kharkov Trial of 1943." *San Diego International Law Journal* 14, no. 1 (2012). digital.sandiego.edu/cgi/viewcontent.cgi?article=1076&context=ilj.

Bisceglia, Louis R. "Lord Ponsonby: Pacifist Peace Campaigner." *Peace Research: The Canadian Journal of Peace and Conflict Studies* 16, no. 2 (May 1984): 38–45.

"Boldt's Escape Suspicious." *New York Times*, November 24, 1921, 20.

"Borden Indignant at Stories of Skulkers." *Toronto Daily Star*, September 3, 1918, 5.

"Boycotting Germany." *New York Times*, July 8, 1918, 10.

"Brazen Germans Say Mine Sank Hospital Ship." *Vancouver Daily World*, July 3, 1918, 1.

"Britain Aroused." *Sydney Morning Herald*, July 4, 1918, 7.

"British Admiralty's Graphic Report of Sinking of the Llandovery Castle." *New York Times*, July 2, 1918, 1.

"British Solicitor-General to Watch Leipzig Trials." *Globe* [Toronto], May 13, 1921, 1.

"Canada and German Murderers." *Globe* [Toronto], July 3, 1918, 4.

"Canadian Hospital Ship Sunk by Sub." *Ottawa Citizen*, July 2, 1918, 1.

"Canadian Nurses Are Drowned When Hospital Ship is Torpedoed." *Toronto World*, July 3, 1918, 1.

"Canadians in Leipzig to Tell of War Crimes." *Toronto Daily Star*, July 13, 1921, 1.

"Canadians Known on Hospital Ship." *Ottawa Citizen*, July 3, 1918, 2.

"Celebrates Fourteenth Anniversary." *Saskatoon Daily Star*, June 8, 1918, 3.

"Chronology in the Imre Finta Case." *Globe and Mail*, May 26, 1990, 13.

"City of Saskatoon — Police Department Tenders for Automobile." *Star-Phoenix* [Saskatoon], May 6, 1913, 14.

"Col. Bell States Only Medicals and Crew Aboard." *Ottawa Citizen*, July 3, 1918, 2.

Crane, Dr. Frank. "Lest We Forget." *Arizona Republic* [Phoenix], April 13, 1922, 4.

Cropley, Ralph. "Nurses and Wounded as Targets for Hun Torpedoes." *Evening Mail* [Halifax], May 29, 1918, 11.

Cummings, A.C. "German War Criminals Will Not Escape This Time, Says War Crimes Chairman." *Ottawa Citizen*, February 3, 1945, 12.

"Death of Captain A.E. Sylvester." *Kent and Sussex Courier* [Royal Tunbridge Wells, U.K.], July 16, 1920, 3.

Demers, Daniel. "The Sinking of the Llandovery Castle." *Canadian Naval Review* 11, no. 2 (2015): 25–28.

"Details Lacking in Loss of Canadian Hospital Vessel." *Ottawa Citizen*, July 4, 1918, 5.

Doucet, Jay, Gregory Haley, and Vivian McAlister. "Massacre of Canadian Army Medical Corps Personnel After the Sinking of the HMHS Llandovery Castle and the Evolution of Modern War Crime Jurisprudence." *Canadian Journal of Surgery* 61, no. 3 (June 1, 2018): 155–57.

"Duty Overseas, Says Borden." *Globe* [Toronto], August 2, 1918, 5.

Egan, Kelly. "Survival Came at a Cost for Soldier." *Ottawa Citizen*, November 8, 2018, A3.

"The Eighth Outrage." *People* [Dallas, TX], July 7, 1918, 5.

"England May Rage at Mild Sentences for Sea Atrocities." *Globe* [Toronto], July 16, 1921, 1.

"Ex-Officer Shackled." *New York Times*, June 30, 1921, 19.

"Fighting Men Are Quite Disgusted with Politics." *Vancouver Daily World*, October 13, 1917, 2.

"First Direct Blow Ferocious Hun Has Struck at Canada at Sea." *Ottawa Citizen*, July 3, 1918, 2.

"500 Wounded Veterans Welcomed At Halifax." *Globe and Mail*, January 10, 1945, 13.

Forrest, Wilbur. "Bloodiest Defeat for Germans Since Struggle Before Verdun." *Evening Mail* [Halifax], June 17, 1918, 4.

"4 Years for Sinking a Hospital Ship." *New York Times*, July 17, 1921, 17.

"Free Man Who Sank a Hospital Ship." *New York Times*, June 5, 1921, 1.

"German War Crimes." *Daily Telegraph* [London], July 2, 1921, 12.

"German War Crimes." *Daily Telegraph* [London], July 14, 1921, 12.

"German War Crimes." *Daily Telegraph* [London], July 15, 1921, 10.

"German War Crimes." *Daily Telegraph* [London], July 18, 1921, 9.

"German War Offences." *Times* [London], January 12, 1921, 10.

"German War Trials: Judgment in Case of Lieutenants Ditmars and Boldt." *American Journal of International Law* 16, no. 4 (October 1922): 708–24.

"Germans Suspected All Hospital Ships." *Toronto Daily Star*, July 14, 1921, 1.

"Germany's Crimes." *Sydney Morning Herald*, July 4, 1918, 7.

"Germany's Latest Atrocious Crime." *Philadelphia Inquirer*, July 3, 1918, 10.

"Germany's Latest Crime." *Sydney Morning Herald*, July 3, 1918, 11.

"Handsome Tablet in Stewarton Church." *Ottawa Citizen*, November 15, 1920, 2.

"Heroic Nurses are Honored." *Globe* [Toronto], July 15, 1918, 10.

"Honour Nurses Lost on Hospital Ship." *Toronto Daily Star*, July 15, 1918, 13.

"Hospital Ship Attack Hideous in Ferocity." *Toronto Daily Star*, July 2, 1918, 4.

"Hospital Ship Britannic Sunk; 50 Lives Lost." *New York Times*, November 23, 1916, 1.

"Hospital Ship Crime." *Daily Telegraph* [London], August 8, 1921, 10.

"Hospital Ship Crime Faced by Germans." *Philadelphia Inquirer*, July 13, 1921, 2.

"Hospital Ship, Plainly Marked, Sunk by Huns; Llandovery Castle With Canadian Medicals." *Globe* [Toronto], July 2, 1918, 1.

"Hospital Ship Sunk." *Times* [London], July 2, 1918, 7.

"Hospital Ship Trial at Leipzig." *Guardian* [London], July 13, 1921, 7.

"Hospital Ship Victims Honored." *Daily Standard* [Kingston, ON], July 22, 1918, 4.

"Hun Barbarism Revealed in Conduct of Sub. Crew." *Globe* [Toronto], July 2, 1918, 1.

"In the Leipzig Court." *Guardian* [London], July 18, 1921, 7.

"Indignation in America." *Times* [London], July 3, 1918, 20.

"The International Criminal Court Issues an Arrest Warrant for Putin." *New York Times*, March 17, 2023.

"Italians Take 2 More Asiago Peaks, Have 2,000 Prisoners; First American Army Corps in the Field, Ready for Foe; U-Boat Sinks Another British Hospital Ship, 234 Missing." *New York Times*, July 2, 1918, 1.

James, Edwin. "Silesian Line Left to League Council." *New York Times*, August 13, 1921, 3.

"John Jackson Seriously Ill." *Saskatoon Daily Star*, November 7, 1918, 3.

"King George Hears Experiences of Llandovery Castle Survivor." *Des Moines Tribune*, July 5, 1918, 16.

"The Leipzig Farces." *Evening Standard* [London], July 18, 1921, 4.

"Leipzig Trials." *Daily Telegraph* [London], July 16, 1921, 12.

"Leipzig Trials Dwindle Down to Poor Farce." *Globe* [Toronto], May 24, 1921, 1.

"Leipzig Trials Farce." *Birmingham Gazette* [U.K.], July 12, 1921, 1.

"Leipzig Trials of 'War Criminals.'" *Guardian* [London], December 21, 1922, 8.

"List of Guests Invited to Attend the Unveiling of Nurses' Memorial." *Ottawa Journal*, August 25, 1926, 5.

"List of Missing Grows in Llandovery Castle Outrage." *Daily Standard* [Kingston, ON], July 3, 1918, 5.

"List of People on Llandovery Castle Arrives." *Calgary Herald*, July 4, 1918, 1.

Livesay, J.F.B. "See America Brought in By Sinking of Athenia." *Globe and Mail*, September 5, 1939, 3.

"The 'Llandovery Castle.'" *Evening Mail* [Halifax], July 14, 1921, 5.

"The Llandovery Castle." *Globe* [Toronto], July 16, 1921, 4.

"The Llandovery Castle." *Guardian* [London], July 8, 1918, 4.

"The Llandovery Castle." *Toronto Daily News*, July 2, 1918.

"Llandovery Castle — Berlin Story of British Mine." *Times* [London], July 4, 1918, 6.

"'The Llandovery Castle' — Canadian Memorial Service for Victims of Hun Murder." *Canadian Daily Record*, July 26, 1918.

"Llandovery Castle Outrage." *Leicester Mercury* [U.K.], July 12, 1921, 1.

"Llandovery Castle Outrage." *Times* [London], July 3, 1918, 20.

"Llandovery Castle Survivors are Not Witnesses at Trial at Leipsic, Germany." *London Advertiser* [London, ON], July 14, 1921.

"Londoner Saved." *London Free Press*, July 4, 1918.

"Lost at Sea?" *Saskatoon Daily Star*, July 3, 1918, 3.

Lucas, Robert. "The Farce of Leipzig." *Evening Standard* [London], October 10, 1944, 6.

"Mail and Shipping News." *Nottingham Evening Post*, August 5, 1914, 2.

"Major Lyon a Scotsman." *Daily Record and Mail* [Glasgow], July 3, 1918, 3.

"Major Lyon Says U-Boat Had Beforehand Information." *Globe* [Toronto], July 3, 1918, 1.

"Martyred Nurse Honored." *Gazette* [P.E.I.], July 2, 1919, 1.

McReady, James. "Imre Finta 1912–2003: 'The Lord of Life and Death.'" *Globe and Mail*, January 14, 2004, R7.

"Memorial Hospital Honors Brave Nurse." *Ottawa Citizen*, June 27, 1919, 7.

"Military Appointments Listed." *Victoria Daily Times*, June 17, 1920, 9.

"Mine Explosion Recalls Tragedy." *Globe* [Toronto], March 17, 1937, 7.

"Mine Sank Britannic; 24 Dead or Missing." *New York Times*, November 24, 1916, 1.

"Moscow's Press Tells of Nazis' Kharkov Terror." *Chicago Tribune*, December 18, 1943.

"Movements of Steamers." *Guardian* [London], July 15, 1914, 5.

New Masses 7, no 5 (October 1931).

New Masses 7, no. 7 (December 1931).

"New Union Castle Liner." *Newcastle Daily Journal* [U.K.], January 8, 1914, 2.

"No Further Survivors from Llandovery Castle." *Ottawa Citizen*, July 3, 1918, 1.

"No List of Victims Yet." *Toronto Daily Star*, July 3, 1918, 2.

"No New Trial for Finta, Court Rules." *Leader-Post* [Regina], March 25, 1994, 13.

"No Use Arguing, Kill the Beasts." *Toronto Daily Star*, July 2, 1918, 1.

"Nurse 'Nan' M'Kenzie Is Believed to be Lost." *Toronto Daily Star*, July 3, 1918, 14.

"Nurses Put Up Memory Tablet." *Globe* [Toronto], June 28, 1920, 10.

"One Toronto Man Is Rescued from Torpedoed Boat." *Toronto Daily Star*, July 2, 1918, 1.

O'Neil, Gerry. "Scandal of the Baralong Incident Was Hidden in Veil of Secrecy." *Iris na Mara: Journal of the Sea* 1, no. 4 (Spring 2006): 8–10.

"Orchestra Leader." *Saskatoon Daily Star*, June 8, 1918, 3.

"Ottawa Ignorant of Hospital Ship's Staff." *Toronto Daily Star*, July 2, 1918, 1.

"Patzig to Ask for Trial." *New York Times*, August 7, 1921, 14.

"P.E.I. Technical School." *Gazette* [P.E.I.], August 28, 1920, 6.

"Pioneer Dies." *Saskatoon Daily Star*, November 9, 1918, 3.

Platiel, Rudy. "Court Upholds Finta Acquittal of War-Crimes Charges." *Globe and Mail*, April 30, 1992, A8.

Platiel, Rudy. "Man Called Imre Finta Caused Terror, Trial Told." *Globe and Mail*, January 23, 1990, A3.

Platiel, Rudy. "Prosecutors Launch Appeal of Finta Acquittal." *Globe and Mail*, June 15, 1990, A8.

Platiel, Rudy. "Supreme Court to Hear Challenge of War Crimes Law." *Globe and Mail*, December 11, 1992, A9.

"Pledges of Victory at London Meeting." *New York Times*, July 5, 1918, 7.

"Port of Plymouth." *Western Morning News* [Plymouth, U.K.], February 13, 1915, 3.

"The Probable Ottawa Victims; Praise of Ship and Staff by Returned Men." *Ottawa Citizen*, July 3, 1918, 2.

"Pte. G. Nash Believed Lost." *Toronto Daily Star*, July 3, 1918, 8.

"Random Notes on Current Sports." *Toronto Daily Star*, July 3, 1918, 18.

"Reds Convict 4 at War Trials; Decree Hanging." *Chicago Tribune*, December 19, 1943, 8.

"The Rena McLean Memorial Hospital." *Charlottetown Guardian*, February 23, 1920.

"Requiem Mass Was Impressive." *Globe* [Toronto], August 10, 1918, 7.

"Returned Heroes Who Are Now at Pine Hill Convalescence Home." *Evening Mail* [Halifax], July 12, 1918, 4.

"Ruling on Finta Case Stands." *Globe and Mail*, June 24, 1994, A4.

"Says Neumann Case Is Decided Before Hearing." *Globe* [Toronto], June 6, 1921, 2.

"Search for Survivors Fails; 234 on Red Cross Hospital Ship Are Lost." *Edmonton Journal*, July 3, 1918, 11.

"Second Act in Leipzig Farce." *Globe* [Toronto], May 30, 1921, 1.

"Second Sea Disaster Fatal to Maj. Davis?" *Toronto Daily Star*, July 5, 1918, 11.

Seldes, George. "German U-Boat Officers Face Their Accusers." *Chicago Tribune*, July 13, 1921, 3.

Seldes, George. "Heart of 'Frightfulness' Is Laid Bare in Evidence at German Sailors' Trial." *Globe* [Toronto], July 14, 1921, 1.

Seldes, George. "Travels 7,000 Miles to Denounce Submarine Captain Who Shelled Boats After Sinking Hospital Ship." *Washington Herald*, July 16, 1921, 2.

Seldes, George. "Van. Man Assails 'Sub' Commander." *Vancouver Sun*, July 16, 1921, 1.

"Shipping News." *Birmingham Daily Post* [U.K.], July 8, 1914, 10.

"Shipping Notices." *Western Morning News* [Plymouth, U.K.], December 26, 1913, 1.

"Sink Hospital Ship, Then Blame a Mine." *Victoria Daily Times*, July 3, 1918, 1.

"Sinking a Hospital Ship." *Gloucestershire Echo* [Gloucester, U.K.], July 13, 1921, 4.

"The Sinking of H.M.H.S. 'Llandovery Castle.'" *Bulletin of the Canadian Army Medical Corps*, August 1918.

"Sinking of Hospital Ships." *Evening Despatch* [Birmingham, U.K.], July 4, 1921, 1.

"Solemn Notes of Last Post Resounded Through Hall at the Unveiling of Memorial." *Ottawa Journal*, August 24, 1926, 1.

"Spies at Work in Halifax." *New York Times*, July 4, 1918, 8.

"Spies Thought Responsible for Sinking of Can. Hospital Ship." *Daily Standard* [Kingston, ON], July 3, 1918, 1.

Spray, Leonard. "Germans Angry War Murderer Is Put in Irons." *Globe* [Toronto], June 30, 1921, 2.

Stone, I.F. "Will They Escape?" *Gazette and Daily* [York, PA], February 24, 1945, 15.

"Stranger Brings Word About Son." *Saskatoon Daily Star*, May 25, 1918, 3.

"Sunday Band Concert." *Saskatoon Daily Star*, June 6, 1914, 9.

"Sunk Hospital Ship." *Daily Telegraph* [London], July 5, 1921, 5.

"Survivor Tells Story of Sinking." *Globe* [Toronto], July 5, 1918, 3.

"Survivors Accounted For." *Daily Mail* [London], July 1, 1918, 5.

"Sympathy Expressed." *Charlottetown Guardian*, July 8, 1918.

"Tablet Was Unveiled in Memory of Nurses." *Toronto Daily Star*, March 29, 1920, 12.

Thompson, Eric. "Canadian Fiction of the Great War." *Canadian Literature* 91 (Winter 1981): 81–96.

"Three Nurses and Six Men Perished, Ottawa District." *Ottawa Citizen*, July 5, 1918, 1.

"Three Toronto Men on Torpedoed Ship." *Toronto Daily Star*, July 4, 1918, 5.

"Three War Criminals." *Nottingham Evening Post* [Nottingham, U.K.], January 12, 1921, 6.

"To Try War Criminals." *New York Times*, March 24, 1921, 3.

"Toronto Nurses Erect Tablet to Huns' Victim." *Toronto Daily Star*, June 28, 1920, 10.

"The Torpedoing of Hospital Ships." *Guardian* [London], July 3, 1918, 4.

"Trial of German War Criminals." *Guardian* [London], January 12, 1921, 8.

"Trial of German War Criminals." *Times* [London], February 18, 1921, 16.

"Tribute to Valiant Nurses Is Unveiled in Presence of Distinguished Canadians." *Ottawa Journal*, August 25, 1926, 5.

"Tried to Murder All Witnesses." *Globe* [Toronto], December 2, 1918, 7.

"Try U-Boat Officers Who 'Submarined' Llandovery Castle." *Globe* [Toronto], July 13, 1921, 1.

"12 Nurses Die When Lifeboat Is Shelled." *San Francisco Examiner*, July 2, 1918, 1.

"Two German Officers Each Get Four Years." *Toronto Daily Star*, July 16, 1921, 1.

"Two More Germans Acquitted in Leipzig." *Globe* [Toronto], July 11, 1921, 2.

"Two Peaks Won by Italians; Hospital Ship Willfully Sunk." *San Francisco Examiner*, July 2, 1918, 1.

"U Boat Murders." *Western Daily Press* [Bristol, U.K.], July 13, 1921, 8.

"U-Boat 'Hero' Escapes." *Toronto Daily Star*, November 19, 1921, 7.

"U-Boat Officer Who Fired on Lifeboat Flees Prison." *Chicago Tribune*, November 20, 1921, 3.

"U-Boat Officers' Difference." *Evening Standard* [London], July 13, 1921, 2.

"U-Boat Officers Face Leipsic Court." *New York Times*, July 13, 1921, 3.

"U-Boat Officers Get 4-Year Sentence." *Morning Call* [Allentown, PA], July 17, 1921, 1.

"'Under Orders' Plead Accused U-Boat Men." *New York Tribune*, July 13, 1921, 4.

"Union-Castle Line to South and East Africa." *Birmingham Daily Mail* [U.K.], December 29, 1913, 1.

"Union-Castle Line to South & East Africa." *Western Morning News* [Plymouth, U.K.], May 4, 1914, 1.

"Unique Newspaper on Hospital Ship." *Ottawa Citizen*, July 3, 1918, 2.

"Unspeakable Outrage." *Sydney Morning Herald*, July 4, 1918, 7.

"Unveil Nurses' Tablet on Monday Afternoon." *Toronto Daily Star*, March 27, 1920, 2.

Vance, Jonathan. "The Soldier as Novelist: Literature, History, and the Great War." *Canadian Literature* 179 (Winter 2003): 22–37.

Vienneau, David. "Finta Ruling Belittles Holocaust, Says Jewish Congress." *Ottawa Citizen*, April 3, 1994, 10.

Wallace, Terrance. "Memorial Plaque: She Died (One of 61 Canadians) Part 3 — Gladys Irene Sare." *CSMMI* (Canadian Society of Military Medals & Insignia) *Journal*, Summer 2021.

"War of the U-Boats." *New York Times*, July 28, 1918, 38.

"War Passion at Sea." *Daily Herald* [Chicago], July 15, 1921, 3.

Ward, Bruce. "Clearly Marked Hospital Ship Won No Mercy From U-Boat in 1918." *Ottawa Citizen*, November 10, 2006, 59.

"The Weather." *Evening Mail* [Halifax], June 17, 1918, 2.

"The Week in Review." *Journal of Education* 88, no. 2 (July 11, 1918).

"Went from Vancouver." *Victoria Daily Times*, July 3, 1918, 1.

"West Toronto Nurses Are Reported Safe." *Toronto Daily Star*, July 3, 1918, 13.

"Wife of General on Supreme Council." *Evening Mail* [Halifax], March 2, 1918, 16.

"William Jackson Writes of Work of Medical Corps." *Saskatoon Daily Star*, December 19, 1914.

"Won't Tolerate Leipzig Parody." *Globe* [Toronto], June 18, 1921, 13.

"Yesterday's Hearing." *Guardian* [London], July 16, 1921, 11.

Opera

Martin, Stephanie, composer; Ciufo, Paul, librettist. *Llandovery Castle*. Canadian Music Centre, 2018.

Opera Laurier, Wilfrid Laurier University Faculty of Music. *Llandovery Castle*, Final Dress Rehearsal. February 26, 2020. Video, 1:19:49, tinyurl.com/2r9e4ecn.

Service Records

Campbell, Christina. Library and Archives Canada. Canadian Expeditionary Force (CEF), RG 150, Accession 1992-93/166, Box 1424-41.

Clint, Mabel. Library and Archives Canada. Canadian Expeditionary Force (CEF), RG 150, Accession 1992-93/166, Box 1803A-57.

Cooper, Frederick. Library and Archives Canada. Canadian Expeditionary Force (CEF), RG 150, Accession 1992-93/166, Box 1970-33.

Davis, Lena. Library and Archives Canada. Canadian Expeditionary Force (CEF), RG 150, Accession 1992-93/166, Box 2351-21.

Douglas, Carola. Library and Archives Canada. Canadian Expeditionary Force (CEF), RG 150, Accession 1992-93/166, Box 2620-18.

Dussault, Alexina. Library and Archives Canada. Canadian Expeditionary Force (CEF), RG 150, Accession 1992-93/166, Box 2779-42.

Follette, Minnie. Library and Archives Canada. Canadian Expeditionary Force (CEF), RG 150, Accession 1992-93/166, Box 3172-18.

Fortescue, Margaret. Library and Archives Canada. Canadian Expeditionary Force (CEF), RG 150, Accession 1992-93/166, Box 3217-3.

Fowlds, Helen. Library and Archives Canada. Canadian Expeditionary Force (CEF), RG 150, Accession 1992-93/166, Box 839-62.

Fraser, Margaret. Library and Archives Canada. Canadian Expeditionary Force (CEF), RG 150, Accession 1992-93/166, Box 3287-53.

Gallaher, Minnie. Library and Archives Canada. Canadian Expeditionary Force (CEF), RG 150, Accession 1992-93/166, Box 3377-2.

Hearn, James. Library and Archives Canada. Canadian Expeditionary Force (CEF), RG 150, Accession 1992-93/166, Box 4213A-51.

Hickman, George. Library and Archives Canada. Canadian Expeditionary Force (CEF), RG 150, Accession 1992-93/166, Box 4321-30.

Hoskins, Clifford. Library and Archives Canada. Canadian Expeditionary Force (CEF), RG 150, Accession 1992-93/166, Box 4519-27.

Jackson, William. Library and Archives Canada. Canadian Expeditionary Force (CEF), RG 150, Accession 1992-93/166, Box 4757-13.

Ker, Dr. Robert Harold. Library and Archives Canada. Canadian Expeditionary Force (CEF), RG 150, Accession 1992-1993/166, Box 5109-39.

Knight, Arthur. Library and Archives Canada. Canadian Expeditionary Force (CEF), RG 150, Accession 1992-93/166, Box 5222-40.

Knight, William. Library and Archives Canada. Canadian Expeditionary Force (CEF), RG 150, Accession 1992-93/166, Box 5230-32.

Lafountaine, Joseph Francis. Library and Archives Canada. Canadian Expeditionary Force (CEF), RG 150, Accession 1992-93/166, Box 5303-58.

Lowe, Margaret. Library and Archives Canada. Canadian Expeditionary Force (CEF), RG 150, Accession 1992-93/166, Box 5768-43.

Lyon, Thomas. Library and Archives Canada. Canadian Expeditionary Force (CEF), RG 150, Accession 1992-93/166, Box 5816-25.

MacCallum, Henry Reid. Library and Archives Canada. Canadian Expeditionary Force (CEF), RG 150, Accession 1992-1993/166, Box 6608-34.

Macdonald, Katherine. Library and Archives Canada. Canadian Expeditionary Force (CEF), RG 150, Accession 1992-93/166, Box 6748-49.

Macdonald, Thomas. Library and Archives Canada. Canadian Expeditionary Force (CEF), RG 150, Accession 1992-93/166, Box 6765-16.

McDiarmid, Jessie. Library and Archives Canada. Canadian Expeditionary Force (CEF), RG 150, Accession 1992-93/166, Box 6689-18.

McKenzie, Mary. Library and Archives Canada. Canadian Expeditionary Force (CEF), RG 150, Accession 1992-93/166, Box 6979-40.

McLean, Rena. Library and Archives Canada. Canadian Expeditionary Force (CEF), RG 150, Accession 1992-93/166, Box 7051-22.

Moore, Joseph. Library and Archives Canada. Canadian Expeditionary Force (CEF), RG 150, Accession 1992-93/166, Box 6332-39.

Pilot, William. Library and Archives Canada. Canadian Expeditionary Force (CEF), RG 150, Accession 1992-93/166, Box 7838-75.

Sampson, Mae Belle. Library and Archives Canada. Canadian Expeditionary Force (CEF), RG 150, Accession 1992-93/166, Box 8626-49.

Sare, Gladys. Library and Archives Canada. Canadian Expeditionary Force (CEF), RG 150, Accession 1992-93/166, Box 8647-55.

Scribner, Clement. Library and Archives Canada. Canadian Expeditionary Force (CEF), RG 150, Accession 1992-93/166, Box 8743-55.

Spittal, John. Library and Archives Canada. Canadian Expeditionary Force (CEF), RG 150, Accession 1992-93/166 Box 9199-22.

Stamers, Anna. Library and Archives Canada. Canadian Expeditionary Force (CEF), RG 150, Accession 1992-93/166, Box 9225-32.

Taylor, Shirley. Library and Archives Canada. Canadian Expeditionary Force (CEF), RG 150, Accession 1992-93/166, Box 9548- 21.

Templeman, Jean. Library and Archives Canada. Canadian Expeditionary Force (CEF), RG 150, Accession 1992-93/166, Box 9567-18.

Wake, Gladys. Library and Archives Canada. Canadian Expeditionary Force (CEF), RG 150, Accession 1992-93/166, Box 9989-48.

Radio

Siegel, Alisa, producer. *Sunday Edition.* "To Prepare a Place for You." Aired June 17, 2018 on CBC Radio.

Websites

Adams, Sharon. "The Sinking of the *Llandovery Castle*." Legion: Canada's Military History Magazine, June 26, 2019. tinyurl.com/3tu9h8hy.

Annison, Edward S. "Spurlos Versenkt." Temple University Libraries. tinyurl.com/34ddu3p5.

Avalon Project. "The International Military Tribunal for Germany: Contents of the Nuremberg Trials Collection." Yale Law School. tinyurl.com/5e5zm64t.

Avalon Project. "Laws of War: Adaptation to Maritime War of the Principles of the Geneva Convention (Hague X); October 18, 1907." Yale Law School. tinyurl.com/2p973cpu.

Avalon Project. "Laws of War: Adaptation to Maritime Warfare of the Principles of the Geneva Convention of 1864 (Hague III); July 29, 1899." Yale Law School. tinyurl.com/ycs4ryam.

Avalon Project. "Laws of War: Amelioration of the Condition of the Wounded on the Field of Battle (Red Cross Convention); August 22, 1864." Yale Law School. tinyurl.com/bde5snp5.

Avalon Project. "Laws of Warfare. Convention (I) for the Amelioration of the Condition of the Wounded and Sick in Armed Forces in the Field, August 12, 1949." Yale Law School. tinyurl.com/3wvv4as7.

B & C Staff Register. "Union-Castle Mail Steamship Co. Register." tinyurl.com/37tms23u.

Bell, Angie. "Review: The Llandovery Castle Brings 'Real Emotional Power' to Premier Performance in Toronto." Opera Canada, June 27, 2018. tinyurl.com/3uytpjy3.

Caledonian Maritime Research Trust. "Scottish Built Ships: Llandovery Castle." Caledonian Maritime Research Trust. tinyurl.com/4pv9vayy.

Canadian Armed Forces. "Record of Service: C.A.M.C. Medical Units: H.M. Hospital Ship 'Llandovery Castle.'" Government of Canada. tinyurl.com/bded2s52/.

Canadian Encyclopedia. "Timeline: Women's Suffrage." Canadian Encyclopedia. Updated 2023. tinyurl.com/2j9e3ddf.

Canadian Great War Project. "CAMC Hospital Ships." Canadian Great War Project. tinyurl.com/ynmcjrk8.

Canadian Military Engineers Association. "Military Abbreviations Used in Service Records." Canadian Military Engineers Association. cmea-agmc.ca /sites/default/files/abbreviations_used_in_service_records.pdf.

Canadian War Museum. "The Halifax Explosion." Canadian War Museum. tinyurl.com/52dsnvpz.

Canadian War Museum. "Propaganda: Canadian Wartime Propaganda. First World War Propaganda Poster. Victory Bonds Will Help Stop This: 'Kultur vs Humanity.'" Canadian War Museum. tinyurl.com/4v2wyjay.

CBC News. "Opera Telling Story of HMHS Llandovery Castle Premieres in Waterloo." CBC News. Posted February 28, 2020. tinyurl.com/3kp58mnp.

City of Saskatoon. "Woodlawn Cemetery." City of Saskatoon. tinyurl.com /2asmv7xf.

Commonwealth War Graves Commission. "Tower Hill Memorial." Commonwealth War Graves Commission. tinyurl.com/3tdneb7p.

Cook, Tim, and William Stewart. "War Losses (Canada)." In 1914-1918-online. International Encyclopedia of the First World War, edited by Ute Daniel, Peter Gatrell, Oliver Janz, Heather Jones, Jennifer Keene, Alan Kramer, and Bill Nasson. Berlin: Freie Universität, 2017. encyclopedia.1914-1918-online.net /article/war_losses_canada?version=1.0.

Cornell Law School. Legal Information Institute. "Geneva Conventions and Their Additional Protocols." Cornell Law School. Legal Information Institute. tinyurl.com/56uzbwn4.

Crew List Index Project. "Ship Whose Official Number Is 135302: Llandovery Castle." CLIP. tinyurl.com/5n8pnt2c.

Dauphinee, Lieutenant-Colonel (Retired) Wayne. "The Sinking of HMHS Llandovery Castle, 27 June 1918: 100th Anniversary Commemoration Ceremonies Held in Ottawa and Halifax June 2018." Royal Canadian Medical Service Association. tinyurl.com/vjvdwe3s.

Department of National Defence. "Cyrus Wesley Peck." Government of Canada. tinyurl.com/k66hmjf6.

Department of National Defence. "First World War Nurses Mark the Beginning of Women in the RCN." Government of Canada. tinyurl.com/muvc6scf.

Department of National Defence. "Record of Service: C.A.M.C. Medical Units: H.M. Hospital Ship 'Llandovery Castle.'" Government of Canada. tinyurl.com /49e98u3b.

Department of National Defence. "Record of Service: Overseas Military Forces of Canada Medical Units." Government of Canada. tinyurl.com/4k7fryx8.

Dunley, Richard. "The 'Live Bait Squadron.'" *The National Archives*, Blog, September 22, 2014. tinyurl.com/mr5jr3bx.

English, John R. Updated by Daniel Panneton. "Wartime Elections Act." Canadian Encyclopedia. Updated May 7, 2021. tinyurl.com/yy99brhj.

Government of Canada. "Canada and the International Criminal Court." Modified July 20, 2023. Government of Canada. tinyurl.com/yps6tre6.

Government of Canada. "Daily Data Report for June 1918. Halifax, Nova Scotia." Government of Canada. tinyurl.com/yuuch3ku.

Government of Prince Edward Island. "Vimy Oak Tree Planting Ceremony." May 29, 2017. Government of Prince Edward Island. tinyurl.com/229szey4.

Grace's Guide to British Industrial History. "Barclay, Curle & Co." Grace's Guide to British Industrial History. tinyurl.com/3ebr376m.

Graham, Roger. "Arthur Meighen." Canadian Encyclopedia, March 4, 2015. *Historica Canada*. tinyurl.com/yfv5emx4.

Great War Centenary Association, Brantford, Brant County, Six Nations. "We Remember: Katherine Maud Macdonald." Great War Centenary Association, Brantford, Brant County, Six Nations. tinyurl.com/2p8ektyj.

Halifax Military Heritage Preservation Society. "Halifax Memorial." Halifax Military Heritage Preservation Society. tinyurl.com/43p4ywra.

Hall, David J., and Donald B. Smith. "Lougheed, Sir James Alexander." Dictionary of Canadian Biography. tinyurl.com/5d3epy63.

Hankel, Gerd. "Leipzig War Crimes Trials." 1914-1918-online. International Encyclopedia of the First World War, edited by Ute Daniel, Peter Gatrell, Oliver Janz, Heather Jones, Jennifer Keene, Alan Kramer, and Bill Nasson. Berlin: Freie Universität Berlin, 2016. tinyurl.com/ysbt456e

Harris, Stephen. "Sir Archibald Cameron Macdonell." Canadian Encyclopedia. tinyurl.com/28ncxum8.

Heritage Canada. "Timeline: Canada's National Flag." Government of Canada. tinyurl.com/324hdre3.

History.com. "This Day in History 1865: Henry Wirz Hanged for Murder." History.com. tinyurl.com/49k6bfph.

Hoover Institution, Library and Archives, Stanford University. "'Spurlos Versenkt' (Sunk without a trace)." Hoover Institution, Library and Archives. tinyurl.com /acm8nnk5.

Identify Medals. "What Is a *Cross Pattée* and Why Are so Many Military Medals This Shape?" IdentifyMedals. tinyurl.com/2ex6ycbp.

Imperial War Museums. "Lives of the First World War: We Remember Edward Arthur Sylvester." Imperial War Museums. tinyurl.com/355bypse.

Imperial War Museums. "Lives of the First World War: We Remember William Robert Pilot." Imperial War Museums. tinyurl.com/cydy4v66.

International Criminal Court. icc-cpi.int/.

International Humanitarian Law Databases. "Additional Articles Relating to the Condition of the Wounded in War. Geneva, 20 October 1868." International Committee of the Red Cross. tinyurl.com/3er56s5d.

International Humanitarian Law Databases. "Convention (X) for the Adaptation to Maritime Warfare of the Principles of the Geneva Convention. The Hague, 18 October 1907." International Committee of the Red Cross. tinyurl.com/27tb7uu2.

International Humanitarian Law Databases. "Convention for the Amelioration of the Condition of the Wounded in Armies in the Field. Geneva, 22 August 1864." International Committee of the Red Cross. tinyurl.com/4mrdk4b8.

International Humanitarian Law Databases. "The Geneva Conventions of 1949 and their Additional Protocols." International Committee of the Red Cross. tinyurl.com/23h4fd2a.

Johnson, Jonathan. "Canadian Military Hospitals at Sea 1914–1919." Royal Canadian Medical Service Association. tinyurl.com/mr47wapr.

Johnson, Jonathan. "HMCHS Prince George: Hospital Ship." For Posterity's Sake. A Royal Canadian Navy Historical Project. tinyurl.com/4a7eceed.

Kernaghan, Lois, and Richard Foot. "Halifax Explosion." Canadian Encyclopedia. tinyurl.com/54azubh4.

Latitude. "Latitude and Longitude of HMHS Llandovery Castle." Latitude. tinyurl.com/4fszcvh9.

Library and Archives Canada. "Canadian Army Medical Corps." Library and Archives Canada. tinyurl.com/2creksux.

Library and Archives Canada. "Courts Martial of the First World War." Library and Archives Canada. tinyurl.com/5fh6d8fs.

Library of Congress. "Today in History: November 10. Henry Wirz and Andersonville Prison." Library of Congress. tinyurl.com/msk5jb5d.

LlandoveryCastle.ca. "The Llandovery Castle: A New Canadian Opera." Landoverycastle.ca. tinyurl.com/bdzz5vby.

Lyon, Dan. "Major Thomas Lyon, Canadian Army Medical Corps." Royal Canadian Medical Service Association. tinyurl.com/3csr9pvb.

Milward, Jennifer. "SS Warilda: Troopship, Hospital Ship, Ambulance Transport, Wreck." Australian War Memorial. tinyurl.com/y7hujy2w.

Montreal Litho Co. Ltd. "Photo, Print, Drawing. Victory Bonds Will Help Stop This. Kulture vs. Humanity." Library of Congress. tinyurl.com/yc3y847v.

National Archives. "Ship Llandovery Castle." National Archives. tinyurl.com /ym28vjmc.

Parks Canada. Directory of Federal Heritage Designations. "Next of Kin Memorial Avenue National Historic Site of Canada." Parks Canada. tinyurl.com /36dynnef.

Pate, David. "100 Years Ago Today, a Ship Carrying 546 Wounded WWI Soldiers Ran Aground off Halifax." CBC News. Posted August 1, 2017. tinyurl.com /mwwtzy2h.

Princess. "Princess Cruises." Princess.com. tinyurl.com/29nv6hpw.

Roll of Honour. "HMHS Carisbrook Castle." Roll of Honour. tinyurl.com /9rrjchck.

Royal Museums Greenwich. "Llandovery Castle." Royal Greenwich Museums. tinyurl.com/3kn9mjjr.

St. Andrew's Church. "The History of St. Andrew's." St. Andrew's Church. standrewstoronto.org/about-us/history-of-st-andrew/.

St. Etheldreda's Church. "History of the Church." St. Ethelreda. tinyurl.com/2nafcbj9.

St. Thomas's Church. "St. Thomas's Church, Toronto." St. Thomas's Church. tinyurl.com/yc7urujd.

Stifftung Deutsches U-Boot-Museum. "Type U." Stifftung Deutsches U-Boot-Museum. tinyurl.com/yra78fv6.

Townshend, Adele. "McLean, Rena Maude." Dictionary of Canadian Biography, Vol. 14, accessed March 10, 2023. tinyurl.com/y67wu4c7.

Trent University Archives. "Nursing Sister Helen L. Fowlds: A Canadian Nurse in World War I." Trent University Archives. tinyurl.com/yc6pt2et.

Uboat.net. "Ships hit during WWI: Torrington." Uboat.net. tinyurl.com /53vne5hb.

Uboat.net. "Ships hit during WWI: USS Covington." Uboat.net. tinyurl.com /2p9efxc5.

Uboat.net. "WWI U-boat commanders: Alfred Saalwachter." Uboat.net. tinyurl.com /yf949smx.

Uboat.net. "WWI U-boat commanders: Helmut Patzig." Uboat.net. tinyurl.com /89nkdp48.

Uboat.net. "WWI U-boat commanders: Wilhelm Werner." Uboat.net. tinyurl.com /3p7ebudx

Uboat.net. "WWI U-boat types: Type U 81." Uboat.net. tinyurl.com/3r3jscrn.

Uboat.net. "WWI U-boats: U 27." Uboat.net. tinyurl.com/5x9mhecf.

Uboat.net. "WWI U-boats: U 41." Uboat.net. tinyurl.com/47b9h83s.

Uboat.net. "WWI U-boats: U 86." Uboat.net. tinyurl.com/yc7rb4ut.

U.K. Parliament. "Arthur Ponsonby (1871–1946)." U.K. Parliament. tinyurl.com /2s883tvj.

U.K. Parliament. Hansard 1803–2005 — People (J). "Sir William Jowitt." U.K. Parliament. tinyurl.com/4z63tvkr.

U.K. Parliament. Hansard 1803–2005 — People (L). "Bonar Law." U.K. Parliament. tinyurl.com/yxrwjdsr.

van der Heyden, Ulrich. "An Unatoned War Crime of the First World War: The Sinking of a Hospital Ship by U-86." International Journal of Naval History. Posted December 30, 2020. tinyurl.com/yn8y7pvk.

Vance, Jonathan F. "Commemoration and Cult of the Fallen (Canada)." In 1914-1918-Online. International Encyclopedia of the First World War, edited by Ute Daniel, Peter Gatrell, Oliver Janz, Heather Jones, Jennifer Keene, Alan Kramer, and Bill Nasson. Berlin: Freie Universität Berlin, 2015. tinyurl.com/4tkrxcjk

Veterans Affairs Canada. "Canada Remembers: The Battle of Passchendaele." Government of Canada. tinyurl.com/3sjf8bbu.

Veterans Affairs Canada. "Canada Remembers: The Battle of Vimy Ridge." Government of Canada. tinyurl.com/bdfm7sss.

Veterans Affairs Canada. "Halifax Memorial." Government of Canada. tinyurl.com /4nm4mp7c.

Veterans Affairs Canada. "Memorial Cross." Government of Canada. tinyurl.com /4u2tjfej.

Veterans Affairs Canada. "Nurses' Memorial." Government of Canada. tinyurl.com /y7869r4k.

Ward, Melony. "Radio Pioneer." Canada's History. September 13, 2017. tinyurl.com /msmkz2n5.

Wartime Memories Project. "HMHS Carisbrooke Castle." Wartime Memories Project. tinyurl.com/mvy8nzrj.

WRECK Site. HMHS Llandovery Castle (+1918). WRECK Site. tinyurl. com/2arueus2.

Image Credits

Index

About the Author

Nate Hendley is a Toronto-based freelance journalist and author. He has written several books on topics ranging from wrongful murder convictions to cons and hoaxes and organized crime. His last book, *The Beatle Bandit*, published by Dundurn Press, won the 2022 Crime Writers of Canada Award of Excellence for Non-Fiction and was nominated for a 2022 Heritage Toronto Award. Nate's website (natehendley.ca) offers more details about his books and background.